Ethnic Literatures of America

Diaspora and Intercultural Studies

AMERICAN Studies

Ethnic Literatures of America

Diaspora and Intercultural Studies

edited by

Somdatta Mandal

Himadri Lahiri

Prestige

an international publishing house

Published by
Prestige Books
3/28, East Patel Nagar
New Delhi 110 008
Ph. 9818755529

ISBN: 81-7551-163-X

Printed at Chaman Offset Press, New Delhi 110 002

Contents

III: AFRICAN AMERICAN VOICES

IV: INDIAN AMERICAN VOICES

Introduction

The invisibility of ethnic characters and their lived experience in the cultural representations of the United States has long been an issue of contention. Even in the late 1980s Bharati Mukherjee in a *New York Times* article (28 August, 1988) entitled "Immigrant Writing: Give Us Our Minimalists" points out that despite a perceptible change in the demographic scenario of the nation the experience of the ethnic communities remain outside the purview of literary representations. Her anguish and anxiety is quite evident in her questions: "But where, in fiction, do you read of it? Who, in other words, speaks for us, the new Americans from non-traditional immigrant countries?" (sec. 7: p. 1) Today, the literary-cultural picture of the United States has undergone changes and the ethnic presence can be distinctly perceived. A number of factors can be attributed to this, one of these being the emergence of different organizations which filled up the vacuum or contested stereotyped representations of the ethnic communities and gave new perspectives to the American literature(s) by adding new dimensions to it. The foundation of the MELUS was one such effort. MELUS-India, on its part, has also been performing its role in the same direction, from the Indian perspectives in the main.

The present volume is a collection of papers selected from those presented at the MELUS-India International Conference held in Hyderabad in January, 2004 on "Scene, Space, Scenario: Contexts of Multiethnic Literatures in the Americas" and at the national seminar held in Chandigarh in April 2003 entitled "South Asians in the United States: The Diasporic Experience." These papers raise important issues relating to American Studies in general and Ethnic Studies in particular and also try to project the directions these studies might take in the future. They capture the dynamics of the ethnic literary works and comparative studies, in particular, explore commonalties that might serve for a closer inter-ethnic understanding.

The articles included here are about writers from different ethnic origins and their themes are varied and often community-specific. The editors of this volume were faced with the problem of classifying these and hence the groupings have been done from the point of view of ethnicity which is the dominant idea running through the articles. Also, while doing so, the metaphor of the 'voice' has been used because the struggle for voicing their concerns is clearly evident in most of the authors dealt with. Protest elements are also very strong. The metaphor also carries a sense of agency and urgency. We have, however, deviated from the criterion of 'ethnicity' in the section entitled "The Performing Arts" which contains two articles that could have been accommodated in the "Indian American Voices" section. We felt that since these are emerging areas where the ethnic creative efforts can be perceived, we should highlight this by creating a new section on the performing arts. This book thus offers a kaleidoscopic view of the ethnic world of the United States that is essentially heterogeneous but nevertheless has meeting grounds for its myriad communities. The sections on different ethnic voices are preceded by one on theoretical paradigms which will provide the readers with a road map as to how ethnic and diasporic literatures are now theorized. The last section, which contains only one article written by Mohan Ramanan, offers a projection of how the 'ethnic studies' programmes in organizations like our own should shape up in future.

The first section, "Theoretical Paradigms," has four articles, all dealing with literary implications of migration and ethnicity. Mohan Ramanan's "'Eat Me America': Some Aspects of Indian Writing in America," which was originally the Presidential Address of the 2003 MELUS-India Conference, sets the tone by taking up some South Asian writers like Salman Rushdie, Indran Amirthanayagam and Agha Shahid Ali and offering theoretical insights into their works produced in the new space. He mentions early migrations of indentured labourers to countries like Fiji, Trinidad and Mauritius, distinguishes such migrations from the postcolonial ones, and elaborating how 'relationships'—though problematical—have developed over the decades. He feels that the "original relationships with America" will mature into a more meaningful one, with the acceptance, and not rejection, of the 'other.' In the next article "Political Realities and the Colors of Imagination" the noted critic Jasbir Jain explains the terms 'scene,' 'space' and 'scenario,' terms which figured in the proposed theme of the 2004 MELUS-India International Conference, in the context of human relationships and identity politics, and argues that the centre-margin relationship is basically unstable. The concepts of belonging and unbelonging in relation to that of 'space,' real or utopic, have profound impact on the diasporic subject. She also asserts that 'ethnicity' is not something fixed; it evolves and is the result of the lived experience of the migrant.

In her well-researched article "Travelling with Walls: The South Asian Intellectuals in the United States," Manju Jaidka problematizes the location of the migrant who is essentially viewed as a "man without frontiers," as one who leaves behind the old culture and at the same time carries it with himself. She argues that the intellectual migrant himself remains suspended between two worlds but acts as an interpreter of, and mediator between, cultures. Himadri Lahiri's article "Crossing Borders: In Search of a Location" approaches the problem of the location of the diasporic subject from the point of view of hybridity which is reflected in the stylistic aspects of a work like Amitav Kumar's *Passport Photos* which blurs boundaries of genres. Lahiri feels that despite the liminality of the diasporic subjects, there is among them a tendency to settle down. In "The Text as Narrative: Reading Ideology" Sukalpa Bhattacharjee analyzes Chitra Banerjee Divakaruni's *The Unknown Errors of Our Lives* and Bapsi Sidhwa's *The Pakistani Bride* as narrative productions and as 'socially symbolic acts,' as a process of collaboration and contestation of cultural and historical forces that determine the course of the narrative. She contends that although narratives represent the 'ontological emptiness' of knowledge, subjectivity and cultural productions, they also represent 'historical fullness' by uncovering the 'hidden transcripts' of language and subjectivity.

Stereotyping helps prolonging marginalization, and stereotyped images of the Chinese American community were created through works like Fu Manchu and Charlie Chan films to perpetuate a sense of 'otherness' of the community. In the section on "Chinese American Voices," Gulshan Rai Kataria demonstrates how certain myths related to the community were contested in the works of David Henry Hwang, Maxine Hong Kingston, and Amy Tan. Gönül Pultar examines narrative strategies employed by Amy Tan in her novel *The Joy Luck Club* (1989) to bring out the dynamics of patriarchy, racism and cultural conflict in the Chinese American community. The older generation of women preserves patriarchy in the name of preserving the old culture. Pultar brings out the narrative strategies by analysing the method of Eastern story-telling and oral narratives and Tan's avoidance of traditional Western plot and denouement. These narrative strategies help Tan to interrogate the ideologies and identity politics of both the centre and margin.

In the section entitled "African American Voices," Jap Preet Kaur Bhangu reviews the development of African American drama in the post-Civil Rights period and analyzes how it came to reach the centrestage. Mina Surjeet Singh in "Ballad of a Dream Deferred: Blackness and Bleakness in the Poetry of Langston Hughes" maintains that understanding of Black literary tradition is central to the understanding of American literature in general. She examines Hughes' contribution to American literature from this point of view. Punam Gupta's article on Zora Neale Hurston demonstrates how she employs folk creativity as a 'subversive gesture' in her book *Their Eyes Were Watching God.* R.G. Kulkarni's short article on Ralph Ellison's *Invisible Man* places the book in the tradition of Black protest literature and examines how the act of writing can be an ennobling and liberating act.

The long section on Indian American writing explores the multifaceted aspects of this relatively new area of American literature. E. Nageswara Rao and Nila Das have written on Meena

Alexander, the former on the images of the fire in her works, exploring its myriad implications and the latter on Alexander's positing of 'otherness' in *The Fault Lines* as a positive situation that leads to cross-cultural and cross-national dialogues, as one that can construct personal identity in a larger framework. Anil Raina's article on the title story of the same name in Vijay Lakshmi's *Pomegranate Dreams* (2002) is a valuable contribution on one of the emerging Indian American writers. Vijay Lakshmi as an immigrant writer shows her young protagonist as straddling two worlds. It is, as Raina shows, a story which depicts immigration not only as a loss but also as a gain. Anu Celly examines two stories of Bharati Mukherjee—"A Wife's Story" and "The Tenant"—and demonstrates how the 'integrity' and the sensibilities of the female protagonist undergo individual transformations through a process of trauma and courage. The way the characters negotiate the new space also has its impact on the contours of American culture. Ila Rathore examines how prominent women writers of the Indian diaspora represent the trauma and conflict in interpersonal relationships among their characters, and also shows how gender and culture mediates such relationships. Alka Saxena writes about the cultural displacements in the short stories of Anjana Appachana and Shauna Baldwin. Eami Mathew examines the dynamics of relationships between fathers and sons in the Indian immigrant community as represented in Prem Chopra's *Salaam New York* (1993). Chopra, as pointed out by Mathew, has approached the problem exclusively from a male point of view.

The "Other Voices" section contains articles on Native American, Arab American, white American voices. Mukul Sengupta's focus is on the invisibility of Native American female voices that need to be foregrounded. I.H-Shihan shows how Robin White represents the Indian socio-cultural reality. This is an interesting article in the sense that its focus is on 'reverse navigation' as in White's case the navigation was from the U.S. to India. Indrani Dutta Chaudhuri's article on the poetry of some Arab American women throws light on a relatively less explored area. Though not directly related to multi-cultural studies,

Pratibha Nagpal re-assesses some short fictional works of Katherine Anne Porter and Eudora Welty in the light of Southern literary tradition.

"Intercultural Studies" explores the space where both commonalties and differences are found. Of the articles in this section K.B. Razdan compares Ellison's *Invisible Man* and William Styron's *Sophie's Choice* and discusses how ideology operates in the texts. Both Ellison and Styron transcreate the text as the cultural given. Their works raise important issues about class, ethnicity and race and their protagonists become architects of a process of meaning creation in an odyssey of existential reconstruction. S.S. Kumar finds similarities in the poems of the African American poet Claude McKay (1889-1948) and the revolutionary poet of Tamil Renaissance Bharathidasan (1891-1964). He discusses their poems in the context of their early fascination with the ideology of Communism and their attitude to nature and relationship between man and nature. Deepshikha Kotwal makes a comparative study of Toni Morrison's *Paradise* and Chitra Banerjee Divakaruni's *Sister of My Heart* by embedding the texts in the feminist critical traditions. She feels that "politics of complexity" is an effective tool to neutralize totalising systems and the "maze of dualisms" and to ensure differential relations in culturally and historically specific ways. She shows how Morrison's *Paradise* displays dialogic encounters between conflicting codes inherent in the binaries of social constructions and how it dialogically "poaches" the "malestream" America. Divakaruni, by contrast, fails to do this adequately through her monologically oriented text. Shukla Saha examines the 'feminine' and the 'other' in Toni Morrison's *The Bluest Eye* and Maxine Hong Kingston's *The Woman Warrior* from the cross-cultural perspectives.

The two articles in the section on the performing arts are equally interesting. Somdatta Mandal throws light on the emergence of *bhangra,* the folk music of Punjab, in the documentary films of diasporic filmmakers like Gurinder Chadha, Tejaswini Ganti, Pratibha Parmar and Nandini Sikand. Her article shows how *bhangra*, through a mix of the old and the new, becomes symbolic of universal cultural transformations for new generations. Manpreet Kaur Kang analyzes Manoj N. Shyamalan's film *The Sixth Sense* to suggest how the 'image of an old-fashioned apologetic Indian' has been replaced by that of a 'newly prosperous non-resident Indian.' While emphasizing that there is a difference between the first generation and the second generation migrants with regard to the 'trauma of homelessness,' she asserts, through the analysis of the film, that acculturation can be a positive transformation.

The volume ends with Mohan Ramanan's "MELUS: Where Shall We Go from Here?" in which he re-examines the relevance of doing multi-ethnic studies of America in India. He feels that our approach should promote the inter-disciplinary and cross-cultural studies that link the particular with the general, and that connect one identity with another. He also strongly feels that in the spirit of connectivity we should also pay attention to the Indian scenario, Dalit writings, Indian *bhasa* literatures, and translations from regional languages. There is also a need to study white writers as well. In short, he advocates for the exploration of commonalties that exist among communities which should naturally be reflected in our studies of a wide range of writers and literatures.

Somdatta Mandal **Himadri Lahiri**

'Eat Me America': Some Aspects of Indian Writing in America*

MOHAN RAMANAN
University of Hyderabad

I must at the outset apologize for the innuendo in my title but it is hardly original and I have borrowed it very appropriately from Salman Rushdie in his American novel, *Fury*. Malik Solanka who is his protagonist in this grim book about New York is Indian and he feels overwhelmed with America and cries out for America to swallow him into her capaciousness, an outcry which of course has sexual overtones. Rushdie is only one among an increasing number of Indians living and writing in America. Rushdie continues to look to India for his inspiration even though he has time and again spoken of his need to grow out of India. *Fury* seemed to have done it at last, but as a discerning reader will see, Rushdie's chief character is a take off from the Himachali town called Solan where Rushdie had ancestral property and had at the time he was composing *Fury* just won a protracted court case for possession of it. In *Step across the Line: Collected Non-fiction 1992-2002,* Rushdie speaks feelingly of Solan and about his return there with his son and their mixed experiences on returning home.

This business of returning home is one of the main themes in all Indian Diasporic writing. The question of Home and Abroad, (Tagore called it *Ghare Baire)* the pain of exile and the need for a local place and habitation in exile is an urge which is natural to writing by diasporic writers anywhere and it is so with Indian writers in America. Of course there is a difference between the exile of the older subaltern workers who were displaced by colonial policy and experienced the pain and humiliation of being treated as less than human in South Africa or in the colonial estates elsewhere and the exile experienced by Non Resident Indians (NRIs) in America. The former had no agency of their own and were in a sense, victims of history, helpless participants in colonial discourse. The latter did have a choice and opted to go abroad in search of a more comfortable life and many of them do live reasonably comfortable lives away from the grinding poverty of India and easy in their cushy jobs. In particular those who theorize about 'Home and Abroad,' about 'exile,' about 'diasporic consciousness,' are the ones most comfortable in their tenured academic positions from whose vantagepoint they can interrogate their Third world origins. I do not wish to minimize their sense of loss. Of course it exists but it is qualitatively different from that of the ancestors of say a writer like Naipaul or the workers of Jamaica, South Africa and Fiji. And yet the writers whom we are concerned with are all NRI types and they have produced an impressive body of work which merits attention if only because they have an international reputation and vogue. I am thinking of writers like Salman Rushdie, Vikram Chandra, Meena Alexander, Jhumpa Lahiri, Bharati Mukherjee, and also writers of an older vintage like Raja Rao and R. Parthasarathy, not to speak of A.K. Ramanujan. Even if we have some reservations about their genuineness and sincerity we cannot ignore such an impressive body of work that is characterized by thematic variety and linguistic and stylistic brilliance. They are good storytellers and it would appear that America has opened them up in ways which staying home might not have happened.

But first some contexts. While it is true that these writers have contributed to the prestige of Indian Writing in English (IWE) and indeed seem to dominate our tradition, the fact that they are located in America is of sufficient importance to speak of them as American writers as well. In fact an aspect of their writing is precisely how to make themselves at home in the West and in America. That they dominate IWE is undoubted. Even in the famous Trinity of IWE, the novelists Narayan, Anand and Rao, we find that Rao has been long in the West and as we move down the tradition we find that for every three Indian writers who seem to be rooted to India there are at least one or two who have moved on and who operate from the metropolitan capitals of the world—Sydney, Melbourne, Toronto, London, Copenhagen, New York and elsewhere. In the period after *Midnight's Children* (1980), the exodus abroad has been steady and a quick count tells us that for every Arundhati Roy or an Ezekiel who has stayed behind saying "My Backward Place is where I am," there are writers like Agha Shahid Ali or Sudeep Sen or Rohinton Mistry who have moved on risking loss of innocence, patria and identity. I would not want to berate them for their choices. These have been made and that has made all the difference.

A natural context for the study of work emanating from America is the paradigm shift that has taken place in America. Around the time of the Civil Rights Movement in the late 1950s and the 1960s multiculturalism became an important watchword in cultural discourse. Crucial in this respect was of course the idea of the 'melting pot' and the dominant metaphors to describe American life emerged from Crevecoeur's famous query as to Who was an American. The shift in consciousness came about as a result of an increasing assertiveness on the part of the Blacks and very soon other ethnic groups—Hispanics, Chinese, Korean, Indian, Amerindian—began to show signs of self-consciousness. In American Studies discourse the 'melting pot' metaphor gave place to the idea of the 'salad bowl' where all the ethnic strands and the differences were acknowledged, albeit in a larger American context. We now have the idea of the hyphenated American where ethnic differences and local and specific cultural traits moved into the centerstage of academic debate. The hyphenation is now gone and it is a sign that multiculturalism in America is the dominant discourse. I hasten to add that I am not suggesting that America is a wonderful Utopia but rather I freely acknowledge the resilience of the American spirit which in its most advanced and progressive aspect has the power and energy, in the face of prejudice and discrimination, to continue to say yea. This yea saying represents those features of American character that at one point in history made her a model for the project of decolonisation. Indian Writing in America participates in this carnival of difference and the Indian American Writer takes his or her place in a braided world of ethnicity and cultural pluralism. At the same time Indian Writing in English in America cannot be seen as an exclusive cultural group with no connections with other cultural groups. Indeed they are part of a coalition of multicultural groups including Hispanic, African, Chinese and Amerindian groups and a proper context for a consideration of their work is the Multicultural Literatures of the United States which is our special concern in this forum.

Before I explore the provenance of Indian Writing in English in America I should like to focus on one extraordinary talent who is only tangentially connected to the Indian writers I am concerned with though in the context of ethnicities and plural cultures he is in many ways intimately connected to IWE in America. This is the Sri Lankan Tamil American poet Indran Amirthanayagam. He is a career diplomat and had served in Chennai and knows the IWE scene well. He continues to publish in Indian forums even though he is now in Monterey, California. He is a good example of the displacement I see in our own writers but I have chosen him for particular attention because even though he shares some of the expatriate experiences of our Indians abroad, he writes about these things with a kind of passion and sincerity which I sometimes find lacking in the Indian writers. I believe a brief analysis of this particular poet with a particular and unique cultural provenance will serve to contrast our writers and to put them in perspective. The two volumes Amirthanayagam has published are *Ceylon RIP* and *Elephants of Memory*. These are American poems and he writes to the multicultural provenance of America, but they are something more. They are also Sri Lankan Tamil poems. The poet is torn between his roots and the haunting memory of his childhood spent in Sri Lanka and the loss he now experiences as a result of his American location and, what is more, as a consequence of his international travels which leave him little time to get attached to any one place. This seems to be a peculiar American problem, the innocent abroad and the constant destabilizing effect of the experience generated from travel. He is committed to American values, to values of democracy and openness to experience and to experiment, to making it new. And yet after all is said and done, as an American Foreign Service diplomat, he can only say this much. He has to be reticent. This for Amirthanayagam is not an obstacle but an opportunity. Out of his conflicts he is able to produce poetry and indeed he does suggest that it is his Americanness that allows him to write at all. He enjoys the flexibility and creativity America offers and allows this to inform his verse, even though the verse is about the Sri Lankan Tamil situation. For Amirthanayagam there are two kinds of nostalgia. There is the Sri Lanka which he left when he was barely eight and there is the America he can never stay put in because of the peripatetic nature of his job. He is the citizen perpetually in exile: "You must love the land, love the tongue" and you must "love the other side of the sea." One could ask why he should feel this angst and why he left his home in the first place and the poet answers that leaving home paradoxically allowed him to write better poetry. This emphasis on the aesthetic is after all a post-modernist feature and one must not minimize this in our contemporary quest for a committed literature, committed that is to narrow partisan ends like ethnicity, gender, race and nation. I am arguing for what Wordsworth called the widest commonality of Man.

If the task of poetry is to preserve, then Indran does it by "gathering essences." Of Sri Lanka he writes:

> That undiscovered country
> Now a common item on the 24 hours news
> 40,000 residents of Jaffna about
> to leave the scene.

For Indran his original home is "Paraiso ensangrentado," the "Bloodied Paradise." In "Beyond the Beautiful House," Indran declares:

> I do not know if I will see Jaffna
> Again, the North Pole of my cosmos,
> Where my father was born; this poem
> Has become a speech before the mirror

He celebrates the Tamil Boys

In small boats
The firstcraft of the young wood called Eelam
The boys who left their mothers
By night in silence in fate
To creep by the lanes of Jaffna town
Arm in arm, by twos and threes, alone
To run to the boats and training camps,
of the Tiger, the Cobra, the young boys
Come back to meet the metal whips
Tails, lashing bullets, helicopter
Gunships flying their mandate
To level the sea, (and tear the eyes out
Of a few 'dirty' boys

Here is a sensitive poet who, while he laments his loss of home and what history has made of his home, is nevertheless, able to see clearly that were it not for his location as an American Foreign Affairs man he would hardly have the opportunity or freedom to speak his mind in this way. I think what makes Indran so convincing is his sincerity and authenticity and the tenderness of his verse. Indran then in a way provides us with a suitable context to read our own writers in America.

I shall begin with Salman Rushdie and the *frisson* his opening paragraph in *Midnight's Children* presents us with. It is not a novel written from America but it is a novel written in exile in Britain. It has perhaps one of the finest beginnings in Indian English fiction and has all the hallmarks of distinction. First is the interpenetration of the personal and the public, the individual and the societal, and the private and the historical, which Saleem Sinai's hands handcuffed to history implies. What happens to Sinai is what happens to India and India's destiny is seen as interlocked with Sinai's family history. Rushdie uses the conventions of the Family Saga genre and transforms it into a fine example of postmodern historical fiction. This means that Rushdie, while he may adhere to the conventions of the classical historical novel like *The Heart of Midlothian,* is nevertheless going to experiment with postmodern practices like magic realism, pastiche and parody. And that is what happens here when time and space are deployed to blur distinctions and to create a space for Sinai's meditations on nationalism. Rushdie 'chutnifies' English and he 'chutnifies' history and this is what all his novels do. *The Moor's Last Sigh* is about peppercorn and spice producing families and the union which ensues between them which produces, the novel's protagonist, Moraes Zogoiby. Rushdie is suggesting that this hybrid creature is also representative of India, even though it is the product of an unlikely union of a Jewish family and a Syrian Catholic family from Kerala. The Moor is a party of one, a church of one, if you like, and that too is India. Rushdie has been preoccupied with India, and the early novels in a way set the agenda for our Diasporic writers by in a deep way exemplifying the point Frederic Jameson made with respect to Third world narratives being national allegories. Indeed Rushdie can be seen as initiating from his vantagepoint in Britain a whole series of novels written to Jameson's prescription. One recollects Allan Sealy's *Trotter Nama,* Mukul Kesavan's *Looking through Glass,* Boman Desai's *Memory of Elephants*, Nina Sibal's *Yatra* and even the monumental *Suitable Boy* of Vikram Seth. And so when in *The Ground Beneath Her Feet* Rushdie declares that he has been done with India, one takes it with a pinch of salt: "And now I must sing the last song of India, goat-song, a tragic song"—We realize that Ummeed Merchant is after all a forerunner of Malik Solanka, that this book characterized by fine writing, exciting descriptions, interesting insights, anecdotes, jokes, tall-tales and word doctoring is after all a forerunner of *Fury.* This last novel is Rushdie's first as an Indian American but it is nonetheless Indian in its inspiration. Solanka cries, "Eat Me America and Give me Peace" and this apart from the sexual innuendo is also a cry of the Diasporic writer asking for sources of energy and renewal.

Rushdie has been prolific also in non-fictional writing and he published *Step across this Line*: *Collected Non-fiction 1992-2002* around the time *Fury,* his American novel, appeared. It is an extraordinary collection and contains material already familiar to his readers because it is his journalistic exercises of a decade but what is important for us is that it throws out suggestive comments pertinent to Diasporic writing and in particular it is intimately related to Indian American concerns as well. Rushdie is concerned with the uses of memory and he appreciates the celebratory tone of Hannan Al Shaykh's *Beirut Blues* which mourns the past unsentimentally. This is clearly a quality that one can detect in the NRI writing of Meena Alexander or Agha Shahid Ali. Rushdie also expresses his admiration for Arthur Miller who spoke in Rushdie's defense during the dark days of the Fatwa. The importance of intellectual liberty without which there is no literature is a value he shares with Miller. Clearly our NRI writers do have the freedom to invoke their memory and while not all is well with America it still, at its most advanced levels, does value these freedoms. Not that any of the other Indian writers in America have had anything like Rushdie's experience of living at the edge of life but surely a Vikram Chandra can tell stories with abandon partly because of the ambience he enjoys in America. On a different tack Rushdie speaks of writing and how for him it is inseparable from imagining a nation. For him India is his main theme and he remembers her with fondness, exasperation, sadness, and at times in despair. His is no narrow conception of the nation and he remarks with rare perspicacity: "If writing turns repeatedly towards nation, it just as repeatedly turns away." And speaking of someone like Naipaul he writes: "The deliberately uprooted intellectual [Naipaul] views the world as only a free intelligence can, going where the action is and offering reports. The intellectual uprooted against his will (a category that includes, these days, many of the finest Arab writers) rejects the narrow enclosures that have rejected him. There is great loss, and much yearning, in such rootlessness. But there is also gain. The frontierless nation is not a fantasy." From Rushdie's remark I should imagine that our NRI writers can make common cause with Naipaul because they are uprooted not against their own volition but are willing migrants. The Arab angst is something our writers could not possibly have and perhaps that accounts for the ultimately superficial surfaces of their work, a superficiality which is deliberate and willed into existence. Rushdie also comments on the international nature of diasporic writing and suggests that since much of this literature is in English there is inbuilt into the nature of this writing a liberation from a narrow parochialism. Literature, he asserts, has no need of Partitions. For him India is an obsession: "I have left India many times," he says, but not leaving is also true because he has "a dream of glorious return." He goes on to say: "This, perhaps, is what it means to love a country: that its shape is also yours, the shape of the way you think and feel and dream. That you can never really leave." Of Solan, his ancestral place, he remarks, "Even though I've hardly ever been here in my life, and not at all since I was twelve years old, I feel like I'm home." I find Rushdie's journalistic writings having important resonances and I do see them as explaining much of the work being done by our NRI writers, not to speak of the point that they are after all an important context for the study of Salman Rushdie himself. And Rushdie repays study. He seems to have delineated the contours of the proper discourse to study himself and his NRI children and literary grandchildren, for that at least is how one was tempted to see the relationship between Rushdie and the other NRI novelists proudly appearing in *The New Yorker*.

An important diasporic writer who has a relationship with Rushdie is Agha Shahid Ali. A Kashmiri Muslim by origin, Ali lived and died in the U.S. and is a deeply lamented figure because of his premature demise. He has, taking off from Rushdie's culinary metaphor of the *chutnificatio*n of the English language, spoken of the *biryanification* of it to reinforce his sense of a profound bilingualism at work in his poetry. He finds that his poems are informed by the rhythms and cadences of Urdu and these impinge on his English syntax making for an excellent blend of voices. This surely is an important aspect of good diasporic writing. His remarkable poem "Cracked Portraits" is a good example of this mixed or hybrid sensibility at work:

> My grandfather's painted grandfather,
> son of Ali, a strange physician
> in embroidered robes, a white turban,
> the Koran lying open on a table beside him.

The poem begins with this invocation and in unsentimental manner with just a touch of tenderness Ali writes:

> I look for prayers
> in his eyes, for inscriptions
> in Arabic.
> I find his will:
> He's left us plots
> in the family graveyard.

This is the first movement of the poem and the second elaborates on the character of the painting of this Great Grandfather:

> Great-Grandfather? A sahib in breeches.
> He simply disappoints me,
> his hands missing in the drawing-room photo
> but firm as he whipped the horses
> or the servants.

This patriarch was a drunk lover of music and wept at the loss of youth. In the third movement the scene shifts to the album photo of Grandfather, who was handsome but mad:

> In a dim-lit shop he smoked hashish,
> reciting verses of Sufi mystics.
> My father went to bring him home.

Then follows a moving description of the poet's relationship with the old man and his philosophical temper, his conflation of Plato and Napoleon:

> Sitting in the bedroom corner,
> smoking his hookah, he told me
> the Siberian snows
> froze the French bones.
>
> In his cup
> Socrates swirled.

These intimate confessions of family neurosis and madness provide a context to focus on Father who played tennis and scored with women, "brilliance clinging to his shirt." The poet likes father speaking about Lenin but is cold to any references to Gandhi, Father makes. "Silverfish have eaten his boyhood face." The album of course is moth-eaten and covered with cobweb:

> Cobwebs cling
> to the soundless
> words of my ancestors.

Ali then evokes his past with a mixture of sadness and acceptance:

> No one now comes from Kandahar
> dear Ali, to pitch tents by the Jhelum,
> under autumn maples,
> and claim descent from the holy prophet.

Ali surely is one of our most distinguished poets and Indran Amirthanayagam wrote a suitably moving and evocative tribute to his dead expatriate friend, a tribute which I think, dramatized the true meaning of exile and rootedness in spite of the displacement. Amirthanayagam was only pointing to their affinity and this affinity, I think, is all about sincerity and the expression of true feeling. Ali had hoped that behind his verse readers would "sometimes hear the music of Urdu. Of course, all this has to do with an emotional identification on my part with north Indian Muslim culture, which is steeped in Urdu. I, as I have grown older, have felt the need to identify myself as a north Indian Muslim (not in any sectarian sense but in a cultural sense). And I do not feel that this culture is necessarily the province of the Muslims (after all, Firaq Gorakhpuri was a Hindu) and many non-Muslim Indians can consider themselves culturally Muslim." In any case he considers himself among the very few Indian English writers to have this identity though he would not want it to be a straitjacket identity.

Indeed this multiple identity question is an important one for diasporic writers because they share a rich and varied intellectual provenance. A.K. Ramanujan, for example, puts his finger on the truth, so to speak, when he defines the quality of his own poetic practice. He too has been long in the West and he writes in English like many others with the difference that he anticipates the dialogic dimensions of writing which is an article of faith in our postmodern times. He famously asserted:

> English and my disciplines (linguistics, anthropology) give me my 'outer' forms—linguistic, metrical, logical and other such ways of shaping experience; and my first thirty years in India, my frequent visits and fieldtrips, my personal and professional preoccupations with Kannada, Tamil, the classics and folklore give me my substance, my 'inner' forms, images and symbols. They are continuous with each other, and I no longer can tell what comes from where.

Ramanujan speaks to us about tradition and uprootedness, of exile and nostalgia, of love, death, desire and yearning and speaks of these in a language at the same time taut and ironic, but an irony that does not preclude tenderness. His autobiographical poems are shot through with imagistic precision and a mental toughness that reveals his modernity:

> I burned and burned. But one day I turned
> And caught that thought
>
> He has entered into a liaison with an alien:
>
> And I have no reason to know your kind.
> Bred Brahmin among singers of shivering hymns
> I shudder to the bone at hungers that roam the streets
> Beyond the constable's beat. But there she stood
>
> Upon that dusty road on a nightlit April mind
> And gave me a look. Commandments crumbled
> He succumbs to temptation
>
> Her tumbled hair suddenly known
> As silk in my angry hand, I shook a little
> And took her behind the laws of my land

This exploration of lust and seduction is deeply felt and Ramanujan is able to treat it with a degree of coolness and panache. This comes entirely because of his commitment to writing well and to make his poetry a fit vehicle of this diasporic sensibility because there is after all a hint that this seduction did not have the approval of the laws of his culture and that it was happening elsewhere than in his native land.

Elsewhere Ramanujan displays his capability of describing landscape and the objects therein with imagistic precision. I refer to poems like "The Striders" and "The River," one about a New England insect and the other, a haunting exploration of the poet's Tamil roots, the decadence of that culture, the present moment of that tradition and the continuities and the ruptures between the past and the present. If in a poem like "On the Death of a Poem" he can be absolutely economical in his sententiousness—

> Images consult
> One
> another,
>
> a conscience-
> stricken
> jury,
>
> and come
> slowly
> to a sentence.

He can be more expansive in his treatment of the issues of our time like Bosnia. Here his international dimension is seen to good effect and Ramanujan in a witty way teases out the implications of atrocities in different parts of the world. He speaks of "alphabetized cruelties" and catalogues the various modes of death:

> How file away
> the friend just dead of ovarian cancer;
> a young breast—cigarette—burned by a jealous
>
> husband;

This internationalism is a necessary if not sufficient condition of being diasporic and Ramanujan's poetry speaks out of that experience. The same internationalism is visible in a poet like Chitra Divakaruni whose interest in miniature paintings shows a confident internationalism at work. Poems like "The River" and

"Arches" are a testimony to this quality but I may also draw attention to lines like

> When the last call
> of my body has dissolved, the last cry
> of the lake-birds, I will, once more,
> hear the river inside

where I think the poet is able to write her body itself and there is an interiority of perception which is truly remarkable. A similar kind of quality is seen in the following verse:

> Pattern
> of mosaic—Point of roof. Hieroglyph
> of cloud. My arms are white as stone,
> slender as the hope of love.

There is a great evocative power in this writing and I believe it has something to do with the quality of sadness at dislocation and displacement.

For lack of time I shall content myself by merely mentioning Meena Alexander who left Hyderabad in the '70s to make a living in the U.S. Travel and displacement are not new to her because her father's occupation took the family to many parts of the world, notably Africa, and she herself studied in England. This internationalism has had a healthy impact on her writing and *Fault Lines* must surely be one of the most gripping of expatriate evocations of exile, loss, ecstasy, human relationships, family, race, and above all gender concerns. Alexander has managed to weave a beautiful tapestry in this book and her poems and two novels, *Nampally Road* and *Manhattan Music,* underscore the concerns of her memoir.

Finally to return to fiction, Vikram Chandra in *Red Earth and Pouring Rain* (1995), like Rushdie seems to be in the business of representing India in the West and the novel is a parable of India in the sense that it touches on the interminable urge of Indians to tell interminable stories. This is a book about telling stories and Chandra attempts to tell the story of India by doing what is natural to Indians and to the Indian tradition of Puranic narration—of weaving story after story and story within story.

Raja Rao had drawn attention to this quality in his Foreword to *Kanthapura* when he spoke of the eternal grandmother's propensity to tell stories. Abhay, one of the characters in Vikram Chandra's novel happens to have returned to India after a stint in America and so the Indo-American encounter is very much a motif in the novel and gives context and significance to the other stories which are all tied and bound and fused in tight circles, overlapping with one another. The interlocutors include Indian gods like Ganesha, Hanuman, Yama and several others. This medley of stories told by Parashar, the monkey, Sanjay the poet, Sikandar the warrior, and Abhay the diasporic Indian, then, helps us to draw the contours of Indian history through the classical past, through Islamic times, through British rule and on to the present moment of the variety and complexity of India. Chandra tells us stories about India because he is away in America and America spawns and enables stories. And so there is learning and knowledge, desolation, great despair and intense joy in these stories of Abhay at an American university, fornicating his way to the heart of America (Rushdie's sexual innuendo: "Eat Me America" is not inappropriate to describe Abhay's urges) before returning to India. I am not suggesting that Indian diasporic writers cannot replicate this business of story telling in Fiji or Australia or Canada or New Zealand but only that in our present context of discussing multiethnic literature from the United States it seems appropriate to assert that the overwhelming evidence points to a symbiotic relationship between Indian expatriates and America which has resulted in a great efflorescence of writing and that this writing emanating from America is a version of Indian writing in English and that these writers share a double tradition which is both Indian and American. Also the ethnic quality of Indian writing from America is part of the decentering multiculturalism of America and our Indian writers get their significance in America by their mutual participation in the American experience.

No study of American culture in India can now be done without a genuflection in the direction of this multicultural provenance and if we are seeking an Indian relevance for American Studies which is the academic discipline within which MELUS must have its local habitation and name, then it seems to me that a study of the Indian Writers in English located in America in the various contexts I have outlined is clearly a central endeavor for us.

Thank you.

---

* This is the text of the Presidential Address delivered to the MELUS Conference at Chandigarh in April 2003. As such the flavor of speech has been retained and any substantial alterations or changes have not been made.

Political Realities and the Colors of Imagination

JASBIR JAIN

Emeritus Fellow, University of Rajasthan, Jaipur

> America had rendered us invisible and at the same time awfully conspicuous. . . . "We're guests in this country. And good guests don't upset their hosts." (Cao, *Monkey Bridge*)[1]

> Graffiti was painted across the brick wall of a warehouse: *Save America, Kill an Arab.* (Khan, *Trespassing*)[2]

The concept of the ethnic or the 'ethnos' works on a host of assumptions, some of which have been formed by the economic histories of the world and migrations undertaken in search of survival, and some others which have been generated by the encounters between cultures, often violent and aggressive. These histories and encounters often overlap. Ethnicity constitutes itself on the will to differentiate, to know and define the 'self' as an organic entity and the will to assert one's presence in a world which is not the 'same.' Thus the 'self' and the 'other,' 'difference' and 'sameness,' 'separateness' and 'oneness' (an integrated merger) confront each other in opposition and attraction, thereby creating a tension in the relationship. When the ethnic is located in a context of multiplicities rather than that of a mere polarity, it is both a political and a personal gesture aimed alike at visibility and self-preservation.

Multiplicity also implies a geographical relocation (which may have taken place at some point of history), brought about either through compulsion or choice, by trade winds, conquest or enslavement. Populations and communities have relocated and re-formed themselves since time immemorial, relocations often very traumatic when caused by wars, partitions, persecutions and hostility which force decisions which are not willed but entered into through compulsions. These migrations and travels have led to an intermixture of cultures—and yet ethnicity wishes to defy this very sense of intermixture by acquiring a politically visible face. Its present day visibility (and saleability) calls for a deeper probing of the contexts in which it exists and persists.

True, at this point in history, human expectations have changed. International law provides a protective cover, consciousness of human rights has increased and democratic countries recognize multiculturalism as a value. Increased knowledge of human behavior and psychology along with developed technologies all go to support the idea of human equality. Yet power remains a constant factor which characterizes all relationships whether they be between individuals, peoples or nations. The three concepts which the seminar proposes to consider—scene, space, scenario—are also shaped by power.[3]

Each of the three words—scene, space and scenario—calls for a detailed analysis and evokes a whole set of associations. The word 'scene' calls attention to the present—what's the scene now? What's happening? It localizes and attempts a frame. Space in its turn provides several metaphorical images and brings to mind not only the concept of nation space but the relationship between the center and its margins; it evokes the idea of personal space, of extraterritorial flights, of utopias and heterotopias, of closing-in and opening-out, of distinct separateness, ownership and possession. It also calls forth the idea of temporality. Space carries undertones of rights and claims, denials and rejections. The third word in this theme—scenario—draws attention to the possible. It is speculative and includes the idea of a human agency—an active will, whether individual or collective. Scenarios written by some people like us have inspired revolutions and freedom struggles. The word also signifies the power of analysis, of description and of narration. The act of 'writing' becomes a conduit between the political realities and future developments. It is the literary imagination that gives the much-needed push to political reality as it awakens a dead conscience, acts like a mirror and forces self-reflection. The literary act—the act of writing—is not only a discourse; it is often a counter-discourse engaged as it is in a constant dialogue with the enacted reality of politics and the load of history. It constantly seeks to decipher the meaning of the world in which it is located and more often than not it projects a parallel, hitherto unnoticed reality, the recognition of which will subvert the accepted structures.

Multiethnic literature today is markedly different from what it used to be a hundred or even fifty years ago. For one, the field has moved outside the polarities of black and white and has grown to encompass the different hues of the human skin thus transferring the ethnic into the multiethnic and also simultaneously moving out of Eurocentric ethnicities. Another change reflected is the centrifugal nature of this writing in its horizontal movement, in the present, to other homelands, histories and identities (and not necessarily framed by linear history). It has spread out to include other geographical locations. A third factor is the presence of immigrant communities which have moved into second and even third generations, communities which have a sizeable number of U.S. born writers. Moreover, besides the conscious acceptance and publicity of multicultural policies, there is now a recognition of the difference which black culture and writers have made to the concept of American identity and ethnic writing.[4] Black writers have intervened in the formation of the canon; they have asserted their right to be heard, have legitimized protest and turned writing into an ongoing process of questioning, defiance and subversion and, through these, compelled a shifting of positions in the theoretical formations of Anglo-centric writing.

Multi-ethnicity perhaps first found its most profound expression in the theatre of the Sixties when the theatre truly became vibrant with experiments, directors and narratives from East-European and non-western cultures. The induction of these cultural tropes dislocated the master-slave and oppressor-victim equations that had marked the writing of the earlier phases and went on to simultaneously dismantle stereotypes. The sprouting of Off Broadway and Off Off Broadway not only transformed the theatre scene, it also provided visibility and space to artists of color.

I would like to take up an image from a feminist theoretical text. Chandra Talpade Mohanty in her work *Feminism without Borders: Decolonizing Theory, Practising Solidarity,* refers to a fascinating performance by Yance Ford, an African American studio major and a feminist activist, who based her performance called "The Invisible World" on her three plus years at a liberal arts college. Yance, she describes, "built an iron cage that enclosed her snugly, suspended it ten feet off the ground in the lobby of the social sciences building. She shaved her head and—barefoot and without a watch, wearing a sheet that she had cut up—spent five hours in the cage in total silence" (Mohanty 205). Later, the student explained what had led her to give this disturbing performance. It sought to describe a complexity of contradictory emotions: about trauma, survival, refuge, invisibility, the collapsing of temporal structures, escape and self-image (205-6), all together and simultaneously. Ford's cage can signify different things to different people and at different times especially for the immigrant whose identity is subject to change and can fluctuate in accordance with other variables like color, location and group. Identities on the passport also do not promise any stability. Any shift in citizenship and migration policies can destabilize it.

The experience of being invisible is thrust upon one through the 'eye of power.' My reference here is to Foucault. In a conversation Michel Foucault had with Jean-Pierre Barou and Michelle Perrot, referring to his own *Discipline and Punish* and Jeremy Bentham's *Panoptican,* he elaborated upon the history of controlled surveillance, where placement is defined and transparency ensures a loss of privacy. (Ironically what is most visible is rendered invisible). Foucault observes: "There is no need for arms, physical violence, material constraints. Just a gaze. An inspecting gaze." (Foucault 155). Power is far more complicated than a set of laws. It works through a variety of ways, especially when it works through interiorization of cultural complexes.

Writings from ethnic communities with their origins scattered all over the world take up issues of racism, economic disparity, social discrimination (and segregation); they also take up the difference in cultural responses of different generations and the loosening hold of cultural practices. These writings are both about the American dream and the disillusionment with it. No longer confessional or the voices of the oppressed, they are engaged in the formation of an 'evolving ethnicity.' Allow me to explain it. Ethnicity cannot and should not be treated as a 'fixed,' inherited culture or identity. It evolves, grows and is subject to internal changes irrespective of the outer pressures or alien environment. In this it simply follows a natural law. Ethnic traditions are living and growing ones, they change in response to socio-historical realities and are not entirely produced by their dislocation and replacement within foreign surroundings. Their hardening in terms of ghettoization or in terms of sacrosanct 'frozen' traditions is unnatural.

In a story titled "Two Lives," Shirley Geok-lin Lim writes about the two parallel lives an immigrant begins to live. It is not a schizophrenic existence, but a conscious act of living between the past and the present. Twelve thousand miles away from her home, the unnamed Chinese woman walks through the American city for hours on end. Her memory of her home is like a great mourning, a death of the living. Finally, she forgets what it feels like not to be a stranger and yet the past has its claims on her. She continues to send money to her half-brothers and sisters as a gesture of debt she owes her dead father. She feels that the 'self is paltry, phantasmagoric; it leaks and slips away. It is the family, parents, siblings, cousins that signify the meaning of self and beyond the family, the extended community' (Lim 56).[5] The past retains a ghostly presence. Somewhere along the line there has to be a break with tradition either willed or involuntary. There have to be silences to facilitate a new birth. Another writer, Lan Cao, a Vietnamese, describes the lives of the refugees in her novel *Monkey Bridge*, where the total displacement accompanied by loss of documents of identification renders them nameless and vulnerable, free either to create new histories and identities and free to lose earlier ones.

Histories of communities and nations interrupt the narrative of belonging. The slave and the worker are not seen as part of the recorded history which is seen as the achievement of the white man. In the 1860s when the rail tracks were laid, the Chinese labor was instrumental in laying them at a record pace but written records do not mention even a single Chinese name. This is another version of being invisible. 'They,' the ones in control 'don't want our names in their history books' (Chin 382). Different perceptions of history may tell different tales. There may be histories of hatred, persecution and brutality. Memory and history work in conjunction to preserve the 'ethnic' self, even as the young move away to reinvent their identities. They move away from Buddhist funerals and lunar calendars (see Chang, "The Eve of the Spirit Festival[6]), and move towards the idea of independence and freedom.

Another question which multiethnic literatures raise is a comment on the category of freedom and independence and what it specifies to the immigrant—the freedom to change, to walk out of the ethnic structures, a freedom which even when executed willingly subtracts from the individual's strength. Eva Hoffman in *Lost in Translation* refers to an observation by Adorno. The loss of alienation amounts to a loss of the soul. 'The Soul can shrivel from an excess of critical distance and lead to an arid internal exile' (Hoffman 209). Thus the perpetual problem remains—how much of transformation is necessary for the act of survival to support creativity beyond which it becomes self-destructive.

Political cultures have a tendency to move in a linear direction: economic security, survival amidst competition—a truly Darwinian reality, the passing on of the American dream to hordes of immigrants, motivating them to adopt slave behavior (rendering them into docile bodies), and the continuity of racist practices. As contrasted with this the colors of imagination are varied, they reflect sharing as well as conflict, anguish as well as ecstasy, a sense of discovery as well as being mowed down. These colors are yellow, pale brown, brown and black. Somewhere the search goes on for lost origins. This movement is not linear, not necessarily forward going but oscillates between the past and the present, the dream and the nightmare.

Recent sociological researches reveal that racism is still very much alive.[7] White privilege is taken for granted—it is considered morally neutral, normative and average. The whites have no problems in the exercise of their choices. As Peggy McIntosh has observed in her study "White Privilege/Male Privilege," the whites are free to choose neighborhoods, are easily accepted and find their presence confirmed by the presence of other people like them both in life and textbooks. They escape the responsibility of being treated as representative figures or being trapped within stereotypes. The power which they hold is unearned power (their "ethnic" identity has crossed the banks to become the "norm"). White America discriminate against the US born blacks in a very subtle way preferring immigrant blacks for purposes of employment primarily because the latter have a non-questioning attitude and are eager to make good, work overtime and accept secondary positions.[8]

I refer to this reality in order to draw attention to the context in which contemporary multi-ethnic writing is being done. An important aspect of this writing would be to ask the questions specifically related to the literary act: where does it belong and where does it intervene in the canon formation? Its relationship with the concept of 'Americanism,' with the reader and its place in the academy, its questioning of normative structures and theoretical frameworks.

It would be well nigh impossible to find any clear answers to all these questions but the fact remains that ethnic writing in multicultural societies all over the world compels a reconsideration of established classical approaches. This writing is not a reflection or an imitation of reality, it is a critiquing, it is not concerned with being representative, instead it is often personal. Above all this writing is able to see through the outer layers of reality and reach the contradictions which inhabit mainstream complacency. It, as Toni Morrison has commented, projects "the presence of the unfree within the heart of democratic experiment—the critical absence of democracy, its echo, shadow, and silent force in the activity of some not-Americans" (48). Writing has the ability to perceive and to hit back. Writers are "the most anarchic, most representative, most probing of artists. That ability of writers to imagine what is not the self, to familiarize the strange and mystify the familiar" (15).

The ethnic is a collective self-recognition on part of a community, it is an articulation of the invisible strands which constitute it, it is all about the making of cultures. One of the visible contributions which ethnic writing has made is the disappearing of the hyphen. The hyphenated identity presumed a division, the non-hyphenated is a composite being made of two strands which do not necessarily divide the individual. The labeling, the categorization is both a denial and an affirmation. It denies sameness and affirms presence. The surfacing of postmodernism and post-structuralism have coincided with the acknowledgement of the ethnic presence. Margins cease to define, they decenter; categories do not confine, instead they subvert. The notions of purity and absolutism are finally yielding to the idea of traveling, multiple inheritances. It is difficult to say where this will lead us. There are two possibilities. One is the dangerous trend towards hardening of attitudes, a withdrawal, a hostility—the newfound fundamentalism which lurks behind the new face of modernism. And the other is the possibility of a new humanist discourse emerging out of the new vibrancy of ethnicity.

NOTES

1. Lan Cao (born in Saigon, Vietnam, 1961) arrived in the United States in 1975. *Monkey Bridge* is her first novel (1997). This extract from the novel is from Shirley Geok-lin Lim's anthology *Asian American Literature,* 473.
2. From Urza Aslam Khan's 2003 novel *Trespassing,* 164.
3. This paper was first delivered as a Keynote Address to the MELUS-India International Conference MELUS-India, Jan. 2004 at Hyderabad and the theme of the seminar was "Scene, Space and Scenario: Contexts of Multi-ethnic Literatures in the Americas."
4. For more details refer Toni Morrison 1990 'William E. Massey Sr. lectures in the history of American Civilization' subsequently published as *Playing in the Dark.* There is also an earlier essay "Unspeakable Things Unspoken: The Afro-American Presence in

American Literature" in *Criticism and the Color Line: Desegregating American Literary Studies.* Ed. Henry B. Wonham, 1996. Wonham's Introduction to the volume outlines the literary struggle for Black assertion in the making of the American identity.

5. Lim came to Boston in 1969 and has published both poetry and fiction. Born in Malaysia her work reflects her Chinese-Malaysian heritage. 'Two Lives' is an excerpt from *Among the White Moon Faces* and is included in the anthology of *Asian American Literature* edited by Lim herself.
6. "The Eve of the Spirit Festival" by Lan Samantha Chang, included in *Asian American Literature.* Ed. Shirley Geok-lin Lim.
7. See Rhett Jones's piece (*Providence Journal*, Feb. 17, 2003), 'It's up to whites to end racism." Rhett Jones is professor of Afro-American Studies at Brown University. Jones writes, "Most Americans do not really see us as individuals but as some kind of formless quasi human mass forsaken by God and shackled by all kinds of biologically determined inferiorities."
8. Cendy Rodrigues quotes John Logan, SUNY-Albany sociologist, Philip Kasinitz, another sociologist from City University of New York and Mary C. Waters from Harvard. The assumption behind this discrimination is that American blacks will not work as hard while immigrants tend to have a willingness to leave everything familiar in the hope of a better life.

Works Cited

Cao, Lan. "From Monkey Bridge." *Asian American Literature: An Anthology.* Ed. Shirley Geok-lin Lim.

Chin, Frank. "From Donald Duk." *Asian American Literature: An Anthology.* Ed. Shirley Geok-lin Lim.

Foucault, Michel. *Power / Knowledge. Selected Interviews and Other Writings, 1972-1977.* Ed. Colin Gordon. New York: Pantheon, 1980.

Hoffman, Eva. *Lost in Translation.* 1989. New York: Penguin Books, 1990.

Jones, Rhett. "It's upto whites to end racism." *Providence Journal.* Monday, Feb. 17, 2003.

Khan, Uzma Aslam. *Trespassing.* New Delhi: Penguin, 2003.

Lim, Shirley Geok-lin, "Two Lives" *Asian American Literature: An Anthology*. Ed. Shirley Geok-lin Lim. Lincolnwood, Illinois: NTC Publishing Group. 2000

McIntosh, Peggy. "White Privilege: Unpacking the Invisible Knapsack." *White Privilege and Male Privilege (*1988), A study carried out in the Centre for Research on Women, Wellesley MA.

Mohanty, Chandra Talpade. *Feminism without Borders: Decolonizing Theory, Practising Solidarity*. Durham: Duke U P, 2003.

Morrison, Toni. *Playing in the Dark: Whiteness and Literary Imagination*. 1992. London: Picador, 1993.

Rodriguez, Cendy. "Study shows US Blacks trailing." *The Boston Globe*. Feb. 17, 2003.

Wonham, Henry B. ed. *Criticism and the Color Line: Desegregating American Literary Studies*. Brunswick, New Jersey: Rutgers UP, 1996.

Traveling with Walls: The South Asian Intellectual in the United States

MANJU JAIDKA
Panjab University, Chandigarh

In this paper there are a few points I would like to draw attention to. In particular, I wish to refer to a point made by Salman Rushdie in his recent collection of essays, *Step across This Line* (2002: 407-8), about the wander-lust that compels one to leave the certainty of one's homeland for an indeterminate, uncertain destination. It is a risk that one takes but without taking this risk one cannot hope to gain anything. At some time, someone, somewhere has to take the first step, move out of the security of the Lakshman-rekha, out into the wide world beyond, explore it and come to terms with it. Without taking that awesome first step there would be no widening of horizons, no wanderers, no diaspora—Asian or other.

Among other observations that Rushdie makes in the same essay is that the archetypal figure of today is the migrant, the "man without frontiers." Such a man, he says, "severed from his roots, often transplanted into a new language, always obliged to learn the ways of a new community, is forced to face the great question of change and adaptation; but many migrants . . . retreat from such questions behind the walls of the old culture they have both brought along and left behind" (415). The walls of the old culture they have both brought along and left behind. The point is worth noting because this is something that happens all the time. We leave a certain geographical space behind, but we also carry it with us in our memory. Old ghosts continue to haunt us. Old loves, old memories, old ways of life—all this is part of the baggage that cannot be severed, the samskara that is an inseparable part of our beings.

Moving from one space to another, or deterritorialization, brings with it a number of related experiences—guilt at having left (abandoned rather) the motherland, the soil that nurtured us, the matribhoomi. For our socially and culturally conditioned psyche it amounts to betrayal, making the migrant feel like a traitor, so that he looks back with guilt-tinted vision at the homeland and tries sincerely, even desperately, to keep it alive in his thoughts, in his actions, in his imagination. Simultaneously, there is an "anxiety syndrome" that creates a strange fear in the mind of the exile that civilizations are vanishing, people are dying—an anxiety that makes him search for mooring (thus felt Agha Shahid Ali). This leads to a conscious evocation of the native culture through a backward glance at the time and space left behind. The "homing desire" to go back constructs in memory "imagined communities" (Benedict Anderson 1991), "imaginary homelands," and "Indias of the mind" (Rushdie1991: 10).

Unfortunately, the homeland that the diasporic sensibility reconstructs is not a real one. It is frozen in time, frozen at the moment when the first step was taken out of its boundaries into the outside world. It does not grow, it does not evolve, it is not a living, breathing, pulsating world constantly in a state of flux. So, the cultural baggage that the migrant carries with him—the rituals, the customs, the paraphernalia of day-to-day life—remains stuck like a needle in the groove of an obsolete record, rigid and formidable, not keeping pace with time. As a result, the diasporic Indian community sometimes becomes more traditional than its rooted counterpart in the country of its origin, tradition itself becoming a dead weight that one must, per force, carry like an albatross round the neck. It has not been abandoned yet it is not the same. The migrant, too, is left in a state of suspension, hanging between two spaces, helpless to shake off the past completely, unable to adjust into the present. The walls of old neither get left behind nor do they remain the same in the changed context. They hinder one's assimilation/ acculturation into the new world.

In a changed geographical space, acculturating into a new environment, the effort is to preserve a culture that not only belongs elsewhere, but also becomes anachronistic with the passage of time. It is part of the illusion that one can and will remain unchanged for the very act of crossing a frontier involves a fundamental change in the person, in the widening of perspectives, in the exposure to other systems of belief, other ways of life. A transfiguration takes place so that neither remains the same—not the migrant, not his beliefs, not even the baggage he has traveled with. Despite his desire to cling to his past, he finds himself inescapably sucked into a present that he must now contend with. Crossing the frontiers, "we become the frontiers that we cross" (Rushdie 2002: 410), the artificial, man-made, dividing lines which separate one section of humanity from another, which become bones of contention in the game of international politics, which are invisible from the air but well-defined on the ground, over which power-brokers are forever ready to wage battles of life and death, but which—at the same time—are necessary for maintaining a semblance of discipline, a distinction between man and man. Invariably the subject of controversy ("give me a line and I will give you an argument"—Rushdie 2002: 423), from time to time they trigger off international warfare. Comparable to social and cultural walls, these are barriers in the political sense that demarcate the jurisdiction and control of a given power block.

Coming back to the cultural walls, what happens to the women who cross the frontier? What happens to Sita when she steps across the *Lakshman-rekha*? It has been observed that women adapt more easily to the comparative freedom of the new environment, almost welcoming the lifting of taboos that govern the silent gender of the Indian population. Someone like Bharati Mukherjee, with a sigh of relief, embraces the newfound freedom with exuberance, delighting in the liberation from claustrophobic phallocentric taboos. Meena Alexander analyzes the fault lines that have split her life into half. And second-generation expatriates like Shauna Singh Baldwin and Jhumpa Lahiri, a generation removed from the experience of diaspora, recreate in their writings a surrogate experience of life in India, presumably based on the stories handed down by the older generation. Evident in the works of diasporic writers is the greater flexibility of the female to adapt, to assimilate and acculturate. If the male sensibility looks back with nostalgia at a comfortable patriarchal culture left behind on the Indian shores, the woman is half-glad to leave it behind, particularly the macho, anti-feminist biases.

And yet, the woman writer, too, remains torn between two worlds, living in one but consciously evoking the other. At all times are diasporic writers only too aware of the audience they write for. Theirs is a hybrid sensibility and they write for a hybrid audience as Baldwin (1999: 4) admits, keeping in mind the marketability of their writings. Thus are creative energies manipulated and controlled by the dictates of consumerism. No doubt, it makes the work self-conscious as it consciously caters to the needs of the western reader—the western reader starved for oriental exotica. And so, the walls of the home country, which were never left behind in the first place, are re-erected in the writings, expressing their schizoid selves. Bharati Mukherjee admits making a conscious effort to hang on to her Indiannness (1977: 170). Jhumpa Lahiri is able to see the poignant side of this kind of refusal to let go. The split, the bifurcation, the plural identity, the double vision is evident at all times.

In the changed circumstances, which is the margin and which the center? Who 'belongs' and who intrudes? Each, to the other, is alien, each is suspect. Trapped between two disparate cultures, the uprooted becomes the mysterious 'Other,' neither capable of remaining part of his past nor successfully merging with his present. These are some of the preoccupations of diasporic writing. We encounter them in Asian American cinema, too, in films made by Non Resident Indians. Take for instance, those produced by Nagesh Kukunoor (*Hyderabad Blues*, *Bollywood Calling*), Gurinder Chadha (*Bend it Like Beckham*) and Deepa Mehta (*Bollywood Hollywood*) among others, which speak of the shifting perspectives of relocated individuals. Revathy and Suresh Menon's *Mitr—My Friend* takes a look at the price paid in terms of interpersonal relationships when one set of culturally inscribed values is transposed with another. These films made by Indians, focus on the diasporic experience, on the interaction between the west and the east through the experience of those who have moved from one chronotopic situation to the other. However, by and large, the marginalized sensibilities portrayed in celluloid attract little attention in the west. Occasional forays are made into the mainstream by producers like Manoj Night Shyamalan and Shekhar Kapur who with *The Sixth Sense* and *Elizabeth* have challenged the audience in the west, proving that Indian film producers need not be 'slotted' and placed in a category that the West sees fit for them: they need not be confined to diasporic themes. They, too, can speak of events that transcend the concerns of the diaspora, that cut across borders, whether it is into the metaphysical world (as in Shyamalan's film) or the historical (Kapur's).

I am aware that in the examples I have been referring to belong to a certain section of the diasporic community, which is not the common working class but the intellectual elite. I have also not taken into account the non-intellectual professional, the IT geeks (a la Sameer Bhatia or Vinod Dham) who have made it big in the new world, contributed much to the IT revolution, but have not expressed the diasporic angst (which they may no doubt must have been afflicted with). The subject of my presentation is the thinking and writing segment of the expatriate community that can analyze and express its experience, sharing it with others. They are outsiders in the new world, intellectuals from developing countries who must find their own space in an alien land, begin a dialog with their environment and re-discover their identities. Their narratives tell us that locating a toe-hold in the mainstream, finding a place at the centre, is the biggest challenge before the migrant, a phenomenon that is very much in evidence in academia, too. Take for instance, the third-world intellectual who moves from India to the U.S. What kind of biases does she/he encounter in the new system? Is there any interaction with American counterparts? How do they view the outsider? Do they welcome him/her or do they feel threatened by the intrusion? How does assimilation take place and at what levels? These are some questions that are worth looking into, the answers to which will be illuminating.

The feminist postcolonial intellectual or, the self-defined third-world women who occupy a place within First World feminist academia, are also subjects of critique. Theirs is a shifting position as an academic "subject," simultaneously privileged as elite, even esoteric intellectuals currently teaching in U.S. academia, and marginalized as third-world or hyphenated-American women. Take the examples of women intellectuals like Sara Suleri or Gayatri Spivak, both very third-world yet westernized, very visible, very representative as 'token women' of developing postcolonial countries. Both interrogate the politics of culture from a dual standpoint, taking a marginal perspective (from the "outside") while maintaining the prerogatives of a professional position within the hegemony. On the one hand they arrive in the new world with their baggage of consciously or unconsciously imbibed values—the conventional moorings that defined their existence in the third world, in the tradition-bound "meatless days" of Lahore or the nostalgic growing up in overcrowded Calcutta. Despite the baggage they carry, they need to find a toehold in a new cultural environment. So they adopt a language that enables them to carry on a dialog with the well-entrenched members of academia, an acceptable format that is visible in the critical terminology they adopt—dense, sometimes jargonized to the point of opacity, and with an overt ideological, generally dissident, bias. And why not, for this is the dominant discourse, it is fashionable, it is accepted. The desire to be part of the mainstream overrules all individual traits and casts these new academic settlers in the same mould as the rest of the West. So, from the object 'Other' they come into the Subject position, from 'They,' 'Us.'

Simultaneously, there is a deliberate attempt at a 'translation' of the third-world ethos for the benefit of the western audience, sometimes with startling effect. Take, for example, Spivak's preface to Mahasweta Devi's short story, "Draupadi," (1997) which uses the hegemonic discourse of western academia to describe a narrative about the underprivileged oppressed of the third world. There is no doubt that the story would have remained in limbo had Spivak not translated it into English and presented it with an introduction that is more formidable than the text it introduces. No doubt, the oppressed and the victimized can enter into an intellectual dialog only through the mediating commentary of someone at home in the discourse. The mechanics of the inclusion that Spivak uses are worth taking note of—the significance of her introduction lies in that it is both mediated and the mediator between two cultural spaces. But her intervention also begs a question—where, in this topos, does she position herself? Is she first world or third? Both? Or neither? One gets the impression that the translator-introducer has moved to the other side of the wall, then turned to explain the landmarks in the territory that has been traversed. In her well-known essay, "Can the Subaltern Speak?" Spivak draws attention to the critics' "positionality as investigating subjects" and her central concern is "the possibility that the intellectual is complicit in the persistent constitution of the Other as the Self's shadow" (1995: 25-28). But, for that matter, isn't there a suggestion of complicity in Spivak's own position and is there not an element of contradiction, even condescension, when today's intellectual represents the oppressed? It is hard to shake off the notion that postcolonial intellectuals in the first world are collaborators in the production of social constructions that they ostensibly oppose.

Similarly, Sara Suleri, appears caught in a dichotomy that underscores her role as a mediator. Take a quote from her *Meatless Days*: "When I teach topics in third world literature, much time is lost in trying to explain that the third world is locatable only as a *discourse of convenience*. Trying to find it is like trying to pretend that history or *home* is real and not located precisely where you are sitting." (1991: 19-20, italics mine) Evident here are her main preoccupations which centre around issues like history and home, the viability of the former and the (un)locatability of the latter. Also clearly implicit is a candid admission that ultimately all scholarship is a "discourse of convenience," a mode of communication, a dialog between thinking segments of intellectuals on the unstable relationship between the so-called first world and the rest. Moreover, it is all too clear that intellectual orientation is controlled, not simply by larger issues like ethnic considerations or center-periphery hierarchies, but, more immediately and on a lesser scale, like professional advancement and institutional affiliations.

What critics and scholars from the third world need to tackle is (a) the problem of location—where do they belong, what is their positioning, and (b) how to negotiate with the western Other, and (c) how to deal with the walls they carry with them. The first teeters on the brink of uncertainty; the second is an uncertain, tenuous transaction, and the third is effected only through a compromise. What is never in doubt is their theoretical orientation—which remains undoubtedly western. In their mediating role, they use the hegemonic discourse to 'interpret' so to speak, the third world for the western consumer, an attitude that is very obvious in the introduction to Spivak's "Draupadi" which actually makes a reference to a "first world scholar," the Senanayak who hunts down the female victim. By extension, the victim, Draupadi, later raped and abandoned, is the third-world woman. Which gives rise to an interesting question—Is Spivak trying to tell us that the same game of victim and oppressor is being played out in academic circles, too, between the third-world woman academic and her first-world (male) counterparts? Debate on this matter would be endless.

Other issues come to mind. Why, for instance, are third world scholars generally associated with Asian Studies Departments and not with others—American Studies, for instance? Even in the English Departments in the U.S. their presence is negligible. Why are they most acceptable teaching Postcolonial Studies and not English or European or American Studies? And why are Indian scholars visiting the U.S. generally asked to lecture on some "Indian" subject—some topic relating to Indian society, art, literature or culture—rather than a west-oriented subject? Trinh T. Minh-ha describes what may be the typical response of a western audience to a speaker from the third world: "We did not come to hear a Third World member speak about the First (?) World. We came to listen to that voice of difference likely to bring us what we can't have and to divert us from the monotony of sameness." The western audience considers itself qualified to judge who is 'authentic' and a visitor from the third world is expected to "paint her/himself thick with authenticity." Thus is "authenticity" packaged and marketed (Minh-ha, "Writing Postcoloniality and Feminism" Ashcroft: 266-67). Chandra Talpade Mohanty, on the other hand, critiques the construction of the "third World woman" as a monolithic in western discourse ("Under Western Eyes: Feminist Scholarship and Colonial Discourses" [17]). The image of the third world woman appears to be "arbitrarily constructed but carries with it the authorizing signature of Western humanist discourse," producing a reductive and homogeneous notion of "Third World Difference" (19) which appropriates and colonizes individual differences, fundamental complexities and conflicts in the lives of these women. There is a process of homogenization and systemization of the oppression of women in the third world. These are subtle, unconscious manifestations of a bias that the scholar from the developing country must cope with, stereotypes that need to be confronted and dispelled in the interest of free and unbiased scholarship. These are walls that have to be brought down so that the view from both sides is not obstructed.

"Something there is that doesn't love a wall, / That wants it down," said Robert Frost once. And yet we walk along the dividing line, keeping the wall between us as we go, each one of us conscious of our positioning, negotiating the best we can. Continuing Frost's poem:

> There where it is we do not need the wall:
> He is all pine and I am apple orchard.
> My apple trees will never get across
> And eat the cones under his pines, I tell him.
> He only says, 'Good fences make good neighbors.'

Works Cited

Anderson, Benedict. *Imagined Communities: Reflections on the Origins and Spread of Nationalism*. London: Verso, 1991.

Baldwin, Shauna Singh. "Talking Head.". Interview with Mini Kapoor. *The Express Magazine*, March 7, 1999.

Minh-ha, Trinh T. "Writing Postcoloniality and Feminism," *The Post-Colonial Studies Reader*, ed. Bill Ashcroft, Gareth Griffins and Helen Tiffin. London and New York: Routledge, 1995.

Mohanty, Chandra Talpade. "Under Western Eyes: Feminist Scholarship and Colonial Discourses." *Feminism without Borders: Decolonizing Theory, Practising Solidarity*. Durham and London: Duke UP, 2003: 17-42.

Mukherjee, Bharati. *Days and Nights in Calcutta*. New York: Doubleday, 1977.

Rushdie, Salman. *Imaginary Homelands: Essays and Criticism 1981-1991*. London: Granta, 1991.

_____. *Step across This Line: Collected Non-Fiction 1992-2002*. London: Jonathan Cape, 2002.

Spivak, Gayatri Chakravarty. "Can the Subaltern Speak?" *The Post-Colonial Studies Reader*.

_____. Translator's Foreword to "Draupadi." *Breast Stories*. Mahasweta Devi. Calcutta: Seagull Books, 1997: 1-18.

Suleri, Sara. *Meatless Days*. Chicago: U of Chicago P, 1991.

The Text as Narrative: Reading Ideology

SUKALPA BHATTACHARJEE
North Eastern Hills University, Shillong

Narratives are expressions and representations of lived experiences even though they may not actually have been lived. Narratives essentially link real life form to art. Likewise, narratives of lived experience and folk narratives with their myriad ethnic or cultural experiences are also an admix of real life and art. Irrespective of how a narrative is formed, be it by an individual or a group of individuals, all narratives have an in-built element or universality at least for the domain for which it is intended and therefore circulation of a narrative is a must for its artistic survival and appreciation. Such narratives, if domain specific and therefore coherent, are likely to constitute a community that identifies itself with the narrative in terms of a remembered tradition, event or shared reasons and values. Such narratives derive their sustenance not because they essentially speak of something that is true or false but because they make their listeners feel a sense of shared meaning. As such, if a narrative tells that we will rise again from the dead, it merely describes, using a familiar metaphor, something that people actually expect to happen. Rather than being a simple case of the narrator and the narrative in question engaged in inventing and imposing metaphors of agreement, what perhaps actually guides and determines the character of the narrative to be told is the traces of lived experiences with all its knowable and unknowable elements. The key issue, in this context, therefore perhaps is to look in detail as to how such narratives create the sense it conveys and who are its target audience. In other words who or what can be trusted to represent the 'real' experiences of the group without the fear of misrepresentation? This brings one to the question of narrative construction of identity which in turn calls for an examination of such constructions of identity and the relation between personal experience and public meanings, subjective choices and objective social locations. The relation between experience and identity is a genuine philosophical or theoretical issue in view of the gap between experiences of social actors or individuals and the theoretical construct that we call their identity.

Ingrained within the narratives, the issue, one presumes, calls for a dialogue between a thinking self and a fixed notion of authentic community. Such dialogues are expected to bring into fore all the implicit and explicit elements that account for the space between the narrative, its teller and the target audience. Such exercises basically centre on/in tracing the moments of presence and absence of the self, the world and others in an interlocution between the text and the context. It may eventually lead one to possibly end up finding a number of breaks and interruptions within what has so far looked like a coherent narrative. Consequently, the stable transmission of a fixed essence gives way to a live criss-crossing of signifiers over a dynamic and wide variety of narratives. Narratives, by virtue of an excess over the comprehension of the tradition, often contain an element of ex-centricity, which implies that they are simultaneously culturally rooted and yet produce a counter cultural domain. While it allows one to speak and not just say what one means, it promotes listening to the unheard, interprets the truth of the world and self in a way that is often unique. A constant shift between being and becoming without a realized essence, a realm of the counter factual therefore automatically goes into it signifying a series of contingent, invented and non-narratable ensemble of experiences.

The text as a narrative, thus provides for the necessary double bind of belonging to a unified narrative of life and at the same time not belonging to what the narrative merely says. It opens up a different space of living that looks for different cultures, communities other than its own and engages one with narratives of others.

Narratives of cultural representations inhabit the epistemic construction of the migrant, gendered or ethnic identity. Narratives centred on the oriental as subjects of colonial or imperial canons of white representation has apparently given rise to a (inter)nationalist discovery of 'noble savages' in the theory and practice of politics of recognition and difference. As such, what seems to be present here is a residue of autonomy carefully vested on such colonial and late modern national subjects, indignant in their own counter hegemonic aspirations and yet struggling to discover a place of speaking by /for themselves. Caught in the exchanges between the local and the global, the centre and the periphery, the citizenship and the cultural membership, the private and the public, the subjects here are experiencing manifold challenges to locate their self-definition and the narratives of self-identity. Characterized by this existential dilemma, the narratives of mixed-blood displaced expatriate and identity here is siege from within in a transition seeking to link late modern cultural and social capital with tradition. A look at the self and the other, therefore, constantly poses a crisis in terms of having a stable definition and hence a stable narrative.

In the light of the above, one needs to look at the narrative construction of a text by authors experiencing such conflictual sensibilities. One could perhaps sum up one's inquiry into the narrative construction of cultural or gendered identity in this way:

a. What is the efficacy of personal and cultural narratives within the current conjuncture?
b. Who/what are the voices subdued and are expressive of the pangs of the past and present? In other words how is voice constituted in a narrative? Who speaks what and how constitutes the ideological element of representation in a text.
c. What acquires significance, being politically correct or sensitive to politics of cultural and social knowledge systems? 'Who sees?' is a fundamental cultural question.
d. How is tradition interpreted and looked at? What is the politics of Self-representation and what are the responses to the Other?

A quick browse through narratological discussions of voice shows Gerard Genette's inquiry into how a voice speaks in order to be distinguished from other competing voices in the text. Seymour Chatman tries to categorize types of narrators in relation to audibility of the voice. Again, the search for a voice has been interpreted as a reader's quest for the origin of the text by narratologists.

One can look at Bapsi Sidhwa's novels as an elaboration of this formulation along with Chitra Banerjee Divakaruni. Both live in America and are women of the Indian sub-continent and yet there is an ambience of the locale, and the essences which they intend to generate to give the reader a feel of place and values—"The stifling heat, the poverty and yet the warmth which exists between the families." Chitra Banerjee's other novels like *The Mistress of Spices, Arranged Marriage*, and particularly *The Unknown Errors of Our Lives* are sensuously evocative and a prose filled with images. Her novels have been described as 'intensely touching tales of lapsed communication, inarticulate love and redemptive memories' and therefore her text as a narrative bridges up not only distinct national identities but finds a place within for the dislocated gender. *The Unknown Errors of Our Lives* is particularly significant as a collection of nine stories. In the first story a widow in California, recently arrived from India, struggles to adapt to a world in which 'neighbours are alien people.' In the title story, a painter looks to ancient myth and the example of her grandmother for help in negotiating and coming to terms with her first real crisis of faith. Covering a canvas from California to Calcutta, the narratives in *The Unknown Errors of Our Lives* depict the external struggle of a narrating self to find a balance between the pull of home and the global ethos of change. In one of the narratives entitled "The Lives of Strangers" a sense of ambiguity of a character called Leela is described as:

> She didn't know when it was that she started thinking about India, which she had never visited. The idea attached itself to the underneath of her mind and grew like a barnacle. In her imagination the country was vast and vague, Talismanic. For some reason she associated it with rain, scavenger crows, the changing of orange

> trams, and the purplish-green of elephant-ears. Were these items from some narrative her parents had told her in her childhood? (Divakaruni 2001: 61)

The question of 'who speaks?' in a narrative invites a further question of whether texts can really be said to 'speak' at all. In the case of Leela here a vague link with her 'imaginary homeland' only produces a disjunctive experience and therefore the metaphors which she uses to describe such an experience is disjointed and distorted in turn. What has been narrated is a partial representation of what the displaced sensibility had sought to narrate and this is because of the unrepresentable in representation itself. This can be elaborated from a situation in another story in the same collection entitled "The Intelligence of Wild Things." Here a sister, who lives in Sacramento goes to visit her brother in Vermont to give the news of the sad demise of their mother in Calcutta. The brother is a totally transformed man compared to what he was before he came to the United States. The sister finds a complete stranger in her brother and the contrast looms large as she recalls her mother's letter to her years back about her brother refusing to come to America in spite of getting admission for higher studies. Finally the mother exploits a sentiment called *abhimaan*, to persuade him. In the letter to her daughter she writes:

> Finally I called him a coward, hiding from the world behind his mother's sari, a fool who lived in a fantasy land. . . . I said he was ungrateful and a burden to me. . . . I could see the abhimaan on his face, like a wound—but it was the only thing I knew that would make him go. (Divakaruni 2001: 42)

The sister ponders on the unrepresentability of the emotion called *abhimaan*, which she tries to define as "that mix of love and anger and hurt which lies at the heart of so many of our Indian tales, and for which there is no equivalent in English" (42).

In the same vein, Bapsi Sidhwa, a second generation migrant, narrates the insipid and gory tales of finding oneself in the midst of othering in *The Pakistani Bride*. Like her other novels *The Crow Eaters and Ice-Candy-Man*, the narrative affects a going back to an imaginary postcolonial tribal context in transition represented in the patriarchal protagonist's desire to go back an idyllic life-world and get his adopted daughter married to a groom from his own community which he had left ages back as if that would symbolize his going back to his community in the mountains and reclaiming his lost identity. This is an ontological ungrounding of the writerly self of Bapsi Sidhwa into a contrasting representation of a tribal/pastoral death and displacement in the narrative and the ethos of unbelonging of the American material life in which she lives. Bapsi Sidhwa's *The Pakistani Bride* reveals to the western reader a way of life that is completely alien. Sidhwa writes with a passion that demolishes the smothering rules of a repressive religion and the violence of patriarchy. The narrative exposes the dramaticality of marriage and an 'innocent eroticism' which is touching but ironical of the naivete the children, Qasim and Afshan bring to the wedding bed. The situation is something like this:

> "Are you my husband?" she asked incredulously. Qasim nodded with woe begone gravity. The girl didn't know whether to laugh or cry. She had been told that her groom was very young, but she had thought that he would be like herself at least fifteen. She began to laugh, while tears of disappointment slid down her cheeks. She laughed uncontrollably and Qasim, strung to the quick, rushed for the door. He threw himself against the bolted door and rattling it savagely, shouted 'Open! Open! I want to get out.' A distant sound of tired chatter crept in through the door. Flushed with anger and embarrassment Qasim sidled to a corner of the room. Sobbing angrily, he at last fell asleep. (Sidhwa 1990: 10)

This is how narratives represent an aesthetic of ideological production by uncovering the hegemonic centres of oppressive systems and values, which cannot be always fought in the form of an open combat. Narratives often serve the function of an offstage resistance which is a 'hidden transcript' (James C. Scott: 1992) of language and subjectivity. This mode of a narrative which have ideological content by way of a collaborative process of interrogation (of patriarchal symbolic order) and contestation is in the process of 'becoming' what is known as 'socially symbolic acts.' A narrative text represents the aesthetics of an ideological production when the symbolic and the imaginary get submerged in uncovering the 'historical fullness' through what Frederic Jameson calls an 'ideological analysis' (Jameson 1981: 20).

Texts of the kind discussed here, which have found a place within the framework of the multicultural and multiethnic literatures of the United States, by performing ideological and symbolic functions contribute to debates about community, justice and freedom. Many works by racial and ethnic minorities develop ethical concepts out of particular contexts and experiences and present them from/for transcultural evaluation and application (Ramon Saldivar: 1990). These texts as narratives can offer ethical problems/solutions to members of other cultural groups in a manner of shared 'relative values' which have universal characteristics. In narratives which describe or share specific experiences of colours or gender, the political predicament is judged on the basis of how far an individual can speak for a group. For example, if no one woman or a woman can know and represent the experiences of all women, on what authority can she speak 'as a woman'? At best, she might be able to speak accurately of her own unique experience of being a woman (in this case a woman of the Indian sub-continent). But then she speaks only as a woman. The issue of authority of experience is intimately tied to the problem of representation. If a woman cannot be trusted to speak for/about "women" then how is it possible to speak at all for/about a woman. On the other hand, in speaking for the other women, a representation then takes an ideological role where, by subsuming the experiences of other/marginalized women into the broader category of "woman" one is engaging in the practice of ideological normalization and exclusion.

In attempting at such narrative representations the authors actually put ideology to work, uncovering coercion of forces that tend to silence a text. A text cannot be 'ethically' read as a narrative without reading ideology as a substance of imagination— real and imaginary. Again ideology must always be necessarily narrative in its structure because it involves a mapping of the 'real.' It also underwrites the stories about what one conceives of as real. The aesthetics of ideological production involves a narrative attempt of the subject to inscribe a place for itself in a collective and historical process, as these authors discussed here have done.

Works Cited

Divakaruni, Chitra Banerjee. *The Unknown Errors of Our Lives*. New York: Anchor Books, 2001.

Jameson, Fredric. *The Political Unconscious: Narrative as a Socially Symbolic Act.* N.Y.: Cornell University Press; London: Methuen, 1981.

Scott James C. *Domination and the Art of Resistance: Hidden Transcripts.* Yale: Yale U P, 1992.

Saldivar, Ramon. *Chicano Narrative: Dialectics of Difference.* Wisconsin: U of Wisconsin P, 1990.

Sidhwa, Bapsi. *The Pakistani Bride.* New Delhi: Penguin India, 1990.

Crossing Borders: In Search of Aesthetics

HIMADRI LAHIRI
University of Burdwan, West Bengal

The phenomenon called diaspora has given rise to intense critical and creative activity. Attempts have been made to formulate the diasporic subject and problematize his or her cultural location(s). Crossing geographical borders necessarily implies cultural displacement and a process of negotiation with other culture(s). Breaking out of the 'local' and locating oneself into the global inpart a 'glocal,' hybrid identity which contains traces of both. Homi Bhabha, while discussing Jameson's perception of a new 'international culture' in the 'perplexed passing of modernity into postmodernity,' comments on "the anxiety of enjoining the global and the local, the dilemma of projecting an international space on the trace of a decentred, fragmented subject" (216). He feels that "cultural globality is figured in the in-between spaces of double-frames" (216). The interstitial/liminal perspective is projected as a necessary presupposition for meaning production in the diasporic space.

The idea of the diasporic subject as a rootless being gives birth to the image of a traveller. Amitava Kumar, himself a diasporic writer located in a metropolitan university, asserts, "The writers in the diaspora are a product of movement. They embody travel" (*Away* xviii). Meena Alexander, a noted poet, novelist and critic with multiple diasporic points, similarly contends that identity of a diasporic subject is like a train heading for destination and stopping at stations on its way. She herself does not have any idea about her own destination.[1] Viewed from this perspective, each stoppage is a point for fresh departure. The identity of such a person is in a continuous process of being formed and re-formed. The fixity of belonging, especially to the originary culture/country, is cancelled in the process. The narrator in Salman Rushdie's novel *Shame* terms this movement as one beyond the "force of gravity." Immigrants, he says, conquer this force of gravity and fly like birds. He sometimes thinks of 'roots' as 'conservative myth' designed to keep people in fixed places. But he also admits that it is very difficult for an immigrant to shake himself or herself free of 'roots' as he or she has to deal with a "past that refuses to be suppressed, that is daily doing its battle with the present" (85).

The diasporic condition is thus highly volatile, and is an attractive and challenging field of study for theorization. Ever since the rise of the marginals, the process of decentering as a discursive and creative practice has gained ground, and the intellectuals from the erstwhile colonies, now located in metropolitan universities, have taken up the challenge to formulate the diasporic condition of which they are a part. Many of the scholars, hard-pressed for a foothold in the highly competitive academic market, find in the diasporic literary and critical practices a greener pasture for research and a scope for projecting the world they know best. The state encouragement of the practice of multiculturalism in Western academic institutions—both in the determination of syllabi and choice of faculty members—and the spread of inter-disciplinary studies have of course created a congenial atmosphere for pursuit and theorization of such studies. The publications by writers of postcolonial background coming out of the West have immense dissemination value since the West, as Jasbir Jain asserts, "continues to be the place for exhibition, recognition and judgment" (15). In his radical study entitled *In Theory: Classes, Nations, Literatures* (1994), Aijaz Ahmad also mentions the scholars' tenure-oriented struggle and that of the tenured professors to keep their position intact. The crowding of the faculty by such scholar-professors, who frequent the circuit of conferences and university presses, develop stakes in 'over-valorizing' third world texts. As a result the "East, reborn and greatly expanded now as a 'Third World,' seems to have become, yet again, a career—even for the Oriental this time, and within the Occident too" (Ahmad 94). The new interest in the East is thus linked up with diasporic efforts, and is seen as a well-organized enterprise to prop up an alternative discourse on the formerly non-canonical body of texts.

With this background in mind, we can better understand the academic activism and proliferation of theories in the West. This is not to deny the legitimacy of the new literary and critical ventures in the diaspora. The material, emotional and intellectual conditions in the diaspora have indeed broken new grounds of literary and critical activities which must be given due importance. Jhumpa Lahiri's stories in *Interpreter of Maladies* (1998), for instance, evoked the conditions of immigrants and expatriates in a subtle and suggestive way, in a tone of understatement. But we at the same time need to be aware of the loud, dross, unrealistic elements in the new outputs. The self-conscious attempt to capture the break-neck speed of violent lives represented in Bharati Mukherjee's *Leave It to Me* or *Jasmine* leaves a serious reader exasperated for their unrealistic portrayals, and one is forced to conclude that attractive but incredible story elements and absurd points of view are crafted into the bodies of the texts with certain target reader-groups in mind.

Coming back to the main thrust of our discussion, we need to interrogate the concept of the diasporic subject as an ever-floating individual. Considering the presence of 'borders' everywhere—national boundaries, requirement of passports and visas, intimidating surveillance mechanism and so on—floating like a log or flying like a bird is not easy. Human beings like to settle in places of their choice. Diasporic people, more particularly their children, are no exceptions. The apparently attractive proposition of floating, scattering individuals, belonging to many places, and unaware of their destination, seem to have been floated for its non-traditional, non-canonical content. Aijaz Ahmad critiques such postmodernist persons having their feet on many soils as having an "excess of belonging" because, in his words, "he or she actually belongs in all of them (i.e. cultures), by virtue of belonging properly in none" (130).

The word 'diaspora' etymologically refers to scattering of people. If we look at the modern scenario we will find that the scattering takes the nature of what Amitav Kumar calls a 'gathering, by which we mean community formation on the basis of common origin or interests. Scattering of the seeds leads to taking roots in the new soil and sprouting plants. This aspect is emphasized by the newly arrived women—wives of Sikh immigrants in the USA—who carry some objects to America in Chitra Banerjee Divakaruni's poem "The Brides come to Yuba City":

> Labelled in our mothers'
> hesitant hands, pickled mango and lime
> packets of seeds—methi, karela, saag—
> to burst from this new soil
> like green stars (77-78)

In the same way transportation of cultures across continents and transplanting of the same in the new soil is the result of diaspora. Out of this scattering a sense of commitment and belonging results. The exile may be a state of mind of diasporic persons, but the physical bodies must find a place to root their interests in and to form alliances and communities. In this respect Sau-ling Cynthia Wong's proposition of two perspectives—diasporic and domestic—in the context of Asian Americans seems relevant. She says:

> A diasporic perspective emphasizes Asian Americans as one element in the global scattering of peoples of Asian origin, in context to what I call a domestic perspective that stresses the status of Asian Americans as an ethnic/racial minority within the national boundaries of the United States. (127)

Although the recent tendency is to consider the current influence of immigrants from 'diasporic perspectives,' the relevance of 'domestic perspective' cannot be ignored. This is proved by the fact that thousands of migrants seek green cards and citizenships and claim the new country as their own. Liminality, an unstable in-between period, necessarily presupposes existence of relatively stable states that flank it on both sides. Claiming the new space indicates a mental condition that aspires for settlement, a state leading to the commitment to the new space.

It is during this gradual process of settling down that the new hybrid subject grows up. Hybridity itself is indicative of the small, intervening, space—interstices—of which Homi Bhabha speaks as producing meaning. The binarism of West and East loses much of its force in the presence of this new active group of people in the in-between space. The ambiguities and schisms inbuilt in the liminal subject find expressions in both the content and style of the diasporic Indian American, and for that matter in diasporic writers from different cultures. Cultural schizophrenia comes to the fore. Only a few characters like Bharati Mukherjee's Jasmine in her novel of the same title can launch a determined but unproblematic and pre-programmed action towards assimilation into or integration to the new culture. Although the work shows revisionary ideology, it fails to foreground material and psychological realism needed to represent such a complex issue. In fact, realistic modes of representation may fail to do justice to it. Rushdie's imagistic, magic realism effectively demonstrates the schisms, and Maxine Hong Kingston's constant shifting of spatio-temporal focus in *The Woman Warrior* or *China Men* points out the plurality and simultaneity of points of views. In fact Kingston even blurs the boundaries of genres in her works, mixing biography, autobiography, history, oral literature, dream sequences all in one narrative.

I shall like to end this article by referring to a work by Amitav Kumar whom I have already mentioned. Kumar's representation of the postcolonial immigrant condition in *Passport Photos* (2000) is complex. He problematizes the in-between condition and adopts a style that corresponds to the fragmentary nature of the immigrant experience. He too, like Kingston, blurs the genre boundary of his work by mixing up personal narratives, critical observations, photographs, border signs, poems and so on. Avoiding a monological mode of representation, he indicates the many-sidedness of the problem. He detests an imposition of any unproblematic narrative style. In the epigraph he quotes from Chandra Talpade Mohanty:

> The very process of constructing a narrative for oneself—of telling a story—imposes a certain linearity and coherence that is never entirely there. But that is the lesson, perhaps, especially for us immigrants and migrants: i.e. that home, community and identity all fall somewhere between the histories and experiences we inherit and the political choices we make through alliances, solidarities and friendships. (qtd. Kumar, v)

Kumar adopts the metaphor of 'passport' to suggest the complexity of the immigrant's identity. He quotes in the book Edward Said's comment that "essentially unconventional, hybrid and fragmentary forms of expression should be used to represent us" (qtd. Kumar 224) and observes that he follows Said in presenting juxtapositions of images and words, and also divided sites and subjects. A passport can at best offer some superficial details about an immigrant who is in fact a site of diverse and divided consciousness and history. The impersonal language and superficial details cannot approach the multilayered personal history. The interstitial/liminal perspective is projected as a necessary graph, Name, Place of Birth, Profession, Nationality, Sex, Identifying Marks and so on, and then goes on to delve into a complicated history and experience, the details of which I am not going into for lack of space here. Only this much can be said that he plays on the 'rich ambiguities' of a personal or cultural history which 'resists a plain reply.'

Kumar, like Bhabha and others, believes that in the 'entire narrative of tussle in between' (227), in the 'vast border' that lies between binaries is the 'real life' of the diasporics which gestures towards a third space of possibility' (228). He believes that in the diasporic culture "there breathe possibilities that resist national wills and narrowly nationalist identities. Differences collapse, sometimes out of ignorance, sometimes because of reconfigured conditions, as political choices, or as more mysterious shifts: the white patron in the restaurant doesn't know how to tell a Bangladeshi from an Indian, a Nepali queer activist joins a group of South Asian gay and lesbians, Indians and Pakistanis live and make music together" (229). Here we catch the optimistic tone of an activist who envisages an alliance of the marginals on the broad border in the diasporic space. The scattering of people unmistakably shows the signs of a gathering, a formation of community that can struggle to claim the new space—a struggle for belonging.

NOTE

1. This was stated by Alexander on 15 December, 2002 in her keynote address at a seminar on "Multicultural America" which was organized by the Department of English and Modern European Languages, Visva-Bharati, Santiniketan.

Works Cited

Ahmad, Aijaz. *In Theory: Classes, Nations, Literatures*. Delhi: Oxford UP, 1992.

Banerjee Divakarani, Chitra. "The Brides Come to Yuba City." *The Open Boat: Poems from Asian America*. Ed. Garrett Hongo. New York: Doubleday, 1993.

Bhabha, Homi K. *The Location of Culture*. London and New York: Routledge, 1994.

Jain, Jasbir ed. *Writers of Indian Diaspora: Theory and Practice*. Jaipur and New Delhi: Rawat, 1998.

Kumar, Amitava. *Away: The Indian Writer as an Expatriate*. New Delhi: Penguin, 2003.

——. *Passport Photos*. New Delhi: Penguin, 2000.

Rushdie, Salman. *Shame*. Calcutta: Rupa, 1983.

Wong, Sau-ling Cynthia. "Denationalization Reconsidered: Asian American Cultural Criticism at a Theoretical Crossroads." *Postcolonial Theory and the United States: Race, Ethnicity and Literature*. Ed. Amritjit Singh and Peter Schmidt. Jackson: UP of Mississippi, 2000.

Racist Stereotyping and Contemporary Chinese American Literature

GULSHAN RAI KATARIA
Punjabi University, Patiala

Chinese-Americans since the 1970s have started responding to the racist stereotyping of their community in a way unknown before. Emboldened by the success of Black Civil Rights Movement, which culminated in 1965 guaranteeing constitutional rights to blacks, the ethnics of color especially the Chinese Americans have since decided not to take the racist hostility lying down as their forefathers did. Frank Chin led the way with *Aiiieeee* and then followed it up with the *Big Aiiieeee*. He has been ably supported by several others (like Chan, Inada and Wong) and has hit back in a strident style at all those who thought that they could get away by hitting out at the ABCs or the American-born-Chinese.

Historically speaking the Chinese arrived from the most impoverished South-western Kwagtung area beginning the middle of the 19th century lured by the news of Gold Mountain in California. They were able-bodied farmers from across the Pacific who believed the stories of the sailors and came in hordes leaving their women-folk behind with a single-minded purpose: haul in the maximum of the yellow metal and return home to their families. But their arrival proved the Mountain of Gold to be a hoax. They had nothing to live upon, nothing to eat, and nothing to hope from where they landed. In order to eke out enough to be able to survive and to return home they took up jobs and settled for meagre wages. In doing this, they cut into the menial jobs that the Irish were doing in California and earned their virulent anger leading to 1882 legislation known as the Chinese Exclusion Act, enacted initially for ten years (but repealed only in

1943), asking the existing Chinese to go back, as also put a stop to future Chinese immigration.

What Chinese Americans write today thus stems from the history of racist bigotry and exploitation by the majority community during the years that Chinese Exclusion Act was in force. Their struggle to save themselves, their ethnic identities and heritage was bitter, hard and terrible—fraught with tension, rivalry and humiliation at every step. The grouse of the Chinese Americans against the white Americans has been a perennial source of mistrust and rancor between the two. Chinese American literature reflects it in ample measure. The present paper deals with it briefly.

Before taking up the manifestation of racist discrimination in Chinese-American literature, it would be useful to look at the stereotypes that proliferated and denigrated the Chinese. Sociologists define a stereotype as "a simplified and standardized conception or image invested with special meaning and held in common by members of a group."[1] It can be understood as a convenient tendency of the mind to refuse to recognize the individuality of a person or the complexity of a community. The Chinese also became victims of this stereotyping. Some of the positive ones arose from the fact that all ancient civilizations belonged to the East, the Orient. The Chinese were therefore recognized as wise, sagacious, compassionate as also thrifty, honest and hardworking; clannish, valuing family ties, personal honor and friendship. The negative stereotypes were, however, more devastating in sweep and were strangely contradictory to the positive ones that held the mind of the white Americans. These stereotypes dubbed the Chinese as ignorant, superstitious, unmanly, non-aggressive, inscrutable, mysterious, cunning and untrustworthy.

These stereotypes about the Chinese (and other Orientals) have been fostered and perpetuated over the years through films, television and comics. The films of 1920s and 1930s showed China and Chinatowns in America, as places of mystery and intrigue. The Fu Manchu films of the period were glaring examples of how Asians came to be viewed in such a bad light. Fu

Manchu was a terrifying villain, inhuman in approach and menacing in manners. Whereas Fu Manchu showed Asians as diabolical, inscrutable, villainous and heartless, another character, Charlie Chan, the detective showed them in another light. Chan was shown as a wiser man clever and inscrutable, of unflappable temper, polite and passive in the most provocative of situations. Both Fu Manchu and Charlie Chan, one villainous, the other sweet, showed Asians as one or the other, anything but average human beings. Several films can be cited as instances of this anti-Orient slant. These include *Air Force*, *Across the Pacific, Purple Heat, Little Tokyo, USA, Black Dragon, Behind the Rising Sun, Betrayal from the East*, besides a host of Dragon movies showing ancient black belt fighters destroying single-handedly a whole army of adversaries. Besides the films, the comics have shown Asians as possessing supernatural powers and children have grown up looking at Orientals as exotic creatures capable of superhuman feats.

Another stereotype carefully invented and perpetuated by the white supremacists is by describing Asians as model minorities. This stereotype is not meant so much to praise the Asians as to downgrade the Black ethnics as uncivilized. The media praises the Asians as embodying the highest values of the American Dream: hard work, thrift and success. *Newsweek* was one of the firsts to note the nuances of the label and the politics behind it. The May 18, 1992 edition of *Newsweek* states:

> Asians however rebel against the model minority label as yet another insidious stereotype. It is seen as a subtly racist excuse to not help underprivileged Asians and to hold back even average Asians—on the ground that they already have "natural advantage."[2]

By calling Asians model minorities, the Whites have played off the Asians against the Blacks who resent the success and affluence of the former. Frank Chin, the noted Chinese-American dramatist and ideologue, remarks that as far as the Blacks are concerned the Asians are the "Uncle Toms of non-white people. . . . We're hated by Blacks because the whites love us for being everything blacks are not. Blacks are a problem: badass. Chinese Americans are not: kissass."[3] Philip K. Chiu has summed up the annoyance of Chinese-Americans at being labelled either sub-human or superhuman. He concludes, "It is about time for the media to report on Chinese-Americans the way they are. Some are super-achievers, most are average citizens, and a few are criminals. They are only human—no more and no less."[4]

The Asian Americans, as mentioned above, took their cue from the success of the Black Civil Rights Movement. They began to write stories based on their experiences as immigrants, as Chinese of second or third generation, their life, and business in the U.S.A. The Chinese, who for reasons of convenience had kept out of the way of both whites and blacks, by opening businesses only where they had their concentration and doing jobs both the other races would not be interested in, such as laundry, deli and fast foods, now began to congregate in ramshackle buildings to vent their spleens, as also share their joys and celebrate Chinese festivals. These places in Chinatowns, Japan towns or Little Koreas where they got together as communities, eventually developed into repertory theatres. Some of them have survived despite several vicissitudes and are located at places where the Asian American diaspora has a visible presence. Tisa Chang's *Pan-Asian Repertory Theatre* in Manhattan, New York, Eric Hayashi's *Asian-American Theatre* in San Francisco, and Nobu McCarthy's *East West Players* in Los Angeles are three of them. The purpose of founding the East West Players can be adapted with minor modifications to suit the other Asian theatres as well. It was founded "to preserve and express a language, literature and sound of their own by developing an Asian-American Theatre, that is vital, truthful and alive." Apart from staging plays by, about and with Asian American cast, the *East West*, like the *North West Asian-American Theatre* in Seattle, Washington, extended the abilities of its company by staging productions of the classics of world theatre as well.

Several major Asian American dramatists have had their work produced in one or the other theatres mentioned above. It might be of interest to note that while the actors, directors, stagehands and choreographers are all Asian Americans, the audience aimed at is mixed. A large number of 'others' walk in to get the taste of Asian-American experience in the United States and become aware of their aspirations, frustrations, joys and anxieties. The result is therapeutic for the Asian Americans, achieved through catharsis and is edifying for the "others" through rising awareness about Chinese-Americans.

The Asian Americans, however, are still divided into groups hailing from East Asian origin and South East Asian origin. This paper, however, focuses on the literature of those who are from the Far East i.e. China, Japan, Korea and Vietnam and who, despite barriers of all kinds have managed to form a composite diaspora. The first rumblings of their getting together as a unified diaspora was heard when they decided not to take the racist insults silently. The white producers who probably believed that even Asian actor's roles were best played by the Caucasian provided the occasion. Beginning with Charlie Chan, the Asian roles had been cornered by European actors wearing make-up. However, when *Miss Saigon* was to open on Broadway the Asian American community decided that they had had enough. The silent and model minority jumped the stereotype and took to the streets in New York in protest. Susanne Wah Lee's report in *Theatre Times* (1991) said, "Hundreds of Asians Americans and sympathizers carried placards denouncing the musical as racist and criticizing those attending the premiere."[5] They protested against Caucasian actors wearing "yellow make-up" comprising taped eyelids and sallow complexion in order to appear Eurasian. Not only for Charlie Chan and Fu Manchu, in several other movies as well, a similar make up had allowed the actors to pass for Asian: only Charlie Chan's bumbling sons were played by the real Chinese.

That playing Asian roles in make-up and under big banners on Broadway had been a point of contention with Asians is seen in the fact that the playwrights of the 1990s wrote angry plays on this theme. Philip Kan Gotanda, a Japanese-American wrote *Yankee Dawg You Die (*1990) and David Henry Hwang, a Chinese-American, produced *Face Value* (1993) on Broadway, both showing Asian stereotyping an affront, if it meant to show that Asians lacked either talent or quality to match the white actors. The notion spread by the movies that Asians were good only for certain roles showing swift action as blackbelt fighters, engaged as one man army, or else as effeminate slaves or Gungadins, or shy geisha girls or coy danseuses performing tea ceremony, were accepting the stereotype in toto and not understanding the reality of Asian Americans as a whole.

Another stereotype about the Asian Americans is that of the "high tech coolies," people fit for technical jobs of developing software, but even the best among them as unfit for positions requiring independent decision-making and management as CEO of multinational companies. In the early Nineties Asian whiz kids, better or equally qualified and capable of delivering results in corporations, were frustrated because of the "glass-ceiling" beyond which they could not aspire or reach, because they were not white. This stereotype has been attacked and subverted in the recent years with the sharp rise in the number of Asian CEOs in multinational companies.

David Henry Hwang's *M. Butterfly*, the Tony Award Winning drama for the best play of 1988, along with a host of other rewards took up the racist stereotyping issue in a big way and was able to embarrass the Whites in the way it hurt most. The play is based on a real story in *The New York Times* about a French diplomat Bernard Bouriscot who had lived with his "girl friend" for twenty years in China. It turned out however that the flame of his heart was not only not a Chinese actress but also a spy and male. The highly embarrassed diplomat was quoted as saying that he had never seen his girl friend naked because, "I thought she was very modest. I thought it was a Chinese custom." In the dramatized version Rene Gallimard, the French diplomat, represents how the West is a prisoner of its stereotypes about Asian women as bowing, blushing flowers, as demure and submissive dolls. Hwang in the "Afterword" to the play rightly remarks, "I, therefore, concluded that the diplomat must have fallen in love, not with a person, but with a fantasy stereotype."[6] The play shows that oriental women have always been treated by the Caucasian men as exotic creatures, dumb and docile, obedient and domesticated, trained for the pleasure of men. Through Song Liling, the Chinese male spy masquerading as a female, David Hwang has hit back. He admits that, "*M. Butterfly* has sometimes been regarded as an anti-American play, a diatribe against the stereotyping of the East by the West, of women by men. Quite to the contrary, I consider it a plea to all sides to cut through our respective layers of cultural and sexual misperception, to deal with one another truthfully for our mutual good from the common and equal ground we share as human beings."[7] That the play was a grand success on Broadway shows how the American audience in general appreciated the basic point the play was making, that how fantasy can become a man's mistress, can blind him to the reality of life around. The play has been acknowledged as a work of unrivalled brilliance, illuminating the conflict between men and women, the differences between East and West, racial stereotypes—and the shadows we cast around on most cherished illusions.

David Henry Hwang's other plays take up several other themes such as the Chinese immigrating in search of the mountain of gold in California. Steve in *FOB* says that the white ghosts (all non-Chinese are nicknamed ghosts by the Chinese Americans) promised them all comforts in America, but all these turned into hoaxes. Steve recalls, "One white ghost told how the streets are paved with diamonds, how the land is so rich that pieces of gold lie on the road, and the worker devils consider them too insignificant even to bend down for. They told of a land where there were no storms, no snow, but sunshine and warmth all year around. . . . A land of gold, a mountain of wealth, a land in which a man can make his fortune and grow without wrinkles into an old age."[8] White agents got passengers for the travel companies and cheap labor for rail construction. The lure of easy gold set the Chinese on to find them new fortunes. But America on arrival presented a dismal depressing picture. They found the native white hostile, their dreams shattered and instead of a mountain of gold all they found was a mountain of drudgery, to earn to be able to pay the way back home. Many perished in this struggle but those who survived lived a life of misery and ridicule. In *Dance and the Railroad*, Ma says, "They walk [in America] with their eyes down, trying to find extra grains of rice on the ground." The rampant discrimination, longer working hours for Chinese in comparison to the white, and exploitation, humiliation at all steps make them think of the ancient Chinese warrior Gwan Gung who fought against adversities and emerged a winner. The Chinamen seem to be reassured by their ancient warrior hero in this land of plenty, which has reduced them to most despicable objects. It is a land of broken promises, they conclude, where the only way out, is through sticking to each other, standing by their own Chinese values, observing customs and rituals of the homeland and observing family devotions. America is a country they would not like to leave but cannot feel that they belong to it. The dilemma keeps their identity question in a quandary, thanks to the irritating stereotypes about them.

The essential distress and hatred of white Americans is in their genes now. If the Americans have their stereotypes about people of Asian descent, the vice-versa is as true. Sui Sin Far writes in a short story ironically entitled "In the Land of the Free,"[9] how heartless and cruel can the white be. Hom Hing lived with his Chinese wife Lae Choo in San Francisco's Chinatown. When his wife became pregnant he sent her off to China so that the baby was born on the homeland soil. After the birth of her son, she nursed her dying mother and father-in-law and it was only after their death that she set sail to reunite with her husband. The happy husband waited for the ship at the waterfront but soon the child was whisked away by the U.S. authorities for entering the country without valid papers for the baby. When the wife had left for China she did not have the baby and now that she did, the child was an illegal immigrant who was sent off to the missionaries for care. The parents of the child squander all their life's savings in fighting a legal battle for the custody of the child. At the end, the mother gives away all the gold ornaments to the white lawyer only to be taken to the place where the two-year-old was living. The child by now used to the white missionaries refuses to recognize his mother and tells her, as also the father to "Go away, go away."

The stringent laws against the Chinese and the other ethnics are the crux of the story. The story shows that the United States has one set of rules for the white and another for the ethnics. It is a scathing criticism of the heartless white man who refuses to understand and reciprocate emotions. In "Reparation Candy"[10] another short story by Maxine Hong Kingston, the Chinese hatred for the white man is obvious. A white boy from a nearby drugstore carries a blue box of pills to the narrator's family making her mother rage with anger. She feels that now that the white man has sent them the medicines, even though by mistake, the disease was bound to visit her family. She vows, "Revenge. We've got to avenge this wrong on our future, on our health and on our lives. Nobody's going to sicken my children and get away with it." The superstitious mother sends the narrator, who was a child then, to go to the drugstore to get a "reparation candy." The mother explains that since the white man has sent them the curse and tainted her house with sick medicine, he "must remove the curse with sweetness." Compelled, the narrator visits the drugstore and the proprietor, thinking her to be a beggar Chinese girl, hands her out some lollipops, knowing neither what he had done earlier nor the significance of what he did now. Even when the mother hates the white, the thought of having to leave, on being found without papers, makes her prepare the children with the lies they must tell when confronted by the San Francisco police. The mother tells them, "Give a new name every time you get arrested; the ghosts won't recognize you. . . . Ghosts have no memory anyway and poor eyesight. And the Han people won't be pinned down." (Kingston 102)

The love-hate relationship between the majority and the minority community is not anything hidden now. It is the ground reality. The distrust and discrimination is seen as the key factor when the mother teaches the 'child to commit no crime and report no crime' because in both the eventualities they would be compelled to identify themselves. And Chinaman wants to remain faceless and nameless as long as there is a guarantee that he would not be discriminated by racist laws.

Finally, like any other community the Chinese settled in the United States have their internal dissensions too, because there are several categories and denominations of the Chinese. While there are FOBs (Fresh off Boats), the bumbling, gawky Chinese speaking English with an accent and easily recognized by their shuffling gait, there are the Yuppie ABCs (American-Born-Chinese), who have been born to parents long since settled in the United States and used to Christian and decent life style, educated in the best of the American schools and completely cut off from their Chinese roots and mythology. It would not be any exaggeration to state that a slinging match has been going on between several categories but the two have been the most prominent of late. These two schools of thought have been fighting over the hyphen, to be precise. The battle lines are drawn around the Chinese hyphen American.

While one school represented by Jeffrey Paul Chan, Frank Chin, Lawson Fusao Inada and Shawn Wong ridicules the ABCs like Amy Tan, David Henry Hwang, Maxine Hong Kingston because the latter are more American than the Chinese, they feel that they should be otherwise i.e. more Chinese than American. Frank Chin in a frank discussion with me recorded on tape in 1992, called the latter as fakers of Chinese mythology, as white supremacists, as the Gungadins, who were altering the basics of Chinese thought to suit the American white. "They were no longer Chinese, they were Christians and Christians cannot be Chinese."

The Chinese Americans are no longer the quiet, submissive, demure community living quietly in their pocket boroughs they used to be. They are decent civilized people who know their rights as American citizens. They no longer shy away from being aggressive when needed. They have branched out into trades such as engineering, medicine, information technology, and are cornering the best of the grades in schools and universities. The White Americans can no longer stereotype them and the successive governments led either by Democrats or Republicans have never taken them for granted. They have made their presence felt and the sops doled out to them and the emphasis on multiculturalism in the American curriculum is a clear pointer towards the changing times. Also the rise and popularity of the non-canonical literature has certainly added a colorful dimension to the white American literature. Much of it stems from the ethnics, including the Chinese American, writing back in a retaliatory tone, and not accepting the racist slurs as quietly as they were known to be doing earlier. In doing this, the Chinese Americans like the African Americans have challenged the power structure as it obtained visibility in the society at large. Liberation from the stereotypes in future is always a possibility.

Notes and References

1. Qtd. "Stereotypes: Images and Attitudes," *Emerging Voices: Readings in American Experience*, 2nd ed., ed. Janet Madden and Sara M Blake (Fort Worth: Harcourt Brace, 1993) 435.
2. "Asians in the Promised Land," *Newsweek* (May 18, 1992): 22.
3. Fran Chin, "Confessions of a Chinatown Cowboy," qtd. *Newsweek*, 22.
4. Philip K. Chiu, "The Myth of Model Minority," *Emerging Voices*: 459.
5. *Newsweek*, 23.
6. David Henry Hwang, "Afterword," *M, Butterfly* (Harmondsworth: Penguin, 1988) 94.
7. Hwang, 100.
8. David Henry Hwang, *FOB and other Plays* (Harmondsworth: Penguin, 1990) 36.
9. Sui Sin Far, "In the Land of the Free," *Imagining America*, ed. Wesley Brown and Amy Ling (New York: Persea Books, 1991) 11.
10. Maxine Hong Kingston, "Reparation Candy," *Emerging Voices*, 98.

"American Circumstances and Chinese Character": Narrative Strategies in Amy Tan's *The Joy Luck Club*

GÖNÜL PULTAR
Bilkent University, Turkey

Introduction

In the early 1970s, Kate Millett exposed in her *Sexual Politics* (1970) how the socialization of women into inferior beings in Western Judeo-Christian society had been replicated in the works of such male authors as D.H. Lawrence, Norman Mailer, and Henry Miller. The women she had in mind were of course white Europeans and Euro-centric Americans. The American ethnic women authors who emerged in the fourth quarter of the twentieth century as a result of the multiculturalist paradigm unveiled in their works of fiction the predicament of the "double negative" in U.S. society. It is not that their female characters are disadvantaged both as women and as members of minority groups, which is what the term conventionally denotes. Their protagonists have to fight on the one hand the patriarchal cultural order, so to speak, of the mainstream white, traditionally tending to subordinate them as women and as "ethnics"; and on the other hand, the patriarchal cultural order of the ethnic community itself. What complicates matters is that the patriarchal cultural order of the ethnic group is perpetuated, or attempted to be perpetuated, by women themselves, as a means of preserving the culture, when the community in question is an immigrant one, at risk of losing it by the act of immigration. Thus, patriarchy as an ideology, while constituting an integral element of the racism deployed by the mainstream white, both male and female, towards the ethnic women, is also incorporated into ethnic identity.

In both instances it serves as a weapon of defense against what they see as a threat to their culture. I argue that this constitutes the major problematics of Amy Tan's *The Joy Luck Club (*1989), an Asian-American work of fiction, and that it leads to cultural conflict between the first-generation immigrant women and their American-born daughters.

In this paper, I examine the narrative strategies Tan employs to underscore the dynamics of patriarchy, racism and cultural conflict she is problematizing. In *The Joy Luck Club,* there are eight protagonists, of which one is dead and seven are living; eight women, four mothers and a daughter of each. One of the mothers has passed away as the novel begins, but the monologues of the seven other protagonists recount her life just the same. The novel contains sixteen stories that are structured as a series of personal narratives by and about these protagonists and that are organized around four sections. Relying basically on various techniques such as Eastern storytelling and Western-type flashbacks, inserting parables, superstition and mysticism, connecting the past and the present, ancient Chinese lore and US modernity—a dialogic pattern if ever there was one—Tan lays bare the "otherness" of the immigrant experience on US soil. The conflicts of the generation gap she recounts—underscored by the recurrent alternation of the voices of the mothers and the daughters—hold the added dimension of cultural conflict, itself emphasized by the narration of past events, going back to grandmothers.

Narrative Strategies

By utilizing narrative styles distinct from the mainstream ones, such as elements of Eastern story-telling and oral narration while ignoring considerations of plot and denouement, and introducing features apparently inimical to the Western rational mind, Tan highlights the specificity of the material she is presenting, as well as the ideology she is denouncing. Moreover, to accentuate the otherness, and stigmatize the politics and discourse of the center, she uses incorrect English, along with discursive and narrative elements of the non-American culture she is contextualizing. In *The Joy Luck Club* China is very much present, not only as the site where four of the eight protagonists were born and lived a major part of their lives, and especially underwent the most crucial experiences in their existences; but also as the site which June/Jing-mei, the American-born protagonist with whose story the novel starts and ends, reaches as the novel closes. China is an alternative anchor to be reckoned with, offering, among others, a philosophy of life and *sensibilité* native Americans are devoid of. Yet, this is basically a premodern China, where, for example, gender oppression is the normative behavior, unquestioned and unquestionable. Thus, the narrative strategies Tan employs allow her to engage in and interrogate the ideologies and cultural politics of both the center and the margin.

Although *The Joy Luck Club* is labeled a "novel," it bears little resemblance to a conventional one. Like Maxine Hong Kingston's *The Woman Warrior* (1976), it incorporates a variety of narrative structures, many from oral traditions, as well as myth and factual material, reminiscence and dream vision. It is all but deliberately turning its back to the Western literary tradition, including as it does much material that is alien to the latter, with the superstitions and mystic beliefs it presents. Concerned with the daily lives of housewives, and young women who have not "made it," at least not yet, *The Joy Luck Club* seems an easy read, a self-exoticised domestic novel. Easterners enjoy reading about familiar scenes such as the making of wonton at home that they would not be encountering in white mainstream fiction; and they find themselves and their circle of ethnic acquaintances in various aspects of the characters, as reflected in a myriad of episodes. As such, *The Joy Luck Club* is hilariously funny at times in passages recounting socio-cultural misunderstandings due to discordant perspectives. Yet it leaves a melancholy note in the reader, deploring as it does between the lines the irreparable losses of ethnicity on American soil.

The plot of *The Joy Luck Club* develops through connections between stories, unfolding vignette by vignette, with one anecdote or reminiscence at a time. These alternating and intertwined narratives of the women who represent the immigrant generation on the one hand and their American-born daughters on the other signpost essential differences between the novel's two groups of women. The novel is essentially episodic, with sections and chapters concentrating on different protagonists whose particular stories each reach a climax, the totality of which builds toward the final conclusion in which the stories come together. As stated above, the episodic structure highlights the conflicts between the mothers and daughters through the contrast displayed in stories following each other yet differing in time, space and attitude to life. Each story stands alone, complete and self-contained, yet each also constitutes an element of the overall narrative. Although the novel has seven speakers, no sense of fragmentation is evident. In fact, the clearest partition is the ordering of the sections that separates one generation from another, mothers from daughters. This structure allows for the distinction that needs to be made between the nature of the mothers' stories and that of the daughters'. Nevertheless, the stories are connected to each other through family ties.

The novel's sixteen narratives, interlocking and interrelated, are divided into four sections with four stories (or chapters) in a section. Each section has a symbolic title and is prefaced with a short fable or narrative proverb or vignette, which serves as a metaphor and/or guiding principle for the story that ensues. Except for Suyuan Woo, the mother who dies before the novel begins, and her daughter June/Jing-mei Woo, whose voice opens two sections and closes two others, each protagonist tells two stories about significant events or turning points in her life. To illustrate, "Feathers from a Thousand Li Away" recounts the mothers' early lives in China and the experiences that brought about their emigration to America. "Twenty-Six Malignant Gates," comprised of the daughters' stories, describes, besides their unease as adults unable to grasp what their mothers want from them, their childhood and the way they suffered emotionally while growing up. The picture that emerges is radically different from the congratulatory tone the real-life mainstream usually adopts, believing that life in America is conducive not only to the pursuit of happiness but to its realization as well. The American Dream has eluded these eight women. "American Translation," which continues the daughters' stories, lets transpire that these may eventually come to accept their immigrant mothers for what they are and perhaps start lending an ear to what they are trying to instill in their daughters—or tried, in the case of the dead mother. All of the stories come together finally in "Queen Mother of the Western Skies" which finds the daughters at last receptive to Chinese culture. Thus, with the two outer sections containing the mothers' stories and the two inner sections the daughters', the reader becomes acquainted on the one hand with significant moments in the four mothers' experiences as immigrants or in their relationships with their daughters, and on the other hand with the daughters' aspirations and frustrations as the American-born offspring of immigrants.

The Joy Luck Club trails the journey the eight women find themselves obliged to take almost daily between the Chinese and white American cultures. This is a distance difficult to traverse, in both directions, all the more so as it is mental, and the boundaries are not delineated in the true sense of the word. The novel starts in San Francisco's Chinatown[1]; yet, moving back and forth between two generations, and two different lands and cultures, it takes the reader across the Pacific Ocean from contemporary mainstream life in San Francisco to the China of the 1920s and 1930s. This is a China which seems more fantastic and dreamlike than real, painted as it is through a discourse that is un-English in substance, as reflected in the multitude of non-Western narrative forms the author utilizes. Yet that is the China and its patriarchal order, linked to a racism that considers the white American as the "other," that will dictate both the lives of the immigrant mothers in the U.S. and their conduct towards their daughters. "For many Chinese Americans," writes E.D. Huntley:

> life in the United States is a series of dualities—two identities, two voices, two cultures, and even two names—that represent an uneasy stance somewhere between the traditional culture of their own or their parents' homeland and the contemporary American culture

in which they have chosen to live or into which they have been born. (73)

Dramatis Personae

Born and raised in China, the mothers in *The Joy Luck Club* come to the U.S. as adults, one because she marries an American, the others in order to run away from the devastation brought about by World War II. Through their recounting of their lives in China is revealed a pre-modern, static society, in which gender oppression is a standard course of action, deriving endorsement and authority from centuries-old customs and beliefs. Gender oppression functions to keep intact a patriarchal hierarchical order in which concepts of morality and respectability are crystallized. Polygamy is allowed and girls may be betrothed when they are still toddlers. Women are responsible for the household while men do nothing in their homes but order them around the house. Men will think nothing of deserting their wives for other women if they so wish it, in total disregard of the women's feelings. Women pretend to accept their fate quietly, all the while acquiring the ability to foresee events in their lives, and resorting to cunning to obtain their wishes. They find comfort in mother-daughter relationships extending to grandmothers that are bonds providing inner security and acting as refuge from harsh masculine behavior.

Grabbing opportunities that rescue them from war-stricken China, each of the four women begin their lives anew in the US. In a sense, this makes them come down in life: "I did servants' tasks. I learned the Western ways" (Tan 286), as one of them, Ying-ying Saint-Clair, puts it.

While the mothers are conscious of not having assimilated properly and troubled by it more than they care to acknowledge, they are just as apprehensive of relinquishing the culture that has formed them, and downright fearful they have failed to pass it onto their daughters. I suggest that in *The Joy Luck Club,* the immigrant generation suffers from what I would like to term the "immigrant syndrome." As immigrant, one has to convince oneself—or else life would be unbearable—that one did well to come to this new land that has turned out to be alien, hostile, and disappointing beyond one's wildest dreams. One sees the past worse than it was and finds the present better than it is.[2] As an immigrant, one has to satisfy oneself that the conditions prevailing in the land of emigration had been intolerable and that one was forced to escape. Once in the land of immigration, the compromise, or the concession, that one's superego, formed in the land of emigration, is ready to accept is for one's children born and raised in the land of immigration to acquire the "character" of the land of emigration while enjoying the benefits, the "circumstances" of the land of immigration. In the novel, this is a land—the U.S.—that is industrially more developed than the land of emigration, China; thus the circumstances appear to be inviting.

That is the solution that the four Chinese immigrant women in *The Joy Luck Club* think they have found. However, it does not work quite that way. Their own lack of cultural adaptation prevents them from providing for their daughters the conditions propitious to such a compromise, were it possible to turn it into reality. The enculturation the immigrant women underwent in China proves indelible. Moreover, the four women are unable to forget their past, their "husbands of youth," as Charles Chesnutt would put it, and unable to fit, to find anything congenial to themselves in mainstream U.S., seeing moreover all their hopes shattered by offspring who are not up to standard according to their criteria.

As in all immigrant fiction, memory[3] thus gains significance in *The Joy Luck Club*, as it shapes the past, real or imagined, and drives mothers to persist in retaining their past culture, a patriarchal one if ever there is one, and impose it upon their daughters. The latter, while presented at first as fully integrated into the U.S. mainstream and repudiating all "ethnic" elements in their lives, will over time start searching for a balance between their Chinese heritage and American lifestyle. Pressurized by their mothers to "make it," they have rebelled and successfully failed—yet they come to realize over time that by thus failing, they have failed by mainstream American standards as well. The racism of the Euro-Americans is there as a backdrop that colors their lives, exerting an influence on these American-born daughters they refuse to acknowledge.

And to the end, to their mothers' infinite chagrin, the daughters remain impermeable to Chinese *sensibilité*. This is complicated by the presence in the daughters' lives of white Caucasian men pulling them into nuclear-family-type relationships colored by capitalism and patriarchy as well as racism, merged and enmeshed as one, that further separates the mothers and daughters. The generation gap is amplified by the cultural conflict, and the negative synergy thus generated affects the lives of all the protagonists. It ultimately prevents the daughters from bonding with their mothers or among themselves, as their own mothers did. As a result, while the four mothers have been bonding among themselves in such a natural way in the Joy Luck Club that it has been taken for granted all along, the four daughters, despising Chinese mores and traditions, sometimes to the extent of being ashamed of their origins, are unable to bond either among themselves or with their own mothers.

The four mothers have all fled China in the 1940s because of the war there, and settled in San Francisco where they have remade their lives. However, although "Americanized" on paper, at least become U.S. citizens, they are still more Chinese than American. Each mother has a past that haunts her, a traumatic story she believes was pivotal in her migration from China, "unspeakable tragedies they had left behind in China and hopes they couldn't begin to express in their fragile English," as one daughter, Jing-mei, puts it (Tan 6). Consciously or not, the mothers all more or less thank God they are alive, as the alternative would be lying in some grave in a Chinese cemetery as a war casualty. They thus try to forget the imposition of Christianity on them once on U.S. soil by American missionary ladies who unscrupulously exploited their neediness, and the imperceptible yet all the more incisive racism they were subjected to throughout their lives in the U.S., due to the way they talked and dressed—not any less germane after all than the Amish manner of dressing that is today observed to be such a characteristic element of American folk lore. The racism, although germinating from white behavior and ostracism, is illustrated in the novel most penetratingly by the attitude of the daughters, ashamed of their mothers.

Most importantly, the mothers all feel declassé in the lives they are leading in the U.S., but this is a matter they are unable to verbalize since all the native Americans around them, including their own daughters, have "closed American-born minds," as the self-critical Jing-mei puts it (Tan 31). The Americans the mothers are able to frequent lack their savoir-vivre, and so prove incapable of understanding what is at stake, although Jing-mei, for one, senses that in Kweilin people had more "delicacy" (Tan 21).

"Doggedly clinging to their memories of life in China even as they adapt to American culture," writes Huntley, the mothers "deliberately remain suspended between two worlds and two cultures, embracing—as they believe—the best of each world and creating a new way of life that they hope to pass on as their legacy to their children" (52). Lindo Jong best articulates what all the mothers feel as she remembers sadly that she once dreamt of giving her children the best of their two heritages: "I wanted my children to have the best combination: American circumstances and Chinese character," adding, "How could I know these two things do not mix?" (Tan 289). Blissful "hybridity" exists only in Homi Bhabha's essays.

As they grow older, the mothers start thinking that they have raised completely "Westernized" children, and feel that the culture of their ancestors has proved to be powerless against the domination of the New World culture. In a way, while the mothers have emotionally still not left China, the daughters consider China as a foreign country they have never seen, and think of it as a "shadowy setting of their mothers' stories, an intangible geography for narratives that have—in their telling—taken the aura of dark fairy tales" (Huntley 54). However, that is not exactly so, and as the novel ends, the reader is left with the impression that the daughters have started re-orientating themselves towards the

Chinese culture, or at least have accepted it as part of their heritage.

As Suyuan's death has created an opening at the mah jong table, the surviving three mothers invite Suyuan's daughter June-Jing-mei to join the Joy Luck Club. This is the subterfuge that allows a second-generation member to integrate the older group, a development that launches the rapprochement that takes place as the novel ends. Jing-mei thus finds herself taking part in a ritualized social function that is perhaps the last bastion of Chineseness of the mothers, to replace her mother, but also as a representative of the American-born daughters. Her introduction into the Club, with which the novel starts, paves the way for the entry of the other daughters into the novel.

The fact is that throughout the Club's long existence, the American-born daughters have by choice remained peripheral to the activity. Although they attended meetings with their parents, and savored their mothers' Chinese dishes, they were in tacit agreement in criticizing their mothers for clinging to their Chineseness. The daughters especially blamed their mothers for their attempt to retain a Chinese decorum totally out of place in the lives retailored in the US. A good example is the mothers' wearing traditional elegant Chinese clothes that are, the daughters feel, unfit for everyday life in Chinatown and look too foreign for mainstream America: "dressed up in funny Chinese dresses with stiff stand-up collars and blooming branches of embroidered silk sewn over their breasts. These clothes were too fancy for real Chinese people . . . and too strange for American parties." (Tan 16)

In spite of their Asian features, the daughters are by temperament more American than Chinese. Consciously and deliberately cultivating American ways and turning their back on Chinese mores, the daughters have tried to fashion for themselves an unproblematic identity. Such an identity leaves out altogether any association with aging immigrant women, as they see their mothers, who have been unable to master standard English and are still speaking their native Chinese at home. "The daughters yearn for an Americanization that they can neither define nor describe," writes Huntley, adding that "More than anything else, they are unhappy and unfulfilled; for some reason, they often feel inferior to their mothers and unworthy of the maternal ambitions that have defined and in some cases scarred their childhood and adolescent years" (52-53). The American circumstances may be there for anyone to see and experience, but the Chinese character has eluded the daughters. Yet that is not their only plight.

Racism, Patriarchy and Cultural Conflict

Of the four mothers, only one, Ying-ying, is married to a white Caucasian. It is ironical that of the four, it should be she, the woman coming from the most affluent background, who is settled with a man who so readily belies the putative superiority of the whites. While courting her in China,

> He bought me cheap gifts: a glass figurine, a prickly brooch of cut glass, a silver-colored cigarette lighter. Saint acted as if these gifts were nothing, as if he were a rich man treating a poor country girl to things we had never seen in China.
>
> But I saw his look as he watched me open the boxes. Anxious and eager to please. He did not know that such things were nothing to me, that I was raised with riches he could not even imagine.
>
> I always accepted these gifts graciously, always protesting just enough, not too little, not too much. I did not encourage him. . . . I put these worthless trinkets carefully into a box. . . . I knew that some day he would ask to see them again. (Tan 284-85)

A cigarette lighter that is merely "silver-colored" to someone who as a child thought of nothing of playing with jade in the mud with her siblings! St-Clair is no "ugly American" but his behavior is normative of many "innocents abroad," compatriots of his who, when traveling outside of the U.S. and confronted with a culture much more sophisticated than theirs, are unable to become cognizant of the fact. The patrician streak in Ying-ying cannot be obliterated in her as she moves to the U.S. as St-Clair's bride: "Saint took me to America, where I lived in houses smaller than the one in the country. . . . I did servants' tasks" (Tan 286).

That there is no mention of her relationship with his family or with other Caucasian whites she would inevitably be encountering through him is a major defect of the novel. The overall impression is that St-Clair was not only smitten by the attractive Oriental woman Ying-ying, but needed her to enliven a banal existence. Whether his utter lack of awareness of her socio-economic background is due merely to foolishness and the modesty of his own background leading to his ignorance of such social strata, or whether a whiff of racism, as well as a semblance of patriarchal attitude can be detected in his behavior is to be debated. This is a behavior that seems tacitly to assume the inherent superiority of the Americans vis-à-vis the Chinese and of men vis-à-vis women.

In the second generation, three of the four girls have or have had partners in life and these all are or have been white Caucasians. It is clear that as part of their willed Americanness, the girls are resolved to unite their lives with white Caucasians only. Yet those white Euro-Americans with whom they are obviously mesmerized turn out to be less than heroes. The reader never meets, so to speak, the husband whom Waverly is divorced from, but the other three, Rich, Harold, and Ted, rivalize with each other to surpass Clifford St-Clair in commonness, vulgarity and crass materialism. Furthermore, while in St-Clair's case, the condescension he manifested in making cheap presents might be explained away as reflecting his (lack of) taste if not lack of mundane wisdom, a blatant patriarchy coupled with racism is unmistakably present in the behavior of the other three. It is this amalgam of patriarchy and racism that I wish to discuss in this section through an examination of the conduct of the three white sons-in-law and the mother of one.

It must be stated at the onset that the whole community exposed in *The Joy Luck Club* has suffered from racism in more ways than one. Yet it must be stressed that this has especially and indelibly marked the second generation, in the same way that they have indelibly become Americans. As a result, the self-image they have of themselves and their parents' culture is that of an inferior one—Gayatri Spivak would use the term "subaltern." This is ironical as these Chinese-American girls are all superior to the white Caucasian men in their lives. A case in point is Lena St-Clair who is more intelligent than her designer husband whose success is based on his putting into practice *her* ideas.

There is to be observed in the novel two types of racism. One type of racism, perhaps the more malignant of the two in the way it affects the people targeted, is what may be termed "internalized racism." It is the ingrown feeling the Chinese-Americans have learned to experience. This leads on the one hand to an inferiority complex, as exemplified in the case of Lena St-Clair:

> all I can remember is how awfully lucky I felt . . . about moving in with him, I also dredged my deepest fears: that he would tell me that I smelled bad, that I had terrible bathroom habits. . . . And I think that feeling of fear never left me, that I would be caught one day. (Tan 169)

On the other hand, it also drives the Chinese into behaving the way they suppose the Americans do, with tragic consequences. As Rose Hsu explains, apropos of the death of her brother:

> We were blind with the newness of this experience: a Chinese family trying to act like a typical American family at the beach. (Tan 130)

The four-year-old Bing drowns because everybody at the time is doing something "American." The father is fishing. The daughter shrugs at her mother's suggestion that the boy playing at the beach may be in danger as Chinese "superstition" (Tan 131).

The other sort of racism is that demonstrated by the whites toward the Chinese-Americans. Although both generations are confronted with it in its most insidious form, in other words, with stereotyping, the daughters, the self-identified Americans, suffer the most. To illustrate, when Rose Hsu encounters her future mother-in-law, Mrs. Jordan, the latter is at pains to explain to Rose at first that she and her husband "personally knew many fine people who were Oriental, Spanish and even black," only to add that as "Ted was going to be in one of those professions where he would be judged by a different standard," the patients and/ or doctors he would have to work with might not be that "understanding." It was "so unfortunate the way the rest of the world was." And, to add insult to injury, Ted's mother goes on to remark, "how unpopular the Vietnam war was" (Tan 124-25).

Of course, some other cocksure person would have plainly told Mrs Jordan that she could not dump together Orientals, Spanish, and black, three epithets denoting three different categories of classification. Any seasoned diplomat would know of a hundred ways of rendering the opinionated woman discomfited without in the least departing from civility. Young Rose Hsu uneasy in her skin is unable to do any of that and has to make do with replying that she is not Vietnamese (Tan 125).

Mrs. Jordan thus inadvertently reveals a bigotry that is so ingrained in her that she is unaware of its existence. Her reference to Vietnam suggests further that for her all Asians are interchangeable, not only demonstrating insensibility, but also ignorance. What she is implying is that white mainstream Americans do not like Asians because of the war in Vietnam. She is unaware that in the case of the war in Vietnam it is the Americans who were the culprit, and as the Pentagon Papers were to reveal, the losers as well.

Racism, it must be added, is almost identically reciprocal. Rose Hsu's mother doesn't want Ted either as for her he is a "*waigoren*" (Tan 124), a foreigner who is the "other." The fact is that in this novel racism and patriarchy are enmeshed, one fortifying the other, as well as taking its source from the other. That the Chinese mothers who impose patriarchy on their American-born daughters, to imbue the latter with a Chinese culture they have only known as patriarchal, are also racists is seen to be the order of things.

And so it is with the white Caucasians the daughters are involved with. Rich Schields, Waverly Jong's partner, is the least offensive of the three young men. The attitude he displays resembles, in accentuated form, St-Clair's stance. He appears to be genuinely disposed towards Chinese culture, acting on the surface full of benevolence towards the family he may be joining soon in matrimony. Yet his blunder at the dinner table, taking literally the self-deprecating comment of a hostess about the dish she cooked—that constitutes the prompt that should start guests praising her accomplishment, a ritual probably taking place during meal times in millions of Eastern households—approximates St-Clair's faux pas in offering cheap trinkets. It also smacks of racism and of patriarchy translated as racism. His offering Waverly a cheap fur coat made up of "left-overs" is another step in the same direction, in even more accentuated form.

Both men, St-Clair and Rich, seem to have adopted the same posture: they are superior white men providing for inferior colored women. Blessed with being Americans, residing in the "city upon a hill," the two men may earnestly be feeling that they are endowed spiritually as well as with affluence and are showing largesse in proffering these gifts. While Ted turns out to be no better than his mother in insensitivity, the vulgar streak becomes even more pronounced in the case of Harold Livotny, who makes his wife pay for every expenditure she makes of an item he himself may not be consuming, but also for such items as ice-cream which she does not touch, just because he himself buys it. By Chinese standards, this is no marriage and the absence of children renders the fact conspicuous. Like a slap in the face, the portraiture of Harold conveys mimetically the "manifest destiny" of a nation and a people.

Conclusion

The representation of patriarchy, racism and cultural conflict in Amy Tan's *The Joy Luck Club* is accomplished through particular narrative strategies. Turning her back almost to the tradition of the Western novel and the "rationality" that is implicit in its structure, the author has recourse to Eastern storytelling and mysticism: while the episodic nature of the work (sixteen stories following each other and yet interrelated with each other) seems to highlight the non-Western aspect of the narrative, the parables, myths, superstitions and ancient beliefs that are recounted help create a non-rational universe. The narrative strategies Tan utilizes allow her thus to achieve a balancing act: through contrastive tales that alternate (between rationality and its seeming lack, between discourse in correct English and that in incorrect English), the eight Chinese-American "protagonists" of the novel, four first-generation immigrant mothers and an American-born daughter of each, expose the ideologies she is denouncing.

In *The Joy Luck Club* patriarchy has various faces: that in China, that propagated by the mothers, and that practiced by the native white American husbands and their families. These are all colored by racism. The first-generation women are themselves agents of patriarchy against other women, their daughters, as that is a weapon to retain the culture native to them. That is a culture all the more fragile as it is an immigrant one. For the women of the first generation, losing it in the face of the all-powerful mainstream American culture signifies losing their identity. The "immigrant syndrome" they are all inhabited with, the conviction that emigration was inevitable and indispensable, allowing them to survive in a U.S. society unwilling to understand and/or accept them, nonetheless adds further to their discomfort.

The American-born daughters versed in Western ways are the novel's second batch of protagonists. Raised in the U.S., they are ashamed of mothers who do not speak English well, yet have been pushed by those same mothers to "make it" in American society. The mothers' ambitions, that daughters instinctively thwarted, have resulted in mother-daughter relationships that have generated hostility rather than bonding. The fact is that the mothers have tried to give the best of both worlds to their daughters. Yet the result is not as expected. Lindo Jong, who verbalizes this dual education as wanting to give her children "the best combination," realizes once her children are adults that "American circumstances and Chinese character . . . do not mix." She finds that, of her daughter, "Only her skin and her hair are Chinese. Inside—she is all American-made" (Tan 289). These second-generation women are too much enamored with New World individualism and sense of propriety precluding extended family relationships to be capable of any bonding with either their mothers or other women of their own generation. This renders them also incapable of fighting the dual patriarchy/racism they are subjected to in a mainstream who discerns their physical traits before all else and whose defects they persist in overlooking.

Their mothers are furthermore able to see through those Euro-American men whom these young women, ready to fall for any white skin, so blindly unite their lives with. It is Lindo Jong who shows her daughter Waverly, pretentious yet lacking judgment in ways of the world, that the mink she has received is not of prime quality but made of leftover strips (Tan 186). Ying-ying Saint-Clair indicates to her daughter Lena the fragility of her marriage by dropping a vase of flowers standing on a table that is not solid. "They sit in a room with no life in it," explains Ying-ying (Tan 287). It is needless to add that this is a childless marriage. If by making their wives share expenses, the sons-in-law prove unable to provide for the family, as they must according to Chinese wisdom, it is because there is no family to speak of. The point is that the daughter "sees only with her outside eyes. She has no *chuming*, no inside knowing of things" (Tan 282), no empathy. Moreover, as one of the daughters, June/Jing-mei Woo acknowledges, the daughters are unmindful of all the "truths and hopes" their mothers "have brought to America." So, even if there are grandchildren born, as Waverly's daughter Shoshana, these are or will be "without any connecting hope passed from generation to generation" (Tan 31).

The mothers, on encountering each other in San Francisco's Chinatown, bonded immediately and most naturally, almost instinctively, replicating the earlier relationships with women they had established in China. They even formalized the bonding by the ritualized playing of *mah jong* in the Joy Luck Club. While the Club may have prevented their immersion in mainstream life and acquisition of American mores, it also furnished them with a psychological shield that helped them withstand the abhorrence they had of these American mores, acting as a buffer against the encroachment of a way of life they found inimical.

Not so for the daughters, who are all inhabited by a rage they are unable to define, that hampers their lives both in the Chinese American community and the white mainstream that only perceives their Asian features. The daughters are unable to find any solace either in bonding with their mothers, or among themselves, in a society that favors competition and individual success above all else. Henceforth, they will solve their problems in the isolation that has become the psychological abode of the modern American woman—hopefully sustained by grains of Chinese sagacity they finally, as the novel ends, open their hearts to.

NOTES

1. The novel implies that for Chinese-Americans, leaving Chinatown to reside elsewhere in the city signifies social ascension. Or, put in another way, social ascension, which ineluctably involves inserting into the mainstream, is evidenced by departure from the ghetto that the Chinatown is.
2. Madame d'Épinay (1726-1783), the French authoress, is reputed to have said: "On voit le passé meilleur qu'il n'a été, on trouve le présent pire qu'il n'est, on éspère l'avenir plus heureux qu'il ne sera" (One sees the past better than it was, finds the present worse than it is, and hopes the future will be happier than it will. Translation mine).
3. See Singh *et al* for a treatment of memory in immigrant fiction, and especially the article by Xu for a discussion of its relevance for *The Joy Luck Club*.

Works Cited

Ashabranner, Brent. *The New Americans: Changing Patterns in U.S. Immigration*. New York: Dodd, Mead, 1983.

Bhabha, Homi K. *The Location of Culture*. New York: Routledge, 1994.

Bloom, Harold, ed. *Amy Tan's* The Joy Luck Club. Modern Critical Interpretations. New York: Chelsea House, 2002.

Bodnar, John. *The Transplanted: A History of Immigrants in Urban America*. Bloomington: Indiana U P, 1985.

Chan, Jeffrey Paul, Frank Chin, Lawson Fusao Inada and Shawn Wong, ed. *The Big Aiiieeeee!: An Anthology of Chinese American and Japanese American Literature*. New York: Meridian, 1991.

Chan, Sucheng. *Asian Americans: An Interpretive History.* Boston: Twayne, 1991.

Daniels, Roger. *Coming to America: A History of Immigration and Ethnicity in American Life*. New York: HarperCollins, 1990.

Dinnerstein, Leonard and David M. Reimers. *Ethnic Americans: A History of Immigration and Assimilation*. New York: Dodd and Mead, 1975.

Dinnerstein, Leonard, Roger L. Nichols and David M. Reimers. *Natives and Strangers: Ethnic Groups and the Building of America*. New York: Oxford U P, 1979.

Ferraro, Thomas. *Ethnic Passages: Literary Immigrants in Twentieth-Century America*. Chicago: The U of Chicago P, 1993.

Gleason, Philip. *Speaking of Diversity: Language and Ethnicity in Twentieth-Century America*. Baltimore: Johns Hopkins U P, 1992.

Hawley, John C. "Assimilation and Resistance in Female Fiction of Immigration: Bharati Mukherjee, Amy Tan, and Christine Bell." *Rediscovering America 1492-1992: National, Cultural and Disciplinary Boundaries Re-Examined.* Ed. Leslie Bary, Janet Gold, et al. Baton Rouge: Louisiana State University Press, 1992. 226-34.

Heung, Marina. "Daughter-Text/Mother-Text: Matrilineage in Amy Tan's *Joy Luck Club*." *Feminist Studies* 19.3 (1993): 597-616.

Higham, John. *Send These to Me: Immigrants in Urban America*. Rev. ed. Baltimore: Johns Hopkins U P, 1984.

Hollinger, David. *Postethnic America: Beyond Multiculturalism*. New York: Basic Books, 1995.

Huntley, E.D. *Amy Tan. A Critical Companion*. Westport, C.T. and London: Greenwood Press, 1998.

Katz, Seymour. "'Culture' and Literature in American Studies." *American Quarterly* 20 (1968): 318-29.

Kingston, Maxine Hong. *The Woman Warrior: Memoirs of a Girlhood among Ghosts*. New York: Knopf, 1976.

Millett, Kate. *Sexual Politics*. Garden City, NY: Doubleday, 1970.

Mintz, Sidney W. and Richard Price. *The Birth of African American Culture*. 1976. Boston, MA: Beacon Press, 1992.

Muller, Gilbert H. *New Strangers in Paradise: The Immigrant Experience and Contemporary American Fiction*. Lexington, Kentucky: The U P of Kentucky, 1999.

Nye, David E. and Christen Kold Thomsen, ed. *American Studies in Transition*. Odense: Odense University Press, 1985.

Øverland, Orm. *Immigrant Minds, American Identities*. Urbana and Chicago: University of Illinois Press, 2000.

Payant, Katherine and Toby Rose, ed. *The Immigrant Experience in North American Literature: Carving Out a Niche*. Westport, CT: Greenwood Press, 1999.

Pultar, Gönül. "Painful Rites of Passage: Novels by Ethnic Female Writers," *The TAA Lectures, 1989-1992*. Ankara: American Studies Association of Turkey, 1993. 147-70.

Reimers, David M. *Unwelcome Strangers: American Identity and the Turn against Immigration*: New York: Columbia U P, 1998.

Rothenberg, Paula S., ed. *Race, Class, and Gender in the United States: An Integrated Study*. 2nd ed. New York: St. Martin's Press, 1992.

Schlesinger, Jr., Arthur M. *The Disuniting of America: Reflections on a Multicultural Society*. Rev. and enlarged ed. New York: W.W. Norton, 1998.

Singh, Amrijit; Skerrett, Jr., Joseph T. and Robert E. Hoga ed. *Memory, Narrative and Identity: New Essays in Ethnic American Literatures*. Boston, MA: Northeastern U P, 1994.

Sollors, Werner. *Beyond Ethnicity: Consent and Descent in American Culture*. New York: Oxford U P, 1986.

_____, ed. *The Invention of Ethnicity*. New York: Oxford U P, 1989.

_____, ed. *Theories of Ethnicity. A Classical Reader*. New York: New York U P, 1996.

Sowell, Thomas. *Ethnic America*. New York: Basic Books, 1981.

Spivak, Gayatri Chakravorty. "Subaltern Studies: Deconstructing Historiography." *The Spivak Reader*. ed. Donna Landry and Gerald Maclean. New York and London: Routledge, 1996.

Tan, Amy. *The Joy Luck Club*. 1988. New York: Ivy Books, 1989.

TuSmith, Bonnie. *All My Relatives: Community in Contemporary Ethnic American Literatures*. Ann Arbor: U of Michigan P, 1993.

Wong, Sau-ling Cynthia. "'Sugar Sisterhood': Situating the Amy Tan Phenomenon." *The Ethnic Canon: Histories, Institutions, and Interventions*. ed. David Palumbo-Liu. Minneapolis: U of Minnesota P, 1995: 174-210.

Xu, Ben. "Memory and the Ethnic Self: Reading Amy Tan's *The Joy Luck Club*." *Memory, Narrative, and Identity: New Essays in Ethnic American Literatures*. Ed. Amritjit Singh, Joseph T. Skerrett, Jr, and Robert E. Hogan. 261-77.

African American Drama's Journey towards the Centerstage

JAP PREET KAUR BHANGU
Sant Longowal Central Institute of Engineering and Technology

African American drama, as part of African American literary discourse has been aspiring for recognition as a literary tradition which has roots in the forms, practices and achievements of the African American diaspora. Accused of lacking a literary and cultural heritage, the black dramatists have staged and published plays which taken together intend to create or where required recreate the image of the African American race in the western discourse. In addition, they have sought theatre to provide an opportunity for coming to terms with the cultural difference in a racist society. Calling for a radical reassessment of the function and practice of dramatic art in the dominant society, African American playwrights have looked for ways of modifying the perceptions as also the procedures of performance. Even while continuing with the struggle to establish a separate and distinct identity, African American drama nevertheless, expresses a yearning to cross over and embed itself into the mainstream American culture. The paper focuses on the development of African American drama in the post-civil rights era and attempts a review of its journey towards the centrestage.

"The problem of the twentieth century is the problem of the color line,"[1] predicted W.E.B. DuBois in 1903. And even in the twenty-first century, the racial concerns continue to occupy the central position among other social issues. DuBois's call of the 1920s for a theatre of, by, for and near the black communities was essentially for laying down of certain strategies. These strategies were to constitute a distinct and parallel institutional body of knowledge that would change and enrich the lives of Black Americans. DuBois believed that black literature and political activism must be fused together and pressed into service on behalf of the black people. However it was Amiri Baraka, Larry Neal and other proponents of the Black Arts Movement in the 1960s, who transformed African American drama. Drawing on the theories put forward by Black thinkers such as DuBois, Frantz Fanon, Malcolm X, and others, these writers sought to raise the consciousness of the Black people. They wrote 'agit-prop' plays that suggested new models of human behavior. Their refocusing of the strategies was to contest the existing value-systems which denied participation to the black people as equals.

One of the most intriguing, controversial and enigmatic figures in the recent times, Amiri Baraka entered the "American consciousness not merely as a writer but as an event."[2] Having remarkable clarity of vision, Baraka pointed out the false optimism of the advocates of integrationist poetics who constantly searched for social indicators of pluralism in American life. He began his career with the one-act *Dutchman, The Slave, The Toilet, The Baptism* (all produced in 1964), and then wrote a series of short revolutionary plays. With his works, Baraka brought an increasing sense of racial consciousness and political militancy to black theatre. Under his guidance, black theatre became concerned less with the white society or with the inner, psychological splits and more with examining the black experience from a Black Nationalist point of view. His plays made extensive use of parody, obscenity, blasphemy and violence to lead the spectators on to recognition of the falsity of myths, aspirations and ideologies governing the community heretofore even as they witnessed the black revolutionaries, their victims, or misled traitors on the stage. Moreover, a lot of action was left to be guided by the coming together of the actors and the audience. As short, agit-prop pieces, these plays did not have subtlety of characterization, plot or action. However, when produced downtown, these proved to be powerful rituals aimed at consciousness-raising of the black people. Baraka thus transformed the black theatre into a means for a collective reflection of what it was to be a black American—an identity to be created, a sociological reality to be struggled for.

While Baraka and his fellow playwrights wrote angry militant plays, simultaneously, playwrights like Ed Bullins, Ron Milner, and Paul Carter Harrison etc. were dramatizing Afrocentric images of African American life and sensibility. Bullins, one of the most prolific of black playwrights transformed theatre into a place of communion by highlighting specific problems within the black community. While Baraka's plays depicted victims fighting a racist society, Bullins on the other hand focused on the inner forces that constrained blacks from realizing their potential. As Samuel Hay appropriately observes, Bullins "pays homage to the heavy-partying, loud-talking and louder dressing, low-income people who, for the most part, lived in the alleys, back streets, and the Projects of urban America. [In fact] . . . the very group who along with whites was viewed by the revolutionary dramatists as enemies of the people."[3] His theatre identifies pimps, prostitutes, drunks, addicts, street-smart 'niggers' and the other common folk as facing and fighting racism in numerous ways, thus being worthy of occupying the theatrical space as heroes. Bullins' focus rather is on the misuse of freedom that his black characters exercise when they freely adopt 'white' values and/or betray their black brethren.

Adrienne Kennedy, another significant playwright of the era, with her non-linear surrealistic theatre stands alone without being part of either of the two kinds of plays being written at the time. Kennedy, "the most original writer of her generation and, along with Sam Shepard, the most original, black and white,"[4] focuses mainly on the African American female self entrapped within the structure of race and gender. Her work embodies the quest of the doubly othered self, racially and gender-wise for coming to terms with the internal and external reality governed by white supremacist cultural logic. Incorporating materials from her life, her readings and her cultural and social experiences, Kennedy maintains that what helped evolve her own unique style and brought her to a fuller understanding of the sensibility of the African continuum was her visit to West Africa in the 1960s, where she began writing her first play *Funny House of a Negro* (1962). However, the switchover to an Afro-centric stance in Kennedy's works is neither clear-cut nor complete. Unlike the other black playwrights of the era who assume a more essentialist shift, Kennedy on the other hand, seems to linger, uneasily and painfully, between cultures, on the boundaries, traveling through the hyphenated spaces between African and American, between black and white, between race and gender. Unlike Baraka who concentrates mainly on the external hardships, Kennedy's theatre delves deep into the black psyche to lay bare the most secret emotions, hopes and fears, dreams and nightmares, and above all, the smoldering rage of the Black people.

The Black playwrights of the 1960s and 1970s thus follow a practice, which may be interpreted within the framework of Stuart Hall's theorizing of the two models of the struggle for cultural identity.[5] According to Hall, the first model assumes that there is some intrinsic and essentialist context of any identity which is defined by either a common origin or a common structure of an experience or both. Struggle against the existing constructions of identity thus involves contesting the negative images with the positive ones and of trying to discover the 'authentic' and 'original' content of identity. Basically the struggle over representation of identity takes the form of offering one fully constituted, separate and distinct identity in place of the other, only this time a 'good' one in place of the earlier 'bad' one. Hall's second model however emphasizes the impossibility of fully constituted, separate and distinct identities. According to Hall, the relevant question instead is how identities have become "different" since history has intervened, hence the important issue is not as much as 'what we really are,' as ' what we have become.'

Among the Black playwrights of the era, only Adrienne Kennedy may be seen as following Hall's second model of the struggle for identity. Other Black playwrights of the 1960s and 1970s in general, unconsciously emulate Hall's first model. As they integrate into their works certain cultural elements borrowed from the African oral, musical, religious and ritualistic traditions, African American theatre distinguishes itself from the western dramaturgy. Their projection of an African aesthetic is aimed at reawakening the Black masses to their ties with each other and with their mother culture. That most of them have never been to Africa becomes irrelevant as they try to reconnect with a cultural past and thereby possess a history other than the one that merely tells of slavery. Thus one by one, the stereotypes are taken up, examined and sought to be constituted through representation of the Black subjects in those very roles which the dominant society views as marginal, insignificant and unimportant. African American playwrights of the era thus come closest to the Black theatre's self-proclaimed role of strengthening a parallel space in drama that no longer looks towards the one alongside for confirmation and recognition of identity.

The anxiety to assert a distinct identity however also leads to a kind of patrolling of the literary and the ideological boundaries that seeks to judge African American writing on the basis of conforming to certain styles, topic and positions which alone are considered as authentically black. The explosion of African American women's writing in the '70s and into the '80s brought a much needed focus on the 'woman's space' and also helped in opening out of the boundaries of the black aesthetic. Writers such as Toni Morrison, Alice Walker, Ntozake Shange, Paule Marshall, Rita Dove, Gloria Naylor, Toni Cade Bambara and a host of other did achieve widespread attention as they illuminated the interconnections of race and gender in a variety of literary forms. Revolting against the essentially male, patriarchal nature of Black Nationalist ideologies, these writers represented a community of women who strongly objected to both the exclusion of Black women from the political mechanism of Black protest and to the pressure to sacrifice gender issues for racial concerns. While Adrienne Kennedy as a lone voice amidst the sound and fury of the surrounding male voices had been barely audible, Ntozake Shange, on the other hand, empowered by the sisterhood of the black women writers was loud and clear while delivering her message. Shange's theatre provided a platform for a public debate on issues regarding relations between Black men and women as well as Black writers and their writing.

In the 1980s there emerged a new generation of African American playwrights who though influenced by both the Black revolutionary theatre of the '60s and the theatre of Black experience of the 1970s yet sought to restructure the focus of African American theatre. Playwrights such as August Wilson along with Shange, Charles Fuller, George C. Wolfe, etc., while continuing to write out of the African-American tradition, felt equally comfortable while borrowing and adapting, wherever necessary, the ideas and forms of western dramaturgy. Neither militant nor interested in contesting what 'black' was or was not, these playwrights wrote in an idiom that appealed to black as well as white audience. Among them August Wilson especially represents to quote Paul Carter Harrison, "the culmination of political, social and aesthetic objectives presaged by the Harlem Renaissance in the twenties and the Black Arts Movement of the Sixties."[6] African American theatre may not yet have reached centrestage, however Wilson with his project of 'writing/righting' the black American history surely seems to be close to arriving.

Wilson's plays, each one set in a different decade of the twentieth century, are aimed at challenging the misrepresentations and un-representations of African American people in the annals of American history. The cultural poetics in Wilson's hands shifts away from the gaze of the centrally positioned observing eye towards the expressive speech of the blues music, thus focusing upon the lived experience of the marginalized subjects. The black presence in his plays assumes the position of a speaking subject. What emerges, however, is not a "filled subject" but "an anonymous (nameless) voice issuing from the black (w)hole."[7] Wilson's plays do not celebrate any particular, 'original' or 'authentic' voice, for history, like the blues, has 'always been there.' His theatre utilizes the past to construct a present and to envision a future. Wilson accomplishes this task by using the everyday, vernacular speech of the black people, which he elevates to the level of poetry, infusing into it the power to guide the audience through a variety of emotions. Wilson's dramaturgy, like the blues music thus transcends the boundaries of cultures.

However, even as white America hailed Wilson's success as part of the multicultural movement of the 90s, and as proof of American theatre's accommodation of the African American experience, Wilson shocked and stunned the theatre community by reiterating the 'separate and distinct' identity of African-American people and art thus establishing a connection with the black ideologues of the 20s and the 60s. While marking the boundaries of "The Ground on which I stand,"[8] Wilson placed himself and his art firmly in the black cultural tradition, a projection that led to uproar among the white establishment with many white critics accusing Wilson of practicing "reverse racism."[9] African American theatre circles, however, strongly object to a system under which their construction of identity is expected first to sink its cultural difference to qualify as a universal product.

Thus in African American literary practice one finds precariously co-existing the idea of race as an irreducible biological reality on the one hand, and as a culturally constructed trope or metaphor that challenges social institutions and practices on the other. From DuBois in the 20s to Amiri Baraka and the Black Arts Movement in the 60s to August Wilson in the 90s, the African American theatre continues to pursue its strategic desire to build institutions where the black people may be nurtured and trained to approach the mainstream cultural spaces with confidence and self-respect. That the black theatre today, surrounded by Eurocentric practice which disconnects theatre from the community has moved away from strictly remaining a theatre of, about, for and near the black people, is a matter of immense concern to the African American artists and playwrights struggling to survive in a highly competitive capitalistic society. Facing the limiting reality of its over-dependence upon corporate, foundational and other governmental funding, African-American theatre groups realize that they have to revise strategies for survival and for growth.

The new millennium became an occasion and an opportunity for African American theatre community to take stock of the past achievements and to rethink, replan and redesign the strategies for the future. The continuing focus on the marginalized, deprived and exploited black identity has led to a growing sensitivity towards the issue of race, ethnicity and gender that has transformed the very meaning of many previously held beliefs and values. Hence DuBois's notion of "double consciousness"[10] which at the beginning of the twentieth century was an expression of lamentation today might be regarded as "a useful bifocal lens and not as the crippling diplopia of the past."[11] With their "two-ness" taken as a tool rather than a curse, African American playwrights continue to draw inspiration from their African roots and yet inhabit the mainstream American spaces as doubly-equipped cultural workers, revelling in their special identity.

The debate on American culture however continues to be focused mainly around the choice between demands for cultural separation, on the one hand, and integrationist assimilation, on the other. But yielding to such an either/or oppositional thinking would be to ignore the intrinsically fluid nature of culture; ideas that scholars such as Stuart Hall, Homi Bhabha, Cornel West, Paul Gilory and others put forward as 'hybridity of culture.' The idea of culture as conceived along ethnically absolute lines and as a fixed property of social groups therefore must be understood as a necessary fiction that is used by both the hegemonic and the resistant forces in their complex battles for power. In fact both whiteness and blackness depend on the notion of the other and as Cornel West argues, "race," "ethnicity," and "nationality" are all "profoundly hybrid." What is important is, in West's words, to "construct more multivalent and multidimensional responses that articulate the complexity and diversity of black practices in the modern and postmodern world."[12] African American theatre ideologues, however, still pondering over the directions that the Black theatre should explore continue to follow broadly the already existing, vastly successful models of the Black theatre of resistance and of the Black experience.

African American theatre thus is still in the process of reaching centrestage. African American playwrights have successfully demonstrated to those of the other ethnicities that one does not have to melt one's cultural identity to assume and assert one's identity. At the same time, however, their projection of a 'separate and distinct' identity is essentially political strategy for effecting racial solidarity and a social and aesthetic positionality. The Black playwrights do not aim to occupy the centrestage in the Eurocentric sense which involves a dispossessing, displacing, repressing and silencing of the other aesthetics and traditions. As a leading ethnic theatre, however, African American theatre has become an important part of the American theatrical mainstream. Thus preferring to redefine and re-draw the boundaries of the centrestage itself rather than letting go of their projection of a 'separate and distinct' identity, African American theatre today stands at the crossroads from where it must decide which road to follow. Since they have already given up open confrontation of the mainstream dominant society and have spent fairly long time asserting their specific identity, it is perhaps time for African American playwrights to move on and find newer ways of telling their stories which would also attract the audience from the mainstream and the other communities. Hence, as they have already demonstrated, if theatre can be used as a platform for the community to come together for an assertion of identity, it surely can also be employed to transform the way the world understands the categories of culture, race, ethnicity, gender, etc. To be able to establish the interconnections and the intersections rather than remaining trapped within the points of ruptures between the categories may seem like a utopian dream, however, it is the one worth yearning for.

References

1. DuBois, W.E.B. "The Drama among Black Folk," *Crisis* (Aug. 1916), p. 171
2. Addison Gayle, "Introduction," *The Black Aesthetic* (New York: Doubleday, 1971), p. 7.

3. Samuel A Hay, *African-American Theatre: A Historical and Critical Analysis* (Cambridge: Cambridge University Press, 1994), p. 39.
4. Herbert Blau, "The American Dream in the American Gothic: The Plays of Sam Shepard and Adrienne Kennedy," *Modern Drama*, 27 (1984), p. 531.
5. Stuart Hall, "Cultural Identity and Diaspora," *Identity, Community, Culture, Difference*, ed. Jonathan Rutherford (London: Lawrence and Wishart, 1990), pp. 222-37.
6. Paul Carter Harrison, "August Wilson's Blues Poetics," *Three Plays* by August Wilson (Pittsburg: University of Pittsburgh Press, 1991), p. 316.
7. Houston A. Baker, *Blues, Ideology, and Afro-American Literature: A Vernacular Theory* (Chicago: University of Chicago Press, 1984), p. 5.
8. August Wilson "The Ground on Which I Stand," *American Theatre* (Sept. 1996), pp. 39-42.
9. Robert Brustein, "Subsidized Separatism," *New Republic* 19-26 (Aug. 1996), pp. 39-42.
10. W.E.B. DuBois, *The Souls of Black Folk* (1903; rpt. New York: Penguin, 1969), p. 45.
11. Amritjit Singh, Joseph T. Skerrett, Jr., Robert E. Hongan, ed., *Memory and Cultural Politics: New Approaches to American Ethnic Literature* (Boston: Northeastern Press, 1996), p. 6.
12. Cornel West, "The New Cultural Politics of Difference," *Keeping Faith* (New York: Routledge, 1923), p. 20.

Ballad of a Dream Deferred: Blackness and Bleakness in the Poetry of Langston Hughes

MINA SURJIT SINGH
Punjab University, Chandigarh

What happens to a dream deferred?

> Does it dry up
> Like a raisin in the sun?
> Or fester like a sore—
> And then run?
> Does it stink like rotten meat?
> Or crust and sugar over—
> like a syrupy sweet?
> Maybe it just sags
> like a heavy load.
> Or does it explode?   Langston Hughes: "Harlem." (*MODD* 71)

The division of the world's population into races is now generally agreed upon by scientists to have arisen as a result of climatic and environmental pressures—the darker more pigmented peoples better equipped to withstand solar output than whites. For various reasons, again largely environmental and climatic, the steady advances in civilization came from a temporary ascendancy of whites over blacks or near blacks. Until the early part of the twentieth century, the technological gulf between white and black was so wide that the Europeans held these darker races in slavery. While such a thought might be repugnant to most today, attitudes to colored people still reflect a pervasive hostility and an inherent notion of white superiority which is easy to deny intellectually but difficult to shake off emotionally. In the U.S.A., the most advanced and at the same time the most tormented of multi-racial societies in the world, the role of its substantial black population however, has changed dramatically over the last hundred years with the introduction of cosmetic reforms aimed at a fictional or theoretical equality. Nevertheless, Jim Crow laws, and Ku Klux Klan prejudices notwithstanding, a change in the black community's view of itself has affected an attitudinal change which has set up a powerful counter discourse that finds its ultimate expression in the concept and ideology of Black Power. It is the achievement of this Black Power which is necessarily disruptive of aestheticized and mythologised representations of blacks that becomes an essentially liberating act. However, there seems to be a more or less tacit understanding among literary historians as Toni Morrison suggests, "that traditional canonical American literature is free of, uninformed and shaped by the four-hundred-year-old presence of, first, Africans and then African-Amcricans in the United States" (5). Because American literature has been clearly the preserve of white, male views, genius and power, scholars assume that this presence "which has shaped the body politic as well as the entire history of the culture, has no significant place or consequence in the origin and development of its literature" (5). The contemplation of this 'black' or nonwhite presence however, is central to any understanding of American literature and should not be permitted to hover at the margins of the literary imagination. In this context the work of Langston Hughes, one of the leading and most prolific writers of the Harlem Renaissance, is of special significance. Hughes has not only given us inimitable defining metaphors of the black experience in his powerful analogies of a "dream deferred" and a "raisin in the sun," but has also focused on the conflicts and injustices that launched Black Power.[1] Yet he has often been dismissed by the critical establishment. Denied formal awards and even informal kudos, the poet has often been accused by some critics, both black and white, of not writing enough consciousness-raising material. On the contrary, Hughes was the first black American to write civil-rights protest poetry when it was quite dangerous to do so. Hailed as the poet laureate of his people, he was ready to risk even the then prevailing subhuman act of lynching, a metaphor he used for American injustice, and which he had masterfully equated with the supreme act of martyrdom and crucifixion:

> It would be too bad if Jesus,
> Were to come back black.
> There are so many churches,
> Where he could not pray,
> In the U.S.A.,
> Where entrance to Negroes
>
> No matter how sanctified
> Is denied,
> Where race not religion,
> Is glorified.
> But say it—
> You may be
> Crucified. (*TPTL* 38)

This paper therefore, seeks to explore through his poetry, Hughes' significant contribution to American literature and what it means to live "in a nation of people who *decided* that their world-view would combine agendas for individual freedom *and* mechanisms for devastating racial oppression" (Morrison Preface xiii).

In an essay entitled "An Empire of Poetry," the critic Sydney Burris draws attention to the "intractable dilemma" that Christopher Columbus was faced with when forced to characterize in most *alluring* terms, the culture of the uncharted territories of the West Indies which he had sailed into. Burris informs us that in an account of the islanders sent by letter to Ferdinand and Isabella of Spain in 1493, Columbus wrote, "They exhibit great affection to all and always give much for little, content with very little or nothing in return" (Burris 260). Columbus' "rhetoric of profit," Burris concludes, "prophetically encapsulate[s] the informing structure of colonialist thought" (259-60). To put it differently, these islands offered good profits for a sound investment. This very mechanics of *sound investment* became the governing principle of white American traders who first envisioned the profitable potential of human transactions which led to the subsequent growth of a flourishing slave trade *industry*, that replicated the Victorian racial dichotomies of white man as rational, black man as irrational.

The narrative of Langston Hughes' poetry as of his other works, reflects not only an acute awareness of the ways in which this Columbian perspective survives in the twentieth century, but also his attempts to counter the fragmentary representations of his community, that have been encouraged by this colonial vision. The 1920s were a transitional period in American history for African-Americans, economically and politically, one in which the locus of black presence was shifting northward and urbanward in search of the American Dream. This mass migration resultantly re-mapped the African-American landscape and the American perception of what blackness means in American culture. Alongside reflecting white and black romantic constructions of the Negro's cultural identity Hughes' poetry, more significantly, attempts to provide for his dark brethren, the definitive strengths and comforts of a "black" narrative that recalls Aimé Cesaire's Negritude[2] and Marcus Garvey's 'black is beautiful' cult, with its focus on black agency:

> Negroes,
> Sweet and docile,
> Meek, humble and kind:
> Beware the day,
> They change their minds! (*TPTL* 100)

Again, a poem like "Harlem Sweeties" (*PN* 101-2), is pervaded by monochromatic, dark and intoxicating images of "coffee," "brown sugar," "caramel," "chocolate," "walnut," "cocoa," "cinnamon," "All those sweet colors" that "Flavor Harlem of mine!" Although these conjure up olfactory, palatable and connoisseurial associations, they also act as reminders of the black power that went into the development of the southern plantation economy.

Hughes' literary career begins with a commitment to black cultural resources as one important basis for his art. His unapologetic allusions to black agency inherent in the folk norms and cultural responses of his community, take on Negro spiritual, blues and Jazz forms, which best define an aesthetic constitution and sensibility that is informed by an innate sense of rhythm and spirituality. Hughes' experimentation with the formal structures of the Blues in his verse, exemplified by improvisatory compositions and syncopated rhythms that replicated the silencing of the black voice, was part of his exploration of black representational possibilities. More importantly however, it became an important source of resistance against racial discrimination and definitions of art to which the opposition between races—re-expressed as conflict between a primitive child and rational adult—was integral. These folk norms, as George E. Kent rightly suggests, were in themselves:

> definitions of black life created on the bloody and pine-scented Southern soil and upon the black board jungle of urban streets, tenement buildings, store-front churches and dim-lit bars. The current generations of black writers, who are trying to develop artistic forms that reflect a grip upon realities as they exist from day to day in black communities, discover that Langston Hughes is an important pioneer who has already "been there and gone." (183)

Hughes' experimentation with and assimilation of Jazz rhythms in his poetry is also in tandem with his attitude to his community. Just as jazz simultaneously stresses the collective and the individual, Hughes' poems are individual statements, but are also part of a larger unity. Significantly, as an individual he is de-emphasized in his work, even as various individual members of the community speak and are spoken about. In a seemingly simple form Hughes thus becomes a subtle and sensitive medium for articulating the trials, tribulations and aspirations of a voiceless community. The work's modernity with its focus on post-Reconstruction, north-oriented urbanization of African-American life, lies in the self-reflexive nature of all the voices speaking and in speaking, coming to a consciousness of themselves and their environment. Time and again we hear voices self-consciously grappling with their Harlem realities, which include an international awareness of African-American, West Indian and African bonding. In a poem like "The Negro Speaks of Rivers," the speaking voice transcends racial and tribal divides to express a cultural and racial pride and solidarity with blacks in the African Diaspora, whatever their nationality. When the Negro speaks of rivers, not only does he unfold before us a saga of deprivation and inhumanity, but also an exuberant cultural historiography that recalls to mind the contribution as well as the rich cultural heritage of one of the oldest civilizations of the world:

> My Soul has grown deep like the rivers
> I bathed in the Euphrates when the dawns were young.
> I built my hut near the Congo and it lulled me to sleep.
> I looked upon the Nile and raised the pyramids above it.
> I heard the singing of the Mississippi when Abe Lincoln
> went down to New Orleans, and I've seen its muddy
> bosom turn all golden in the sunset. (*LHR* 88)

Articulating the sentiment of a collective black consciousness and pan-national racial solidarity that survives in black subcultures everywhere, his poetry is a celebration of this blackness as well as a demonstration of the fact that the political impetus of the postcolonial begins well before the moment of independence. For black people the experience of colonialism is a racial experience that proceeds from the idea of race as a major feature of economic and political discrimination. This leads to the creation of "what Irele describes as a 'community of blood,' and what Senghor calls a 'collective personality of the black people'" (Loomba 211). Consequently, Hughes' writing like all other urbane and subtle forms of protest, serves to demonstrate the silencing and marginality of the black voice, the abrogation of an imperial center within the text and the active appropriation of the language and culture of that center. A forceful illustration of assertions that almost appear to border on an inherent superiority, is thus discernible in the subtext of even a seemingly simple poem like "I, Too, Sing America":

> I, too, sing America.
> I am the darker brother.
> They send me to eat in the kitchen
> When company comes,
> But I laugh,

And eat well,
And grow strong.

Tomorrow,
I'll sit at the table
When company comes.
Nobody'll dare
Say to me,
"Eat in the kitchen,"
Then.

Besides,
They'll see how beautiful I am
And be ashamed—

I, too, am America. (*PN* 97)

Hughes thus conveys in a language that is not his own, a spirit that is his own. Even while celebrating racial and cultural difference, his Negritude challenges white constructions of the meaning and value attached to these associations. If a poem like "The Weary Blues" serves to highlight black plight and white apathy, it also becomes an ethnography of his own cultural specificity and its inherent black power, which is conveyed through recurring images of ebony on ivory, black on white:

Droning a drowsy syncopated tune,
Rocking back and forth to a mellow croon,
    I heard a negro play.
Down on Lenox Avenue the other night
By the dull pallor of an old gas light
    He did a lazy sway . . .
    He did a lazy sway . . .
To the tune of those Weary blues.
With his ebony hands on each ivory key
He made that poor piano moan with melody.
    O Blues! . . .
Sweet blues!
Coming from a black man's soul. (*PN* 98)

It is the black man's 'soul' then that is laid bare in poems that reflect Hughes' commitment to blackness. The poem is a rich tribute to the black performing artist through its commanding image of the black musical magician who also serves as a metaphor for the African American experience up to the 1920s. Centuries of confrontation of black lives with the ambiguities of their universe and that of American culture have forced the Negro artist to look more searchingly towards the dominant WASP American cultural perspective. Rejecting what the cultural critic Arthur Berger terms as its "melting pot metaphor of cultural homogenization" (140), Hughes emphasizes not only the importance of maintaining a black sub-cultural identity even while being American, but also demands an acknowledgement of the fact that the white American structure rests on black scaffolding:

> God of dust and rainbows
> Help us to see
> That without the dust
> The rainbow would not be. (Cited from Berry 180)

His text thus becomes an important means of inverting and challenging dominant means of representation and colonial ideologies:

> It's not easy to know what is true for you or me
> . . . But I guess I'm what
> I feel and see and hear. Harlem, I hear you: . . .
> I guess being colored doesn't make me *not* like
> the same things other folks like who are other races.
> So will my page be colored that I write?
> Being me, it will not be white.
> But it will be
> a part of you, instructor.
> You are white—
> Yet a part of me, as I am part of you
> That's American. (*MODD* 40)

Hughes' poetry plunges into Harlem, the ultimate symbolic black cultural space—the city within a city, the "Mecca of the Negro," as Alain Locke, the Harvard University Professor of Philosophy, put it in 1925, to explore the variegated uptown and downtown life of America's very own heart of darkness. "Harlem was like a magnet for the Negro intellectual, pulling him from everywhere" wrote Hughes. "Once in New York, he had to live in Harlem. Harlem was not so much a *place* as a state of mind, the cultural metaphor for black America itself." A cultural and psychological watershed, the Harlem Renaissance was an era in which black people were perceived as having finally liberated themselves from a past fraught with self-doubt. They had surrendered instead, to an unprecedented optimism, a novel pride in all things black and a cultural confidence that stretched beyond the borders of Harlem to other black communities in the Western world. This cultural confidence is best reflected in the spirit of bonhomie, freedom and fellow-feeling that prevailed at the rent-parties, speakeasies, buffet-flats and costume balls that formed the sub-cultural life of Harlem and which Hughes described as "spectacles in color." The inimitable lesbian figures of the Blues great, Bessie Smith and the 250-pound pianist Gladys Bentley whom Hughes called an "amazing exhibition of musical energy," along with other black vaudeville entertainers good timing their way through life, all find a place in Hughes' poetry. Yet, notes of severe skepticism and weariness often percolate the narrative, and even though they are largely resolved by the exuberant cultural historiography that constantly engages the poet, they never vanish from his score. Behind the happy Negro exterior, the boisterous music lies the hurt in the heart:

> You think
> It's a happy beat?
> Listen to it closely:
> Ain't you heard
> Something underneath (*MODD* 3)

Lennox Avenue is thus viewed, as not only the cultural hub of black life, but also as the repository of dreams and aspirations gone awry, of disappointments and betrayals, of 'night funerals' and 'red sun blues.' Harlem is the ultimate "Jim-Crow section/ On this merry go round," which provides "the horse/ For the kid that's black" (*TPTL* 92). Trapped in a matrix of structural repression, and intimidated through a violent repression of opposition, hundred years of supposed black freedom are marked by a progression that can only question the very objectivity of the American justice system:

> From the slave chain to the lynch rope
> To the bullets of Yorkville,
> Jamestown, 1619-1963
> Emancipation Centennial,
> 100 years NOT free. (*TPTL* 15)

Hughes' deepest hope for black militancy and the enfranchisement of his community lay in art. These were large claims but not unrealistic ones as long as art continued to define itself as resistive, as continually aligned against diffidence from colored people who were uncertain about their abilities to participate in the grand ritual of resistance. His poetry with its deepest fund of history inflected through its melodious and regional music, thus lent a discursive dimension to a drama of otherness that took place on a split stage. Two misallied characters had resigned themselves to their hierarchic positions in a culture, which practiced an art of deception that was psychologically debilitating to its subjects. Jazz, Hughes believed, was the instrument "best fitted to express the rebelliousness of a whole people against the unworthy lot that some hoped to impose on them forever" (Wagner 386). If modern poetry tended towards a fusion with painting, Hughes' uniqueness lay in his adapting the rhythms of black music to poetry. If language and writing were to be used as weapons of protest against individual, group and structural repression, he was making use of exactly those capacities that the whites did not expect blacks to possess or even allow them to develop. Jazz with its sense of immediacy, its cultural associations and intellectual foundations, which evoked a "visceral, emotional and intellectual" impact on the listener as Morrison describes it (viii), was thus for Hughes:

> one of the inherent expressions of Negro life in America; the eternal tom-tom beating in Negro soul—the tom-tom of revolt against weariness in a white world, a world of sub-way trains, and work, work, work; the tom-tom of joy and laughter, and pain swallowed in a smile." (Peplow and Davis 475)

Although poems like "Ballad of the Landlord," never entirely assuage the linguistic, social, and political conflicts that Hughes addresses himself to, yet they do assert the overwhelming prominence of the black predicament:

> Landlord, Landlord
> My roof has sprung a leak. . . .
> These steps is broken down. . . .
> Ten bucks you say I owe you?
>
> What? You gonna get eviction orders?
> You gonna cut off my heat?
> You gonna take my furniture and
> Throw it in the street?
> Um-huh! You talking high and mighty.
> Talk on—till you get through.
> You ain't gonna be able to say a word
> If I land my fist on you.
>
> Police! Police!
> Come and get this man!
> He's trying to ruin the government
> And overturn the land!
>
> Headlines in press:
> MAN THREATENS LANDLORD . . .
> TENANT HELD NO BAIL . . .
> JUDGE GIVES NEGRO 90 DAYS IN COUNTY JAIL
> (*MODD* 2)

It is in such poems that Hughes locates much of the trenchant interrogation that sustains his poetry. Now and again uneasy truces are worked out in poems between the blacks and the governing WASP community. He envisions a possible future in which "Martin Luther King is the governor of Georgia" and "Dr. Rufus Clement" the then white president of Atlanta University, his "Chief Advisor." He imagines "Wealthy negroes" in "white pillared mansions" with "white servants" and "colored children" with "white nannies" (*AYM* 8-9). These however, are truces whose terms have misrepresented black biographies. Recording evidence to correct such misrepresentations then, is one of the fundamental purposes of Hughes' works. He has thus succeeded remarkably, in providing for his community a deeply assimilative work that immediately becomes essential to further assessments of the African-American literary tradition.

NOTES

1. In the late 60s, when the Black Power movement was at its most aggressive phase of expansion, there were real fears that open conflict, almost of civil war dimensions would break out in American cities. However, increasing liberalization and better opportunities for the social advancement and education of Negroes, saw a dramatic change in the state of the American Negro in the 70s, with Blacks penetrating middle-class and professional strata of society at a rate, which would have seemed incredible twenty years ago. Although this has slightly dulled the movement's sense of purpose, urban ghettoes still exist and provide numerous flash points for black-white conflict. Nevertheless, most observers now view the future with optimism, for America is fast becoming one of the most integrated countries of the world, a fact that can be partly traced to the injustices and conflicts that launched Black Power into being.
2. Negritude, as Loomba rightly suggests, "is a reactive position, and yet it tries to create an identity free of colonialism's taint." Both Cesaire and Senghor "chart a dichotomy between Africa and Europe in terms that celebrate the former." (212). As Ran Greenstein points out: "Pan-Africanism, Negritude and Black Consciousness have all emerged in the aftermath of the colonial encounter, and not just in their written forms, although they have drawn on and sought to mobilize pre-colonial discourses." ('History and the Production of Knowledge,' *South African Historical Journal* 32, May 1995: 227). Franz Fanon on the other hand, was highly critical of the Negritude movement and proposed against it, a national literature. However, even though "both 'the nation' and pan-national racial essence are contentious conceptions," as Loomba points out, they have nevertheless "helped anti-colonial consciousness" (213).

Works Cited

Berger, Arthur A. *Cultural Criticism: A Primer of Key Concepts.* California: Sage, 1995.

Berry, Faith. *Langston Hughes: Before and beyond Harlem.* West Port: Lawrence Hill, 1983.

Burris, Sidney. "An Empire of Poetry." *Postcolonial Literatures.* 259-68.

Hughes, Langston. *Selected Poems.* New York: Alfred A. Knopf, 1979. Hereafter cited as *SP*

_____. *The Panther and the Lash: Poems of Our Time.* New York: Alfred A. Knopf, 1974. Hereafter cited as *TPTL.*

_____. *Ask Your Mama: 12 Moods for Jazz.* New York: Alfred A. Knopf, 1961. Hereafter cited as *AYM.*

_____. *The Langston Hughes Reader.* New York: Braziller, 1958. Hereafter cited as *LHR.*

_____. *Montage of a Dream Deferred.* New York: Henry Holt, 1951. Hereafter cited as *MODD.*

Hughes, Langston and Arna Bontemps, ed. *The Poetry of the Negro 1746-1949.* New York: Doubleday, 1949.

Kent, George E. "Langston Hughes and Folk and Cultural Tradition." *Langston Hughes Black Genius: A Critical Evaluation.* Ed. Therman B. O'Daniel. New York: William Morrow, 1971: 183-210.

Loomba, Ania. *Colonialism/ Postcolonialism.* London and New York: Routledge, 1999.

Parker, Michael and Roger Starkey, ed. *Postcolonial Literatures: Achebe, Ngugi, Desai, Walcott: Contemporary Critical Essays.* London: Macmillan, 1995.

Morrison, Toni. *Playing in the Dark: Whiteness and the Literary Imagination.* Cambridge, Massachusetts: Harvard UP, 1992.

Peplow, Michael W. and Arthur P. Davis, ed. *The New Negro Renaissance: An Anthology.* New York: Rinehart and Winston, 1975.

Wagner, Jean. *Black Poets of the United States: From Paul Lawrence Dunbar to Langston Hughes.* Urbana: University of Illinois Press, 1973.

Folk Creativity as a Subversive Gesture in Zora Neale Hurston's *Their Eyes Were Watching God*

PUNAM GUPTA
Dev Samaj College for Women, Chandigarh

Black women have been in America since 1619. After having been mercilessly snatched from their homelands and undergoing the de-humanizing ordeal of the 'Middle Passage,' this 'human cargo' arrived well prepared for their new role in America, that is, that of slaves. In slavery black woman was victimized in multiple ways: she was the object of lust of the white man; she was made the breeder of human property by forced mating with the black slaves; she was made to serve as farm-mule—doing arduous jobs on the plantation; she had to be mammy to the white children, when her heart bled to care for her own; she was the object of violent and jealous hatred of the white woman and of the black man. This dehumanization of the black woman was not limited to the period of slavery alone or to the American South. The racial and sexual politics of the post-emancipation period in America that either left the black man unemployed, or made him a family deserter, or lynched him, put the onus of family survival on the black woman for which she was once again sexually exploited by the White man and then dumped as an evil temptress, a bitch or a matriarch.

The main objective of any coloniser/enslaver in so victimizing a people is to beat their language and culture out of them. But it goes to the credit of the black woman that memory and pride persisted in her and it manifested itself in various forms of artistry—writing, communal talking, story telling, growing gardens and quilt-making. June Jordan calls this creativity a miracle:

> Come to a country to be docile and dumb, to be big and breeding, . . . to be turkey/horse/cow, to be cook/carpenter/ plow, to be 5'6" 140 lbs., in good condition and answering to the name of Tom or Mary: to be bed bait: to be legally spread legs for rape by the master/ the master's son/ the master's overseer/ the master's nephew: to be nothing human nothing family nothing from nowhere. . . . How could you, belonging to no one, but property to those despising the smiles of your soul, how could you dare to create yourself: a poet? (87)

To me, this creativity of the black woman is her form of resistance to all the powers that dominated her. Miraculous as it is, it is also subversive in nature. I quote Nghana Lewis, who says,

> Even the most oppressive forms of domination . . . are not hermetic and, in fact, have cleavages, spaces, margins, and gaps that "the other" can search to acquire agency.[2]

My conceptualization of human subjectivity and agency is based on this theoretical foundation.

Phillis Wheatley is the first published Black female poet in America. Sold into slavery at the age of seven, two volumes of her verses were published by the year 1773, when Wheatley was only nineteen years of age. I quote briefly from two of her poems:

> The Goddess comes, she moves divinely fair,
> Olive and Laurel binds her golden hair[3]

> Should you, my Lord, while you peruse my song,
> Wonder from whence my love of freedom sprung,
> I, young in life, by seeming cruel fate,
> Was snatched from Africa's fancied happy seat.[4]

I have particularly chosen these two extracts, because Wheatley has been held to ransom on account of calling Liberty or her white mistress Goddess in the first poem and for the 'contrary instincts' of the second poem, where she is not sure whether the fate which snatched her from her homeland was cruel or not, whether her homeland was really happy or she just fancied it to be happy. Wheatley has been called a traitor and an idiot for writing such poetry.

My point however is, that in the very act of writing poetry, Wheatley has taken a political step, which not only asserts her own humanity, but that of the entire race to which she belongs. We know that the philosophers of history had suggested that the absence of writing among blacks proved the absence of reason, of history, of culture and of traditions. This had been made the most powerful plea in the enslaving of the 'apes' of the 'dark' continent. So, when Wheatley writes poetry in the 18th century, she is creating a counter-hegemonic discourse. It becomes a unique rhetorical strategy to counteract the self-evident relation between blackness and stupidity or blackness and absence. I call Wheatley's poem her cultural space which is an act of self-will and based on her intense creativity with words. And this is not all. Slaves were not supposed to know anything of their age, their genealogy, or their place of origin any more than beasts did. By tracing her origin to Africa, Wheatley has asserted awareness of identity through geography, which in itself, is a subversive gesture.

From the writing of poetry as a radically subversive act, I come to another artistry of the African American woman—communal talking. These triply marginalized (black, female and lower class) women were not the ones to take their invisibility lying down. They fought subversively with the only weapon at their command: the spoken word. In her autobiographical essay, "Poets in the Kitchen" (1983), Paule Marshall recalls how ladies from her mother's and grandmother's neighborhood got together in the kitchen every afternoon and talked endlessly, passionately and poetically on topics like politics, militancy, neighborhood gossip and their homeland, Barbados. This talk restored them to a sense of self-worth. Through language they were able to overcome the humiliations of everyday life. Their exuberant talk also functioned as an outlet for the tremendous creative energy they possessed, because they were women in whom the need for self-expression, as Marshall tells us, was very strong. Marshall attributes her own first lessons in "narrative art" to this "workshop" of the kitchen. I quote Bell Hooks:

> For us [black women], true speaking is not solely an expression of creative power; it is an act of resistance, a political gesture that challenges [the *gender*] politics of domination that would render us nameless and voiceless.[5]

In a 1974 essay, 'In Search of My Mother's Garden,' Alice Walker too has remembered her mother as an artist for her storytelling ability, from whom Alice herself unconsciously learnt not only all her stories but also her mother's performative style in narrating them. But Walker has credited her mother (and all Black mothers) for more than one way of artistry—others being her skill with planting gardens and making quilts. Walker says that the hazards of a sharecropping life constantly kept her family on the move when she was a child. But whatever shabby place they made a new home, her mother planted a petunia garden which counteracted the disruption of their life and helped them have a sense of identity and rootedness. She has also paid a rich tribute to the tradition of quilting by her black mothers. These otherwise overworked mothers and grandmothers stitched quilts very fast so that their family would not freeze, but they stitched them beautifully so that their heart would not break. Mostly patched out of reused scraps that were given to the black women in place of the wages that were due to them for their labour in the white man's house, these women put their creative imagination to use and stitched lovely story quilts that satisfied their sense of artistry. Quilting thus became a way of acquiring agency for these oppressed black women who were denied even basic material survival. Houston Baker, Jr. and Charlotte Pierce Baker see quilting as a paradigm for the effects of the African Diaspora:

> Weaving, shaping, sculpting, or quilting in order to create a kaleidoscopic and momentary array is tantamount to providing an improvisational response to chaos. . . . It constitutes survival strategy and motion in the face of dispersal. A patchwork quilt, laboriously and affectionately crafted from bits of worn overalls, shredded uniforms, tattered petticoats, and outgrown dresses stands as a signal instance of a patterned wholeness in the African diaspora.[6]

Now I propose to make a detailed analysis of what to me is the contestational ethnic creativity of the female protagonist of Zora Neale Hurston's novel, *Their Eyes Were Watching God.* Hurston is a novelist, anthropologist, storywriter, autobiographer and a writer of essays, too. She lived and wrote in the first half of the twentieth century. Hurston's pride in black culture is exemplary and Alice Walker acknowledged her as her literary foremother. Hurston had once said, "I am not tragically colored. . . . How can anyone deny themselves the pleasure of my company?" Her novel *Their Eyes Were Watching God,* written in 1937, has Janie Starks—a cream-colored black woman as the central character. The novel is considered as the quest for identity of a black woman as she goes through three marriages. My point is that at various stages in the novel and even in the end, Janie's acquiring agency is a function of the ways in which she creatively adapts herself to any situation in life by putting to use one of her cultural codes.

In the early part of the novel, Janie a sixteen-year old girl has an orgasmic view of a bee fertilizing a pear tree in bloom and she tells herself, "So, this is a marriage!" Her three marriages then turn out to be a search for this bee-man who can give her ultimate happiness. But at the end of the novel when she returns to Eatonville after burying her third husband, she realizes that there is really no bee-man. But this thought does not make her unhappy. Instead she has a triumphant feeling and tells her best friend Phoeby, "Ah'm back home again and Ah'm satisfied tuh be heah."[7]

Janie's Nanny, who was born and lived in slavery could not think of the black woman as any better than the mule of the world. She did dream of sitting on a 'pulpit' to preach a sermon to black women, but to her this pulpit is the security of marriage. To her Janie's growing sexuality is alarming and she huddles her into marriage with a well-to-do aged farmer, Logan Killicks who is the owner of sixty acres and a mule. While Nanny is extremely satisfied with herself for having done the best she could for her baby girl, Janie is absolutely frustrated. Her vision of marriage as sweet things happening under a pear tree is completely desecrated as there is no love or romance in this marriage and Killicks is ugly and dirty looking. To Killicks, Janie is mere workhorse and he thinks he has done her a great favor by lifting her from the white folks' backyard and by giving her a house of her own.

Janie is young and restless and she jumps at the first possibility of change and chance when she meets the stylish, citified Joe Starks. He too looks much older to the seventeen-year old Janie and does not seem to represent sun-up and blooming trees, but Janie is willing to experiment. She runs away with Joe and marries him.

At Eatonville Joe (or Jody as he is called) becomes a "big voice" very soon and thinks Janie should be very proud and thankful to him for having made her "Mrs. Mayor Starks." To him the cream-colored Janie is just one of the essential pieces of property among his other criteria of success like the big white house, the store, the post office, the paved streets and the street lamps. Janie's frustrations begin and she tells Jody that somehow they are not natural and sweet with each other and always under a kind of strain in the pursuit of ambition. Jody laughs her off. What irks Janie most however is that at the store porch, which becomes the heart and spring of the town, men get together and tell stories, laugh, joke and make merry. While Jody himself takes part in the fun and games, he forbids his 'Queen of the Porch' from having anything to do with the 'laity.' He just wants her to clerk for him at the store. "Janie feels far away from things and lonely," (211) we are told. Only if things had stopped at that, Janie perhaps could have borne up. But it so happens that Jody's sexism begins to manifest in publicly ridiculing her for little faults at the store. He blames her for puny brains: "When Ah see one thing, I understand ten, when you see ten things, you don't even understand one." Then again, "Someone got to think for women and children and chickens and cows. They don't think none themselves" (232). Initially Janie tries to get even with him by fighting back with her tongue but she realizes that it does not get her anywhere. Jody must have her total submission and he does not stop until he thinks he has it. It is here that Janie makes her first subversive move: "She gradually pressed her teeth and learned to hush" (232). No matter what Jody did or said, she said nothing. In this assumption of silence and seeming submission to Jody, Janie has put to use an aspect of her folk legacy—that is, donning a "lying mask." Right from slavery when blacks were unable to fight the atrocities of institutionalized white superiority, they assumed a grinning, lying mask. By doing so, they seemingly fitted the white man's conception of them as stupid and happy and escaped punishment. Why I call Janie's silence 'masking' is because it is clearly a self-division testified by the text. One day when Jody slaps her for cooking a bad meal, she experienced the following revelation:

> She stood there until something fell off the shelf inside her. Then she went inside there to see what it was, it was her image of Jody tumbled down and shattered. . . . She found that she had a host of thoughts she had never expressed to him, and numerous emotions she had never let Jody know about. . . . She was saving up feelings for some man she had never seen. She had an inside and an outside now and suddenly she knew how not to mix them. (233)

Soon after this incident she bathed and put on a fresh head kerchief and went to the store. "That was a bow to the outside of things," the narrator tells us. Further

> Then one day she sat and watched the shadow of herself going about tending store and prostrating itself before Jody, while all the time she herself sat under a shady tree with the wind blowing through her hair and her clothes. Somebody near about making summertime out of lonesomeness.
>
> This was the first time it happened, but after a while it got so common she ceased to be surprised. It was like a drug. In a way it was good because it reconciled her to things. She got so she received all things with the stolidness of the earth which soaks up urine and perfume with the same indifference. (236)

John Lowe says that Janie's silence is pregnant with creativity which becomes manifest in her later tirade against Jody.[8] Thomas Kochman would call this "fronting" which is a mechanism whereby African Americans consciously suppress what they truly feel or believe. This was a daily habit for every American black child since childhood. It represents the prudence of silence when speech would generate risks.[9] I call it Janie's movement into an autonomous cultural space which she is able to create for herself imaginatively. This space becomes empowering for Janie during the traumatizing years of her marriage to Jody.

Yet it is not in her long silence, but in her use of voice finally that Janie acquires agency in her marriage to Jody. Jody had begun to publicly humiliate her for her advancing age by calling her an old hen of forty or "you are no courting gal now," etc. But one day he crossed all limits of decency when he began talking under her clothes in the "Old as Methusalem" speech. Now Janie's patience is exhausted. She takes centrestage on the store porch and begins "playing the dozens" on him, which is an African American ritual of verbal insult. She tells him:

> Humph! Talkin' 'bout me lookin' old! When you pull down yo' britches, you look lak de change uh life. (238)

Roger Abrahams tells us that playing the dozens is a male privilege.[10] So when Janie indulges in this ritualistic insult, she clearly subverts Jody's patriarchal values. Jody feels so humiliated after this that he takes to bed and dies soon after. At the time of his death also Janie's empowering self-division comes handy:

> Then she starched and ironed her face, forming it into just what people wanted to see. . . . The funeral was going on outside. . . . Enough weeping and wailing outside. Inside the expansive black folds were resurrection and life . . . she sent her face to Joe's funeral, and herself went rollicking with the springtime across the world. (246)

After Jody's death, Janie meets Tea Cake, a troubadour who is several years younger to her. She soon finds herself playing checkers with him, fishing by moonlight and displaying affection freely. She thinks that Tea Cake could be a bee to a blossom. She marries him and together they embark for a nomadic existence on the "muck"—the Florida Everglades. Here Janie has full freedom to find the people and gain the sense of community she has always craved for. She listens and laughs and tells big stories herself. It is a life of making money and sheer fun and foolishness. Added to this is the intensity of love in her relationship with Tea Cake. All this definitely helps Janie thrive spiritually. But Janie has not attained full subjectivity even at this point of her life. It is only after Tea Cake's death that Janie attains a liberatory subjectivity by harnessing the power of her vision, her creative imagination and by privileging her own memory, her own experience and narrative authority. She returns home and plants a packet of seeds left by Tea Cake, thereby committing him to memory. She will live on the power of a selective memory of Tea Cake and not be a prisoner to his memory. She shares the story of her life with her best friend Phoeby and through her with her community. She thus passes on her wisdom that she had acquired by her complete immersion in her culture on the 'muck.' She has understood that life is not about sixty acres or about being a 'Queen' or even about deeply loving a 'bee-man.' This consciousness that female dependency on a male is not consistent with the attainment of full agency, is definitely a subversive realization for Janie. Janie has understood that the fact that as long as she can remember, she can think and she can communicate her memory and her thoughts, she is empowered to resist all forces that would seek to suppress her.

NOTES

1. June Jordan, "The Difficult Miracle of Black Poetry in America or Something Like a Sonnet for Philis Wheatley," *On Call: Political Essays* (London: Pluto Press, 1986), p. 87.
2. Nghana Lewis, "'We Must Speak with the Same Weapons': Reinscribing Resistance in Zora Neale Hurston's *Dust Tracks on a Road*," *CLA Journal*, XLV, 3 March 2002, p. 311.
3. Alice Walker, "In Search of Our Mother's Gardens," *In Search of Our Mother's Gardens* (New York: Harcourt Brace Jovanovich, 1983), p. 236.
4. Phillis Wheatley, "To The Right Honourable William, Earl of Dartmouth," *The Poems of Phillis Wheatley*, ed. Julian D. Mason (Chapel Hill: University of North Carolina Press, 1966), p. 83

5. Bell Hooks, *Talking Back: Thinking Feminist, Thinking Black* (Boston: South End Press, 1989), p. 9.
6. Houston Baker Jr. and Charlotte Pierce Baker, "Patches: Quilts and Community in Alice Walker's 'Everyday Use,'" *Southern Review*, 21.3 (July 1985), p. 706.
7. Zora Neale Hurston, *Their Eyes Were Watching God, Novels and Stories*, ed. Cheryl A. Wall (New York: Literary Classics of the US, 1995), p. 332.
8. John Lowe, *Jump at the Sun: Zora Neale Hurston's Cosmic Comedy* (Urbana: University of Illinois Press, 1994), p. 169.
9. Lowe, p. 175.
10. Roger Abrahams, "Playing the Dozens" *Mother Wit from the Laughing Barrell* (New Jersey: Prentice Hall, 1973), p. 305.

Racism and the Literature of Protest in Ralph Ellison's *Invisible Man*

R.G. KULKARNI
N.D. Patil Night College, Sangli

With increasing vehemence from social and economic institutions, African Americans had to live in a society in which the majority was convinced that the Black people were inferior to the Whites. The argument was that they should therefore be consigned to a place of permanent social, economic and political subordination. The bitterness of White racism was a powerful spur to literary activity, as African American writers sought to use their writings to fight against racist practices and ideas. These writers believed that literature could strike a blow against racism and in their works they directly confronted the conditions of an increasingly racist society in everything from their choice of subjects, to the way they portrayed their characters, and the kinds of moods they tried to portray. African American writing not only protested against racism, but created a protest that took account of changing conditions.

As we know, a very cruel slavery was imposed on the African Americans for more than three centuries. The land of liberty locked them in the dark dungeon of slavery. Their racial problem resulted in social, economic, political and cultural problems. The inhuman exploitation of the African Americans has no parallel in the history of mankind. Slavery was institutionalized in the social behavior. The Whites treated the African Americans as per the code ingrained in the minds of both the Whites and the Blacks. J.M. Wagmare rightly says:

> Freedom without bread is meaningless. They [the African Americans] felt that slavery with bread was better than freedom without bread. But it was also true that bread with slavery was poisoned

> bread. The option before them was obvious and clear. They chose freedom because it gave them strength to struggle. "All men were created equal." This was the corner stone of the American constitution. Here all men did not include black men. That was unfortunate reality. (18-19)

The African American writers faced racial dilemma. What was America to them? A deep well of sorrow? A land of travail and trauma? They knew that their forefathers were brought to America in chains and auctioned. Waghmare further says:

> The black Americans have made the land fertile with their efforts and blood. It is because of the black Americans, America is a land of crowning glory. . . . Africa, the land of [black Americans'] ancestors, cannot altogether disappear from their memories, however faint these might be. Africa occupies a special place in their hearts and souls. Their conscious minds are filled with America but Africa struck forever in their psyche. That is the reason why they call themselves Afro-Americans. (20-21)

The history of the African Americans is a long passage of time telling a tale of two continents. They were thrown out of their own history, faith and culture. It is a story of an endless hallucination of agony. They have not lost their hope. They regard this endless hallucination of agony as a kind of liberation through which they regenerate their strength. To understand this we must read Ralph Ellison's *Invisible Man*. It deals with the essence of black identity caught in the crisis. Ralph Ellison has been recognized as a well-known versatile writer of American fiction. He has enjoyed charismatic glamour for the last four and half decades. His only novel, *Invisible Man* (1952) has been recognized as a modern classic. The subject matter of the novel is sociological. The content is moral and its revelation is purely artistic. Social awareness, aspirations of humanism, eternal values with specific reference to art, is explored in this novel. It highlights the pangs, the trials and tribulations experienced by the African Americans. It was the turning point in African American literature because for the first time it echoed the sense of protest. In the novel, the protagonist asks a pertinent question to providence in his baritone voice:

> What did I do?
> To be so black
> And blue?

He is condemned because he is black. What it means to be a black man in this world dominated by the white race? The African Americans have too much to say but the art experience is different from practical experience. Literature tries to give in-depth analysis with generic discipline. So art experience is richer than actual human experience. Ellison clearly says, "People who want to write sociology should not write a novel."

Invisible Man is a documentation of the African American identity. It refers to American culture and iconography. Narrated in the first person, the protagonist is a typical Ellison brand character. He doesn't claim any special name. The story moves around his self. He has not sacrificed his self but his existence has the depressions on White society. The protagonist lives in a basement that is surrounded by 1339 electric bulbs but his existence is not felt. He calls himself:

> I am an Invisible Man. No, I am not a spook like those who haunted Edgar Allan Poe; nor am I one of your Hollywood movie ectoplasms. I am a man of substance, of flesh and bone. Fiber and liquids and I might even be said to possess a mind. I am invisible, understand simply because people refuse to see me. (7)

In America the African Americans were not counted. In the sophisticated world of Whites they have been exploited. Even the protagonist's grandfather on his deathbed told him to continue the struggle for self-esteem. He had further advised him to preserve his identity till his last breath.

The central theme of *Invisible Man* is the quest for identity in a chaotic world, the struggle between hypocrisy and modern idealism, the abuse of political and economic power. Ellison in his novel retains a broad political focus on both racial consciousness and national culture by redefining the terms of social reality. As Thomas Schaub observes:

> As a novel of social reality *Invisible Man* describes a culture in which the difference that separates black from white, both within

society and within the mind that has internalized those symbolic pigments, is a difference of race so vast that Invisible Man is not merely awkward or out of place. He is invisible. Though this condition of being excluded is one that Ellison universalizes, it has its origin in real relations and is the initial and unproblematic meaning of the psychological reality.

> You often doubt if you really exist. You wonder whether you are not simply a phantom in other people's minds. Say, a figure in a nightmare which the sleeper tries with all his strength to destroy. It's when you feel like this that, out of resentment, you begin to bump people back. And let me confess, you feel that way most of the time. You ache with the need to convince yourself that you do exist in the real world. (7)

Thus *Invisible Man* is a tale of the harsh reality of racial segregation. Ellison records the redemptive cultural life of the African Americans. He explores both the meaning of black invisibility in white America and, in counterpoint, the vital culture of African Americans. The novel transcended America's social dilemma and made that dilemma undeniably important. In tracing the development of the protagonist through a sequence of historical events—Black college life in the south, an encounter with veterans of World War I, migrating to Harlem, northern factory work, involvement with a live wing political group, and the advent of a writing career, Ellison has chosen techniques of autobiography.

As the protagonist moves from one tentative role to another, he attempts to cast off the earlier part of his identity that the new roles cannot accept. Simultaneously with becoming a brother, he tries to discard the bank, which is an image of different kinds of dependencies. The Invisible Man's attempt to destroy the bank suggests the corps of jazz musicians who have refused to smile while playing in order to prevent association with the old image from coming back to destroy the dignity of their art. In spite of his attempts, the invisible man cannot get rid of the bank. A white woman and a white man force him to retrieve first out of the garbage and then of the street. So he seals up in the briefcase all the other clues that would help him to identify things which he refuses to accept. The briefcase is an emblem of him, a container of images that he hates but cannot lose:

> "What in that briefcase," they said, and if they asked me anything else, I might have stood still. But at the question a wave of shame and outrage shook me and I run, still heading for jack, but I was in strange territory now and someone, for some reason, had removed the manhole cover and I felt myself plunge down. (455)

Earlier the same question was asked to him by the doctors, and now he is ready to find the answer. In the darkness of his hole he is forced to explore the contents of the briefcase, which are the real clues to his identity. Thomas A. Vogler says: "In this exploration the big issues are the problems of politics, of freedom, of brotherhood, of the rejection of a father and the loss of a mother, the distrust of rhetoric and abstractions which dilute experience and disguise reality."

All of these issues are the elements in the former patterns and structure of the novel. But all of these are tied together by the central problem of finding identity.

The African American writer's confrontation with the disparity in him is a double consciousness that grows out of his investigation of what identity in America means for him. Protest is blended with autobiographical fact to produce allegory. Ellison discovers that to be Black, American, and an artist does not negate being human. The act of writing, out of his experience of 'racism' frees him from its impact and creativity. Such is the case of *Invisible Man*.

The novel is also a satire on racial discrimination and hypocritical elements in American society. America is a country that has lost its soul. It is a country with a mistaken identity. Even though the Invisible Man gets the pleasures denied to the African Americans, Ellison is not happy. He feels that all the teachings relating to humbleness and nobleness have failed. He feels that he lives in the country of his enemy. He does not blame anybody. He does not capitalize the stories of his humiliation. As a reason he is prepared for self-scrutiny. He accepts the facts, the invitations, the passions, the pangs etc. He has no ideology to preach. He has no philosophy to guide the generations. I think he is an existentialist. The novel has a capacity to make us restless and therein lies its greatness.

Works Cited

Ellison, Ralph. *Invisible Man.* Penguin Modern Classics, 1952.

Schaub, Thomas. "Ellison's Masks and the Novel of Reality," *New Essays on* Invisible Man, ed. Rabert O. Mealy. Cambridge: Cambridge UP, 1988: 123.

Vogler, Thomas A. "*Invisible Man*: Somebody's Protest Novel," *Ralph Ellison: A Collection of Critical Essays*, ed. John Hensey. Englewood Cliffs, N.J. Prentice Hall, 1974: 138.

Waghmare, J.M. "Literature of Marginality," *Dalit Literature and African-American Literature*, ed. N.M. Aston. New Delhi: Prestige, 2001: 18-19.

A Forest on Fire: The Literary Imagination of Meena Alexander

E. NAGESWARA RAO
Formerly of Osmania University, Hyderabad

Meena Alexander quotes at least twice in her writings Sankara's words: "The world is a forest on fire" (*River and Bridge* 35). She uses the Buddhist philosopher Nagarjuna's words, "If fire is lit in water, who can extinguish it?" as an epigraph to her first novel, *Nampally Road*. She cites Nagarjuna in "Civil Strife" (2000) again. In her essay, "Exiled by a Dead Script," which was published almost at the beginning of her career in 1977 as a creative writer and which may be taken as a statement of her literary and linguistic credo, she likens language to flame: "Then the language will become flame, threatening in its rage to consume both the self which utters and the objects invoked. The body of the poet, no longer a phantom, now turns into a burning brand, consuming both itself and all that it touches" (3). As a girl in her native Kerala, she attempted to swallow fire by taking a lighted match inside her mouth, thinking she could acquire tongues of flame as in *Revelations*: "I really believed in it, until they thought it was too dangerous and stopped me" (Duncan 27).

It seems to me that Sankara's metaphor of the world as a forest on fire is deeply etched in Alexander's consciousness and informs much of her writing, both poetry and fiction, from the beginning. One of her earliest poems, "I Root My Name," begins:

> Our life is fire but these things remain (20)

The things which remain in her reckoning are the great trees and the river. The poet roots her name between the trees and the ancient timber. In another poem, "Text from the Middle Earth for Two Voices," in the same volume, *I Root my Name*, the speaker repeats:

> My face is burnt into an earth
> I cannot touch or see
> Where I am, I cannot be (27)

House of Thousand Doors includes descriptions in poetry or prose of quite a few heart-rending scenes. The speaker watches:

> Children torn by the winds
> Married women burnt in their own homes (53)

in "Brief Chronicle by Candle Light."

"Hotel Alexandria" describes a pathetic scene which Alexander watched within two weeks after her arrival in New York. An old people's home, Hotel Alexandria, located in the city of New York was demolished. The speaker observes an old woman walk out carrying her few belongings with great difficulty. The author contrasts this scene with the one at Alexandria on the seacoast. The tranquillity and happiness of the city of her childhood and the misery of old people driven out of their shelter on a wintry morning is a painful picture that haunts us. Similarly, "In Divi Seema" is a poignant rendering of the devastation caused by a great cyclone in the East Coast in 1977. The humiliation and suffering of individuals also find a responsive chord in the author. Her prose piece, "Mosquitoes in the Main Room," describes the ordeal of Rameeza Bi who was gang-raped by policemen in Hyderabad in 1976.

The long poem, "The Storm," is a metaphor not only for the "displacement [and] violence, but also [for] the poise of a ritualized order" which are all parts of the feminine world as the poet sees it. She observes the dance of death all over:

> In Baghdad's market places,
> In the side streets of Teheran,
> In Beirut and Jerusalem
> In Khartoum and Cairo,
> In Colombo and New Delhi,
> Jaffna, Ahmedabad and Meerut,

> On the highways of Haryana. . . .
> We mourn our dead (8)

Her song is one of pain and despair:

> Let me sing my song
> Even the crude parts of it
> The decrepit seethe of war,
> Cruelty inflicted in clear thought,
> Thought elided in brutal profiteering
> The infant's eyes still filled with sores. (9)

After narrating the gruesome matricide of Renuka by Parasurama at the bidding of his father Jamadagni, and Abraham's dragging of Isaac up Moriah mountain, the poet concludes with a paradox:

> Such songs of agony
> ravish our hearing. (22)

Alexander's memoir, *Fault Lines*, is an account of her multiple migrations across countries and continents, the consequent dislocation and trauma. Like the San Andreas Fault, she feels there is a crack, a fault line, caused by dislocation. One of the images which haunt her is that of young girls jumping into wells in her native Kerala. Suicide to escape social scandal due to pre-marital sex and pregnancy is a harrowing experience witnessed by Alexander in the impressionable years of her girlhood. The same images which restrict one's freedom and increase misery recur in "Night Scene: The Garden." If her personal dislocations make her feel suffocated by "the barbed wire" and the ferocious alphabets of flesh," she finds an analogy in the larger world: "These spaces [West Bank, Aden, Sri Lanka, Punjab] of radical dislocation are bounded by barbed wire" (*Fault Lines* 129).

Violence anywhere in the world elicits a prompt and sympathetic response from Alexander. In "News of the World," she writes:

> In Cambodia I carried my mother's head in a sack
> And ran three days and nights
> through a rice field (*River and Bridge* 6)

From the rice fields of Cambodia, Alexander's imagination travels to China, to Tiananmen. She dedicates a moving elegy to "The Young of Tiananmen":

> As blood swallowed them whole
> They became our blood
> As the sun swallowed them whole
> They became children of the sun
> What ink can inscribe them now
> The young of Tiananmen? (14)

A recurring feature of Alexander's writing is the vast sweep of history, mythology and literature in it. Sita and Draupadi are wronged and humiliated women who spend a good part of their lives in exile. In Alexander's case, exile is dislocation, albeit self-imposed. "San Andreas Fault" recounts tales of misery and death across the globe: "A Muslim woman in Sarajevo shot to death, Turks burnt alive in New Germany, a man in Somalia locked to his starved child . . . hundreds hacked to death in Ayodhya" (94-95).

Alexander is agonized over a series of racist incidents in New York city. She was herself a target of racial violence in New Jersey; she was the object of racially insulting remarks. She complains of her hyphenated existence, a black woman, and Indian woman, a woman poet, and so on. She hints that her tenure at her college was delayed for these reasons. The bitter personal experience of racial prejudice prompted her to write an important poem, "Art of Pariahs." She invokes the aid of the queen of Nubia and the Rani of Jhansi to put an end to racial discrimination. They shall not stop fighting

> Till tongues of fire wrap a tender blue,
> A second skin, a solace to our children. (80)

Alexander invites the two queens, of Nubia and of Jhansi:

> Come walk with me towards a broken wall
> —Beirut still burns—carved into its face.
> Outcastes all, let's conjure honey scraped from stones, . . .
> Manhattan's mixed rivers rising. (80)

The deep sense of personal humiliation which Alexander experienced because of her complexion and sex makes her lament:

> Arawac or Indian
> The names confine
> There is nothing for us
> In the white man's burden (*Shock of Arrival* 69)

These lines are from "Ashtamudi Lake." On reviewing this poem, the poet asks: "what would it be like to live in a house filled with flames?" (78) [One would choke to death.] This question is perhaps triggered by Sankara's metaphor of the world as a forest on fire, only reduced in scale. Her anguish of living amidst racially unfriendly surroundings makes her speak out in "San Andreas Fault":

> You have crossed a border, never to return
> Stranger in this soil, who will grant you burial? (94)

The multiple forms of violence such as "bombardment, mass shootings, curfews, riots, rapes, the forced exodus of civilians—when crystallized into art, reveal, not merely the extreme, enforced condition, but also the hidden structures of a world in which women have not often been at ease" (*Shock of Arrival* 86).

Meena Alexander's two novels, *Nampally Road* and *Manhattan Music,* also deal with exploding violence that affects civil society very badly. When the lawmakers and the law-enforcers commit heinous crimes with impunity as in *Nampally Road*, where is security for an individual? The rulers are insensitive to the needs and wishes of the people. Brutality, disorder and violence have reached alarming levels in the country. While one extremist group sets a running train on fire without any qualms of conscience, the policemen gangrape a woman in the police station, and the Chief Minister is busy celebrating his birthday in a vulgar display of his power, wealth and vanity. These incidents are symptomatic of a sick society. These are watched at close quarters by Mira Kannadical, the central character, a university lecturer, who carries on a passionate love affair with her colleague, Ramu, during the same period.

If *Nampally Road* deals with violence and brutality in a single city, Hyderabad, *Manhattan Music* is a collage of violence and cruelty across the globe. Alexander seems to be sensitive to violence in all forms anywhere. There are references to Polish gas chambers where thousands of Jews were annihilated. Sandhya Rosenblum's (the heroine of this novel) husband, Stephen Rosenblum, would not have been born if his parents were also sent to the gas chambers. Then, there is a reference to a childbirth in the Kuwaiti desert during the Gulf War. The Irish Republican Army's unsuccessful attempt to bomb Mrs. Thatcher and her cabinet, Rajiv Gandhi's assassination during Sandhya's visit to her home in Kerala, dead Apaches, broken and buried bodies of slaves, LTTE violence and the terror in Jaffna, horror in Bosnia, the Hindutva agenda, the fanatics of Waco, Texas, the attacks by Mullah Omar, Hiroshima—all these and many more reverberate through the imagination of Alexander and she links these disasters to show that the world is indeed on fire. The law of the jungle where might prevails over right seems to govern the course of events. Voices from Bosnia, Rwanda and Sri Lanka disturb Sandhya. Her cousin, Sakhi, comments: "New Yorkers had the Empire State Building and the World Trade Center. Still what good did it do to live staring down from an immense height at poverty and pain crawling on the ground, human beings drugged out of their minds, stabbed each other, shooting, for absolutely no reason except that nothing made sense and there is no reason to stop oneself" (131). Her conclusion is that the "new world is lit by anger" (136).

Manhattan Music was published in 1997, four years before the terrorist attacks on New York. But Sandhya had heard: "Men came from Sudan and Egypt making up bombs with fertilizers, rat poison, a real witches' brew. Men hiding the canisters in little holes in the ground, getting ready to blow up America" (179). Alexander wonders through the persona of the fictional Sandhya: "What if Manhattan were being bombed by an imaginary nation thousands of miles away?" (196) Was it a modern Cassandra warning before the actual event?

Alexander's more recent writings such as "Civil Strife" and *Illiterate Heart* continue to voice the same anxiety, anguish and agony. One of the recurring, but nagging, questions Alexander poses is: "What would it be like to live as an ordinary woman in a war zone, no water, no power, little food and always the terror of a moment by moment existence?" (196)

There may be some underlying themes such as love in *Nampally Road* and sex in *Manhattan Music* but it is a world in turmoil, a world cleft by many San Andreas Faults, a world ablaze, an exploding world that we observe in the poetry and fiction of Alexander. Out of despair and impatience at the course of events she asks: "Was Sankara right?" (*River and Bridge* 35). Her own answer, I rather suspect, will be in the affirmative.

Works Cited

Alexander, Meena. "Civil Strife." *Kavya Bharati*, 12 (2000), 40-41.

_____. "Exiled by a Dead Script." *The Journal of Indian Writing in English* (July 1977) 1-4.

_____. *Fault Lines: A Memoir*. New Delhi: Penguin, 1993.

_____. *House of a Thousand Doors: Poems and Prose Pieces*. Washington, D.C.: Three Continents Press, 1988.

_____. *Illiterate Heart*. Chicago: Triquarterly Books/ North-Western University Press, 2002.

_____. *I Root My.Name*. Calcutta: United Writers, 1977.

_____. *Manhattan Music*. San Francisco: Mercury House, 1997.

_____. *Nampally Road*. New Delhi: Orient Longman, 1992.

_____. *River and Bridge*. New Delhi: Rupa, 1995.

_____. *Shock of Arrival: Reflections on Post-Colonial Experience*. Boston: Southend Press, 1996.

_____. *The Storm: A Poem in Five Parts*. New York: Red Dust, 1989.

Duncan, Erika. "A Portrait of Meena Alexander." *World Literature Today*. 73 (1999) 23-28.

Questioning Otherness along the Fault Lines

NILA DAS
University of Kalyani, West Bengal

> "Night after night, I asked myself the question, what might it mean to look at myself straight. . . ? How many different gazes would that need?" (2)
> "What could I ever be but a mass of fault, a fault mass?" (3)
> "That's all I am, a woman cracked by multiple migrations. Uprooted so many times she can connect nothing with nothing." (3)

The deeply disturbed soul searching words are Meena Alexander's, the renowned Asian American poet and short story writer, who resents the very term Indian American or Asian American, the marginalizing 'ethnic' tag, that brands her as the unwelcome "Other" in the racially discriminating U.S. for all the drum beating of its postmodern multiculturalism and free equal society. Although Meena herself is fully aware that more than any other factor, it is her racial Otherness that has fetched her the much sought after visibility in the United States book market, "a gateway to a life in letters" she cherishes most, she smarts that the imposed Otherness has cost her a "resolute fracturing of sense: a splintering of older ways of being, ways of holding that might have made the mind think itself intact, innocent, without presumption" (1993: 201). Meena is not the only marginalized U.S. writer to feel the tag of racial 'Otherness' a serious impediment to the development of the creative mind.

The inner crisis that Meena speaks of in the lines cited at the beginning, however, has deeper nuances and refers to a more complex situation than what arises from being an "ethnic" American in the contemporary U.S. Meena belongs to the late twentieth century "special generation" of cultural refugees (as Catherine R. Stimpson identifies it), whose life course and mental space are contoured by multiple migrations/uprooting, who are "at home in several continents, in exile from all," who have 'Otherness' tattooed all over them, and yet are unable to come to terms with it. Perpetually in search of a homeland, over boundaries, across borders, the sensitive ones intensely feel they lack a way of being that keeps one in tune with oneself. They are never sure how to make the inner synchronization. Meena's *Fault Lines* (1993), a tenderly preserved, lyrical, reflective, thought provoking memoir, records her search for the tuning in her own terms.

The fascinating literary work vibrates with touching memories flowing through poetic images, dreams crossing the borders of reality, sharp socio-political analysis merging in deep philosophic reflections, as Meena, the person and the persona, strains her every nerve to relate her Indian childhood, African adolescence, British university life, and American present to answer the invariable query in every globe-trotting cultural refugee's "transnational hybrid" mind: "Who are we? What selves can we construct to live by? How shall we mark out space?" (174) "What is there to drop back: inside/outside, mind/body, East/West" (20). In each phase of her inner quest the author-narrator encounters, negotiates with, at times even invites Otherness to find her own voice amidst the cacophony arising from within her fragmented life and self. It is of little wonder that she chooses *Fault Lines* for the title of her book, readily identifying herself with a mass of faults. "I looked it up in the Oxford English Dictionary, it went like this 'Fault; Deficiency, want of something. . . . Default, . . . a dislocation or break in the strata or veins. Example: every coalfield is split asunder, and broken into tiny fragments, by faults. . . . Fragments of the adjoining rocks mashed and jumbled together . . . called . . . fault rock." (3)

Memory takes the Indian American narrator back to her ancestral Tiruvella house in far away Kerala. A house of emotional bonds, it is a soothing shelter to her wandering mind, cut adrift if not way-lost in contrary thoughts, experiences, realizations. Back, for a while, in the "magic of childhood," her imagination flies to the large house of the expanded family, with multifarious visitors, "loose yet formalized functions." Her mind races around the family garden of incense bearing trees, where she "could hide and find "herself again, "crying athe, athe . . . as if I was" (20). To an Indian, an ancestral house stands for an institution that roots one not merely to a geographical site but to a life way, oriented to a value system believed in and lived by people through generations. Considered as one of the four successive stages of an individual's graded course of spiritual growth, a householder's life, lived to the full, keeping true the varied relations, ensures the integrity of relationships, releases one from selfishness, purifies the mind, and paves the way to spiritual fulfillment, the highest attainment of human existence. So said the ancient Indian seers, and the other wise heads down the ages. Indian myths, folk tales, literature, music, painting, sculpture composed in different times at different corners of the country uphold the continuum of the idea/ideal as a lived experience. To an Indian the continuum is the real anchor line.

Meena's musing over her Indian anchor line is repeatedly snapped as she returns to the sharply contrasting reality of her American present, her own life way in a society that compels her to view herself as an outsider. "When she approached me, this Other, who I am, dressed in her bits-and-pieces clothing. . . . I see quite clearly . . . she has no home, no shelter, . . . she is a nowhere person." (30) Touching scenes flood the memoir. Meena, the mother, is more disturbed over the socio-cultural anchorage of her son Adam by her Euro-American husband. She overhears her American neighbor asking her child:

> "So what you, child?"
> Adam, shy as ever. Had just looked at him.
> "You American, child?"
> "No," said my son, boldly.
> "Indian, then. You Indian, child?"
> Adam shifted his weight, "No." . . . I was growing tense. What did my first-born wish for himself? Some nothingness, some transitory zone where dreams roamed, a border country without passport or language? (172)

The agony of Otherness is a predominant feature of recent Indian American writing, including the upcoming literature of the writers of Indian origin born and raised in the U.S. A question raised is not always and necessarily a question answered. It is easier to make a self-piteous exhibition of one's agony than encountering and living through it. It requires one to be a spectator of one's own self. Self-evaluation points to the awareness of a standard or ideal, and an ideal in the context signifies an obligation to work for it. Many of the contemporary Native American writers, yet another marginalized U.S. community with a distinct socio-cultural tradition, readily seek their ideal in their respective tribal heritage. To Meena, and many Asian American writers of her kind who have gone through multiple migrations, the situation is more complex. For all her emotional attachment to her grandparents, parents, and relatives in India, Meena knows that her Indian cultural heritage is too precarious to set her on to a steady life way and life view. She is, in a sense, an outsider to what she interprets as Indian history and tradition in her West-trained outlook. She prefers being the "Other" in India. "After all my life did not fall into narratives I had been taught to honor, tales that swallowed its own ending, birth, an appropriate education . . . an arranged marriage to a man of suitable birth and background somewhere in India" (2), she ruminates in her Manhattan home, evidently happy to highlight her psychic resistance to a custom accepted and appreciated by her ancestors including her own parents in spite of their years of stay abroad. The thought recurs time and again in the memoir.

A social custom of any community and country, reviewed out of its social, emotive, ideational connotations and context, is prone to appear queer to one unfamiliar with the particular country and culture. Being born in a country is not all or enough to know the country. The psychic distance Meena wears as her enlightened Otherness, however, collapses when towards the end of the book she recalls joining her sisters in India to listen to their mother telling them of the much cherished family and community rituals of her own arranged marriage to a man of suitable birth and background. Marriage in India being viewed as mode of living the fullest community life, less emphasis has been given to individual inclination or self will. Her mother's marriage too had been a community celebration. "Not one of us three sisters would enter that old world. But the imagination may draw us into it. The web of our mother's words warmed us as the chill winds began to blow," (219) writes Meena. The warm words count to her. The very thought of the warm bond of the family and the community soothes her deported, disturbed mind. The tale brings the mother and the daughters together.

Memory as a luxuriating nostalgia offers the author-narrator an escape route from her American present that blasts out the past for her: "In Manhattan, I am a fissured thing, a body crossed by fault lines. Where is my past? What is my past to me? Is America a place without memory?" (182) The questions arise in her mind time and again. It is often said in India that as in physical movement, in one's life too one cannot move on unless one has the back foot firm on the ground. Meena's restless search for a firm ground draws her to memory and history. The past, to her, is invariably associated with the memory of her grandfather. "Ilya, the grandfather, drew me back into an India that could only be a history to me" (36). Meena does not read history in the Indian sense of *purā api nava eva*, forever new even if old, but rather in the Western sense of a linear movement, in which each period is viewed as a pattern of life lived and lost forever. Her grandfather's had been "a life of struggle and yearning, travels and disasters in foreign lands, a restless idealism that really believed the earth could be transformed." (36) The granddaughter knows she does not have the grandfather's dreams. She does not own his ideology either. Generation gap coupled with the changed global scenario and the difference in her own circumstance had snapped her ideological anchor line.

The narrator's self-conscious distance once again collapses as she remembers the Khartoum phase of her adolescence, when she used to relate her own ideological standpoint to her grandfather's: "Raised by Ilya on the stories of civil disobedience that finally forced the British to leave India, I was prepared on my own way for the oppositional struggle my friends were embarking on in Sudan. I felt that it must be possible for all human beings to struggle towards equality and social justice" (117). That of course has been another form of the same dream that the earth could be transformed. Perhaps the narrator's real heritage of her grandfather has been her very mental make up. In invisible letters the past had written the tales of her ancestors at the core of her being.

Sudan had made Meena realize herself as the Other in a different way. For all her active involvement in the students movements related to the current political situation in Sudan, she knew she was an outsider. She had always been looked upon as an "expatriate Indian child" too distant and different to share Sudanese ordeals. Another major alienating factor had been her fluency of the high-pedigree British English, the language of the Other she had been compelled to learn as her mode of "survival" in a foreign land. English distanced her not only from the Sudanese people she had been growing up with, but also from her own mother tongue, the language of her rich culture. "As I became a teenager, I realized the forked power in the language I had acquired: English alienated me from what I was born into" (116). Meena has a mixed reaction to the alienation. At times she tries to rationalize her refusal to learn the Malayalam script. The script would have confined her to an "exclusionary canonical language" of "a traditional hierarchical society" (119). At other moments she endorses that her vernacular stores the ancestral wealth of wisdom that sustains the mind of her community. The utterances in Malayalam cannot be transmitted in English. "Why would I ever . . . turn those words of the language where I lived and moved my inmost being into English that would never carry that emotion, that would only distort it?" (121) The ambiguous standpoint, her fault line, had made her shaky to tread what would have been her natural inroad to a cultural ground.

Meena's painstaking efforts at finding her own voice in a language not her own ("I was an outsider confronting it" (111) often erupted in various modes of resistance. She recalls how she reacted to reading history in English, and took to "reading poems day and night" instead, so that "history might not consume me, render me dumb" (123). In postcolonial India a sharp line of criticism towards the use of English, the language of the colonizer, as a medium of education centered round the standpoint that exposure to English without any access to the vernacular would turn the mind of the child to the West for inspiration, thought pattern, culture that an Indian can never be in close touch with in life. Too young to be confident of her Indian ideational and cultural heritage, the expatriate Indian girl, nevertheless, chose her own mode of reading history, a poet's mode of finding a personal space in the continuum: "I depended on the poems, irruptions of the imaginary to make an internal history for me."

Meena's days in England made her conscious of what she "actually was, a female creature from the third world, with no discernible history" (141). The stereotypical image of Indian womanhood created and nourished in the West marked her Otherness with an inherent inferiority she had never experienced in Sudan. The persistent assault on her "human dignity, identity and sense" made her seethe with "a violence from within." For all her cultivated ease with Western ways and taste, she decided to break with her Dutch fiancé Maxim: "If I stayed with Maxim, I felt I would have lost India" (141), although she was not sure what exactly made her psychologically anchored to the country and culture she had been consciously distancing herself from in many respects.

In America, while frequently shifting locale with her Euro-American husband, Meena found it hard to orient herself to the life pattern of her adopted nation. "I did not understand what it meant to keep house in this inconstant fashion, to hold on, to keep going. Often I did not recognize myself, I felt I had lost my soul: that it was sucked into the vortex of an Otherness I had no words for" (104). Living in the contemporary U.S. is to live in a nation given to transnational exchange in global trade and digital culture. "The old notions of exile, that high estate are gone; smashed underfoot in the transit lounges, in the supermarkets, in the video parlors of the world. . . . History is maquillage. No homeland here." (193) The voice of the narrator does not ring in tune with the U.S. media fanfare over "new internationalism." The harsh reality of getting along in the U.S. has taught her a different lesson. To be a person with multiple cultural anchorages is to find oneself hyphenated in every respect. "Everything that comes to me is hyphenated. A woman poet, a woman poet of color, a South Indian woman poet who makes up lines in English, a postcolonial language. A third world woman poet, who takes as her right the inner city of Manhattan." (193)

Meena's creative mind parches for a homeland that will not turn her into a marginalized inferior Other, who can be "bought in, brought in" with magnified images, to be "bartered in the high palaces of capitalist chic" (195). The homeland of her dream is not India she has in her memory, a land "touched by hierarchy, and authority, and the great weight of the centuries" (198). Nor is it the U.S. with its "dazzling quickness, its breathless exhilaration" of a culturally collusive present. "After all for such as we are the territories are not free. The world is not open. The endless space . . . is worse than a lie" (199). The process of elimination, not this not this, *neti, neti*, has been upheld by the Indian philosophers as a way to truth. Meena's mode of questioning Otherness is a process of elimination of a kind.

If Meena the person is unable to cross over the fault lines in her life, Meena the poet does in her wistful dream of a world where "the head can be held high," and each individual can find space in human dignity and freedom. "The struggle for social justice, for human dignity is for each of us. It is shaped by forces that . . . turn us towards light, a truth whose immensity . . . casts all our actions into relief, etches our lines into art" (203). The relocation of the home and the world Meena speaks about, matches with the thoughts of India's first Nobel Laureates. Some three-quarters of a century back, Tagore wrote the famous poem regarding the future of his country reeling under British rule:

> Where the mind is without fear and the head is held high
> Where knowledge is free
> Where the world is not broken up into fragments
>   By narrow domestic walls,
>   Where words come from the depth of truth

> Where the mind is led forward into ever-widening thought and action
> Into that heaven of freedom . . . let my country awake.
>
> (*Gitanjali*, 36)

Whether an exclusively socio-political struggle for justice, visibility, and reciprocal recognition of human dignity can meet the inner crisis that Meena's memoir brings to the fore, is a debatable issue. The "endless space" she dreams about, that can turn one from ignorance to truth, darkness to light would need what Tagore calls "world consciousness," a larger frame of mind beyond the bonds of personal desire. The consciousness of universal humanity enables one to reach out to the others in respect and love. It is said in India that to be united in knowledge, love and service with all beings is the essence of freedom. One requires an inner discipline to reach it. Homi Bhabha speaks of a "radical revision in the concept of human community itself." What is needed is a radical change in human consciousness to frame a world community and culture. Human life like a river strikes its banks not to find itself closed in by them, but to realize anew that it has its unending opening towards the sea. Meena's life-course too strikes its banks in confronting Otherness in different forms, and dimensions. In each phase she opens out to a larger consciousness. The process continues.

Works Cited

Alexander, Meena. *Fault Lines: A Memoir*. New York: The Feminist Press, 1993.

Bhabha, Homi. "The Location of Culture," *Literary Theory: An Anthology*, ed. Julie Rivkin and Michal Ryan. 1998.

Tagore, Rabindranath. *Gitanjali.* In *The English Writings of Rabindranath Tagore,* Volume I, ed. Sisir Kumar Das, Sahitya Akademi, 1977.

Straddling Two Worlds: Diasporic Dislocation in Vijay Lakshmi's *Pomegranate Dreams*

ANIL RAINA
Punjab University, Chandigarh

> Two landscapes and two houses—one familiar, and the other unknown—had fused into one. . . . I was in two places at the same time, straddling two worlds. I didn't know then that it was just the beginning of the kaleiodoscopic formations and reformations that my mind was always going to be subjected to. (18)

This is how Juhi, the first person narrator of *Pomegranate Dreams* sums up her plight in the first section itself of the 144-page long short story that has been described by Paule Marshall as "a novella longing to be a novel." The author of *Pomegranate Dreams* Vijay Lakshmi is a recent entry on the Indian American literary scene, dominated as it is by women writers, particularly of short stories, like Bharati Mukherjee, Chitra Banerjee Divakaruni, and Jhumpa Lahiri. This paper will analyze the title story of Vijay Lakshmi's collection of stories *Pomegranate Dreams and Other Stories* (2002) in terms of the diasporic dislocation i.e. the experience of straddling two worlds.

Reviewers have been mostly unanimous in praising *Pomegranate Dreams* as an expression of the Immigrant experience. Anne D. Ulrich and Eric Kennedy see it as dealing with the isolation of immigration. Richard Wertime sees in it "touches of loss" and Simone Zelitch feels that it is about "what people lose when they come to America." J. Birjepatil describes it as being about "diasporic dislocations" in the "transnational space." If the *Tripod* reviewer thinks that Vijay Lakshmi interprets and critiques the newcomer's experience of living in America, the reviewer for *Hindu* believes that it is about the issue of lost cultural identity and the peculiar dilemma of uprootedness. Maneesha

Sane writes that the author "weaves themes of east meets west, bridging Indian and American lifestyles, beliefs, hopes, and dreams."

Pomegranate Dreams, like most diasporic narratives, then, is about displacement and the consequent reconfiguration of identities. Memory and nostalgia are often an integral part of such narratives, particularly the ones that focus on the characters' alienation. Simultaneously one also witnesses what Bharati Mukherjee calls the middle class Asian American themes of relocation, immigration, un-housement, and re-housement that characterize the narratives that are concerned more with acculturation and assimilation. Though the overall tone and tenor of *Pomegranate Dreams* is nostalgic, its strength lies in the fact that it explores the various diasporic choices in terms of its narrative. It is as much about assimilation and adjustment to new values and new ideas as about alienation, uprootedness, and the lost cultural and ethnic identity. While exploring what it means to be an American and what the American dream means to the fresh immigrant, it simultaneously puts into question the perceived homogeneity of India, whether by an Indian or an American.

Technologically and economically, the contemporary world may be turning transnational, yet the individuals/communities that occupy the ever-increasing transnational spaces are psychologically and culturally still rooted in and nurtured by the idea of the mother country or the mother-Nation as something sacrosanct. Thus, in spite of the voluntary nature of most contemporary migrations in contrast to the earlier forced ones, the present day diasporic experience continues to be a mournful experience, an experience often of more loss than gain, and consequently of memory and nostalgia.

In contrast to Bharati Mukherjee, who consciously focuses on assimilation into the culture of the place migrated to, and the gains thereof, Vijay Lakshmi's *Pomegranate Dreams* on the face of it seems more about the sense of loss generated by the desire for an absent topos, i.e. India, which always remains a point of reference for her protagonists. When the narrator of the short story "Distances" bemoans, "How I wish I could celebrate what I have and block out that which is gone" (217), one suddenly feels that it is not only the narrator but the author also bemoaning the inability to "block out," something that Bharati Mukherjee, perhaps, succeeds in doing.

In order to counter this unsettling experience of being neither here nor there, the diasporic writer often takes recourse to what may be called ethnicity. Commenting on ethnicity, Thomas C. Greaves writes:

> Factors which build ethnic solidarity include origin myths, oral tradition, pride in the achievement of heroes, distinctive foods and dress, a separate religious history, a strong identification with a homeland, sacred sites and localities of past events, artistic and musical styles, and language. These factors may be conserved from the past, embellished, or fabricated anew to support the desire for group solidarity. (182)

The passage applies very much to *Pomegranate Dreams* except that one needs to replace the term "group solidarity" in the end with the term "individual identity." Most of the factors mentioned above are on display in the story, which has been described by the *Hindu* reviewer as a study in the "peculiar dilemma of uprootedness." They are all an attempt to counter the self-doubt expressed so poignantly by Anu in the story "Distances": "What is this place? Why am I here? What am I?" (217) Juhi's first impression of Brinkroad, the place they were going to stay in as "one step more, and we would plunge into empty space" (9) is more prophetic than literal. Among the things that Juhi feels sad about leaving behind are not only toys, dresses, *koel*, friends, cousins, festivals, grandmother, storehouse, garden, the pomegranate trees, and monkeys but also significantly "a sense of belonging" (28). At the time of Diwali, she is disillusioned by the darkness around prompting her to exclaim, "Inscribed on the tablets of our memory alone, it didn't exist for others" (72). And she protests, too, "Going to America couldn't mean dismantling our past and abandoning it like a charred building" (27), a different response from that of Chacha who like Vikings initially believed in "making a clean cut with the past. Beginning a new life" (39). At the same time, *Pomegranate*

Dreams is not only a story of "what people lose when they come to America," but also the story of what America does to its immigrants, both in a positive and a negative sense. The movement of the story is a movement away from the initial response: "Coming to America. What for, if not for material wealth" (26).

On the face of it, what *Pomegranate Dreams* seems to say, then, is this: An imperfect India could be replaced by a dream America but as the dream America, for most migrants, is just a mirage, an illusion, it necessitates a return to a dream India, largely a creation of memory and nostalgia. The nostalgia with its roots in the selective memory, then, is used to underplay the idea of an imperfect India, to hide from one's own self the real India from which one has tried to escape. However, on a deeper look, *Pomegranate Dreams* may be described as exploring a set of oppositions centered on the basic contrast between two imagined categories—America and India. The two are further divided into dream America and real America, and dream India and real India respectively, the real America and real India being further subdivided into the good and the bad ones. On the basis of these divisions, a set of oppositions is possible, some of which are explored in more detail than the others. The oppositions dealt more thoroughly in the story relate to the ones between dream America and dream India, real America and dream India, and dream America and real America. The ones that are casually glimpsed at are the ones that relate to the opposition between real India on the one hand and the real America, dream America, and dream India on the other. This is so, because as a careful analysis of the story will show, while a lot of energy goes into expressing the dream India, the real India, except for a few passing references, is largely left unexplored. Vijay Lakshmi works within a limited range, and as she claims to have written a short story and not a novel, one may ignore her inability to penetrate the subjective constructs of India to arrive at the deeper social reality, something a great writer would have achieved imperceptibly.

The India-America oppositions mentioned above are worked out in terms of the various elements of the story, i.e. characterization, plot, and language and imagery. The contrasts permeate the whole fabric of the story: the sanitized ghost of a rich American lady is put against the scary ghost of the tamarind tree in Jaipur; long hair versus hair cut short; schools in India versus "here, in this new country, school was chaos" (55); Panchvati against Merlin's Forest; the lights of Diwali in India versus the Diwali in America where there was darkness all around leading to Juhi dreaming of a hybrid Halloween-Diwali; or the comment on dying: "No one could die alone in India. Or lie undiscovered for days. It was only in America that people died alone" (112), and so on.

At the level of characterization, the various characters seem to be the markers of various positions in this set of oppositions. For example, the restricted or false notion of the dream America as only opulence and material wealth is represented by early Juhi, Mrs. Singh, Suraj Mehta, Gopi, etc., while the true notion of dream America as self-fulfillment and self-realization through individual effort are epitomized by Mom, Chachi, and Bansi in the later half of the story. The good real America is represented by Grandpa and Grandma Miller and Jack, and one need not wonder why these characters are either already dead (Jack) or die during the story. Plenty of space is given to the bad real America symbolized by the American school-kids (other ethnic writers like the Lebanese-American Elmaz Abinader and Julia Alvarez of Caribbean origin, too, have not forgotten the schoolyard racist epithets hurled at them), Chip, the Psycho Lola, the Indian convert Priya, and finally the molester in the park. If Dadi represents the absent dream India, the good real India is briefly represented by Shantabehn (the maid Juhi wants to make a movie about), and the bad real India by its beggars, lepers, and female foeticiders. The experience of straddling two worlds prompts an individual crisis in almost each character. Some of them like Mom and Chachi emerge as more mature while others like Papa get unmasked. The story has some strong women characters but men like Papa are devastated by their entry into a more radical world. He complains: "America does strange things to women. They see the Statue of Liberty and they think it means liberation from womanly duties" (122). And when Bansi decides to join the navy, his mother supports him but Papa refuses to forgive him. In a violent outburst he asks Bansi, "Who gave you the authority to make decisions" (146). The reader's response to such outbursts should determine how far he thinks the story moves beyond the ever-look-back nostalgia. I feel that Vijay Lakshmi by contrasting the Mom's response to Bansi's decision with that of Papa, is exposing the priggishness of the father, and thus making the point that America may have something positive to offer to the immigrant.

The images for the dream America are those of the 'Enchanted/Promised land.' As Bansi puts it, "Freedom is what America is all about" (55). Its false notion is defined in terms of villas, dresses, jewelry, taste, "gorgeous rooms, marble bathrooms, cast-iron balconies, crystal chandeliers, and so much more" (44). The images of porches, driveways, vast lawns, huge mansions, tall columns, wrought-iron balconies, opulence, polished mirrors, gilt-framed paintings, oriental rugs, crystal fixtures, and Jacuzzis keep haunting Juhi who cannot but exclaim, "this should have been my house." She cannot but feel frustrated when she compares the quiet hallway, living room with ivory walls, whipped cream carpet, spotless, sun-filled kitchen, and recessed windowsills of the America-born Indian kid Debyani's house with her own house. The good real America is seen as "clean air, vast playgrounds, shining hallways, free books of the American school" (55); the bad one as grizzly cherry tree, and "ghosts of real life—single mothers, delinquent kids, crazy men and women haunting the streets" (35). Commenting on the dream India-imperfect America contrast, Juhi says, "I couldn't believe that we had exchanged that bounty for a tiny house with a grizzly cherry tree whose gnarled roots were splayed like fears unleashed in the dark" (28). The dream India momentarily is reproduced in the United States through *tablas* and *tanpuras,* but it primarily dwells in the world of memory, whether in Shobha Chachi's nostalgia for servants, friends, and comforts in India, or in Juhi's dream of being the princess of India with Ganga Ram carrying her school bag, or the papayas, mangoes, guavas, bougainvilleas, and flowering shrubs of Jaipur. The bad real India is mostly ascribed to the wrong perceptions of the Americans. The looney kicking at the door calling them monkey chasers prompts Juhi to ask herself, "Now why on earth did I come here?" (37) When Mrs. Thompson shows the school kids a documentary on India with nothing but beggars, *sadhus* and death in it, Juhi exclaims, "is that how they view immigrants." Juhi's childhood dream is to counter this negative perception of India with one which sees it not as the abode of lepers, beggars, maharajas and palaces, but of people like Shami, their maid and her seven daughters, none of them a victim of female foeticide.

Pomegranate Dreams, with its first person narration, may also be read as a *bildungsroman*, a novel of initiation into adulthood, as being about the growing up of its teenage narrator-protagonist Juhi. To quote Maneesha Sane, "What makes this story interesting is that it is told from the unique perspective of a grown woman who has not forgotten the confusion, chaos, and innocence of being a child. The teenager, who initially lives in a world of pomegranate dreams, finally awakens to a world where there are no fairy-tale endings, and where dreams often need to be deferred. In *Pomegranate Dreams*, the world is seen through the eyes of a young girl, but we should not forget to add that Juhi is a round character who develops as the story unfolds. And Juhi herself realizes it:

> I felt sorry for Debby. Despite all her riches, all her friends and comforts, she was a lonely girl. For the first time, the twin house on Brink Road superimposed itself on the red brick house on Lincoln Road. . . . For the first time I realized that happiness, which I had taken to be such a simple affair, wasn't so simple, after all. Life was going to be more like a complex algebraic problem with many equations of infinite relationships. (100)

The development from the initial fascination for villas and bungalows, and the inability to understand her brother Bansi to the final scene where she sees the logic of Bansi's action in cutting himself free from his father's dream can be seen as a movement from the false notion of dream America to the true one of the possibility of self-fulfilment. It is at this point that the true notion of dream America and the good real America become one. The strong women characters of the story like Mom, Chachi, and even Juhi seem to be the bearers of this coalescing. The ending may seem fluid and open, but the point has been already made. Juhi's fascination for houses, whether Indian or American, has to be replaced by Bansi's for boats and ships; the stasis of the former has to be replaced by the movement of the latter. Life, as in Herman Hesse's *Siddhartha*, is to be accepted as a flux. It is like the Jaipur Baba of the story who keeps on moving, because to stop was to cease. Towards the end even Chacha has to admit, "Arrivals and departures. . . . Joy and pain, having and losing—that's the name of the game" (142).

Works Cited

Greaves, Thomas C. "Ethnicity." *A Dictionary of Cultural and Critical Theory*. Ed. Michael Payne. Oxford: Blackwell, 1997.

Lakshmi, Vijay. *Pomegranate Dreams and Other Stories*. New Delhi: Indialog, 2002.

Sane, Maneesha. Review of *Pomegranate Dreams*. *Sawnet* Online. 9 Nov. 2003.

The Hindu Review of *Pomegranate Dreams*. Literary Review Section. Online. 4 Aug. 2002.

Tripod Review. Online. 11 Sep. 2003.

'Stuck in Dead Space': The Sense and Sensibility of the Indian American in Bharati Mukherjee's Short Stories

ANU CELLY
Punjab University, Chandigarh

> O you who love clear edges
> More than anything, watch the edges that blur.
>
> Adrienne Rich

Cross-cultural immigration in today's world has become an irrevocable precursor to the re-negotiation of identity, the re-mapping of boundaries, the re-naming of the self within and a re-structuring of the life without. In the postmodern world the diasporic notion of subjectivity contests the apotheosis of a monolithic, unified and independent construct of identity, taking into account the differential considerations of location, boundary, class, race, gender, ethnicity and transmigration into account. The very mention of the term 'diaspora' conjures up an image of psychological alienation, emotional suffering, physical uprooting, cultural readjustment and financial strife that is inherent in the thematic patterns of the literary works of a few of the writers of the South Asian Diaspora in the US. The new Indian diaspora, in continuum to the old Indian diaspora of indentured labor migrants, to several countries all over the world, comprises one of the most significant demographic shift, dislocation and realignment, now representing a force to reckon with in global culture. The homogeneity of the old Indian diaspora has now given way to a heterogeneity and hybridity which hyphenates human identity and designates the diaspora, as per the opinion of many a diasporic writer, as a kind of parenthesis, a gap in one's history which will never be fully written out. While the old Indian diaspora marks itself off as an historical fact as landless people who became footnotes to the history of imperialism, the new Indian diaspora, according to Bharati Mukherjee, are of a different order:

> But we are refugees and mercenaries and guest workers; you see us sleeping in airport lounges; you watch us unwrapping the last of our native foods, unrolling our prayer rugs, reading our holy books, taking out for the hundredth time an aerogram promising a job or space to sleep, a newspaper in our language, a photo of happier times, a passport, a visa, a laissez passer. (100-1)

In general the act of displacement, in today's world, also connotes the life style of subjects forever on the move, formulating not altogether unproblematic coalitional social formations wherever they live and having a streak of reactionary complexity in their psyche, both with regard to their exilic condition and the notion of homeland as a series of images in their minds. William Safran defines the Diasporas in terms of six characteristics linked to two invariables: exile and homeland. These characteristics are: dispersal of people from center to peripheries; the retention of collective memory, vision or myth about homeland; a feeling of non-acceptance, alienation or insulation in the host society; a strong feeling that their ancestral homeland is their true, ideal home to which to return to, eventually; a responsibility for the maintenance or restoration of the homeland; a self-conscious definition of one's ethnicity in terms of the existence of this homeland.

What is of particular interest in the works of Bharati Mukherjee is that she broaches the problematic and creative nature of the position of the gap or hyphen occupied by her diasporic subjects and most of her short stories or rather "soul studies" reflect, in shades at once subtle and startling, the metaphorical homelessness and the metamorphic transformation which occurs in the life of the South Asian immigrant populace in the United States. What the identity of America does to the South Asian diaspora or the people from the "nothing places," as per her own terminology, is something more complex and more mutual than merely the logistics of re-location. It's all about straddling one's sense and sensibility in a way that connotes a peripheral distancing from one's own cultural moorings and a superficial accommodation to the adopted culture, leading to a state of spiritual anxiety and estrangement that may be conducive to practical survival, but not to happiness, that may lead to acclimatization but not to uncompromised contentment. In an essay in 1983, Salman Rushdie wrote:

> Exiles or emigrants or expatriates are haunted by some sense of loss, some urge to reclaim, to look back, even at the risk of being mutated into pillars of salt. But if we do look back, we must also do so in the knowledge—which gives rise to profound uncertainties—that our physical alienation from India almost inevitably means that we will not be capable of reclaiming precisely the thing that was lost; that we will, in short, create fictions, not actual cities or villages, but invisible ones, imaginary homelands, Indias of the mind. (78)[1]

This paper attempts to capture the dialectic of identities, the crisis in values and the fragmentation of the self under the duress of the duplicitous demands of reality inundating the life of Indians in the United States, as reflected in two short stories by Mukherjee, even as she highlights, with relentless candor, the maladies of civilization and entrapment of mannerisms inherent in both the cultures. As per popular critical opinion, Mukherjee is adept in the intricate patterning of a narrative art that enables her to "trace the split in the diasporic subject, expressed in that sense of being here and elsewhere, of being at home and abroad" (Sudesh Mishra 287). Through an intrusive and sensitive study of snapshots from the lives of women in "A Wife's Story" and "The Tenant," this paper aims to unravel the integrity of the 'sensibility' within the 'inscape' of the women characters, naked and shorn of any hypocrisy, even as their clear-sighted 'sense' of pragmatism surrenders to a spontaneous pursuit of happiness and fulfillment, howsoever aberrant and transitory it may turn out to be. What is significant about the interplay between character and circumstance in these short stories is the fact that the female protagonists, both the flamboyant Panna and the mystical Maya are disarmingly honest and forthright individuals who manage to leave an impressionable dent in the contours of the American culture, even as they themselves undergo a transmutation that is not entirely denuded of the trauma and the courage, the shame and the heroism, the 'dead space' (Mukherjee's term) and the adamantine passion of the human consciousness under the duress of displacement.

"A Wife's Story" by Mukherjee is all about the straddling of the two cultures, the tradition-bound but strife-torn and chaotic reality of life in the Indian sub-continent vis-à-vis the liberated, but fissiparous and ruptured reality of life in the United States. Here is the story of a married woman, one among the millions of Indians on a student visa to the US; yet, an individual in her own right, with a level of intellectual vibrancy and rational felicity that makes her dissect the quintessential "American" way of life, directly to the reader, with a no-holds-barred, fearless verve. As a roommate to Charity, an oriental immigrant and a girlfriend to Imre, a Polish delinquent of sorts, Panna comes across as a survivor figure. If names were significant, one would consider Mukherjee's choice of her name as a signifier for sanctity of womanhood, representing the historical figure of a woman called Panna Dai who connotes maternal nurturance and unflinching loyalty, even as her modern day progeny in this short story feels like a destitute whose inherited legacy is of sterility, the kind that is born out of riots, uprooting, separation and the death of her son. Even the cultural model offered by her homeland is of contamination and not of a sanctified, unified space, carrying with the baggage of racial discrimination, maltreatment of minorities and casteist dissent.[2]

Panna comes across as someone who has acclimatized herself to the quiddities of an "emigrant" culture in America—a ubiquitous mix-up of gestures and mannerisms, which range from the pre-regulated weekly sexual rendezvous of her roommate with a doctor in lieu of his fees, to am impromptu act of hugging her own boyfriend while breaking out in a dance on the Broadway sidewalk. Yet, it is on the landscape of her sensibility where lies the inscription of "an ugly, nasty rage" (26) and a "simple, brutish, partisan hate" (27) over the exploitative displacement that threatens to rob her of her dignity and the blinding racial humiliation inflicted even through the theatre plays that are lapped up by her, that stir up the hornet's nest of an insidious, restive wrath within her. As per an authorial foray into her mind:

> It's the tyranny of the American dream that scares me. First, you don't exist. Then you're invisible. Then you're funny. Then you are disgusting. Insult, my American friends will tell me, is a kind of acceptance. No instant dignity here. A play like this, back home, would cause riots. Communal, racist, and antisocial. The actors wouldn't make it off stage. This play, and all these awful feelings, would be safely locked up. I long, at times, for clear-cut answers. Offer me instant dignity, today, and I'll take it. (26)

On the one hand, Panna relishes the gay and reckless abandonment of mind and body that she rehearses as a part of the American life; on the other, she refutes the patronizing condescension of the elite American intelligentsia that denigrates the worth of the multi-ethnic immigrant populace in America. "I've made it. I'm making something of my life" (29), she muses, as the images in her mind overlap, of the destitutes in India, indistinguishable from the street children of New York city, from the strike and lock out of her husband's factory in India to the Wuchang uprising which has displaced an old man from Chengdu in China to a grocery store in the US. The snapshots from her mind focus on the tableau of her own marriage, arranged after making sure that she knew her husband's taste in food, to the commodification of love as sex by her roommate and her numerous lovers. What strings together the disparate blitzkrieg of such flashpoint revelations is the impact of a critique that unravels the futility of man-made institutions, whether that of marriage or education, even as an authorial perspective targets a harsh reprisal against the entrapments of a civilization which breeds nothing more than the psychosis of anxiety and estrangement in the human condition.

"When I'm down, when I'm lonely for my husband, when I think of our son, or when I need to be held, I think of Charity's uncle. If I hadn't left home, I'd never have heard of the Wuchang

Uprising. I've broadened my horizons" (31), speculates Panna in a mood of self-consolation, even as her spirit veers at the edge of a rebellion amidst the "borough of vice and greed" (33) that has bred a generation of muggers swarming the sub-ways of New York city. As a site for resistance, the trajectory of identity crisis within Panna's sensibility, at this stage, connotes Homi Bhabha's view that, "resistance is not necessarily an oppositional act of intention, nor is it the simple negation or exclusion of the 'content' of another culture, as difference once perceived . . . (but) the effect of ambivalence produced within the rules of recognition of dominating discourses as they articulate the signs of cultural difference" (153).

When Panna gets news of her husband's impending visit to the US, even as her sensibility is steeped in skepticism, Panna decides to play Mrs. Bhatt to the hilt and indulges herself in acts of compliance, in complicity to the normative codification of a married woman's behavior. In this instance, Panna resorts to what has been called "a strategic essentialism," that is, "rather than assuming that one is a particular type of subject and thus a particular type of essence . . . there may be certain circumstances particularly in resistance movements, where it is necessary to adopt a particular type of role and hence subject position strategically. Despite the contradictions inherent in this position, it does entail a position of agency" (Mills 104). Panna bedecks herself with jewelry and traditional Indian apparel when she goes to receive her husband and feels a warring tumult between guilt, shame and loyalty in her sensibility, even as her senses register a scornful disdain with the way in which her husband displays an awe-struck interest in, what appears to her to be merely the exoticized version of the 'high tech' life in America. The guided tour of New York city that she takes with her husband becomes the source of an insight that the flight of ambition which formulates the quest migrants like her in America may just turn out to be a mirage that never actually bears a co-relation to their real talent and aspiration or to the ground reality of options available in America.

"The view of the city from the Circle Line ferry is seductive, unreal. The skyline wavers out of reach, but never quite vanishes. The summer sun pushes through fluffy clouds and dapples the glass of office towers. . . . Tourists and dreamers, we have spent our life's savings to see this skyline, this statue," thus reads a speculation from the psyche of Panna, decoding and demythifying the spurious and illusionary nature of the American Dream which offers to its people merely a farcical vestige of liberty, equality and prosperity. The sheer irony of the fact that America deemed to be the richest country in the world has a tour guide who is vying for a small tip, brings home to Panna the stark disparity in the distribution of wealth as a pronounced feature of the American economy.

A casual remark on the part of Panna's husband about the cheats in New York being akin to the thugs in Bombay strikes her with the dreadful feeling of her own complicity in a design of invidious treachery in not being devoted to her husband. The mere concern that she has for his well being does not detract from her sensibility a level of detachment that has crept into her sensual response to him. Even when they make love, it seems that her husband's new found excitement, which is antithetical to the apathy in their relationship otherwise, has taken off from a level of energy that is in imitation of the American way of life. Yet, it appears to her that the quality of her bond with her husband is such a contrast to the element of adventitious sordidness inherent in the relationships that people share around her. Even the jealous possessiveness of her husband comes across to her as a refreshing change from the prosaic mundanity and indifference of the relationship that she shares with Imre, her Polish boyfriend.

The decision of her husband to return to India unfolds within her the fledgling defloration of a new self that does not have to bother about the keeping up of appearances. The metamorphic transformation within Panna, at least, is now complete as the 'split' in her sensibility is now beginning to melt together into a new pattern of self-perception that is not fettered by considerations of convention within marriage and conformity outside marriage. "In the mirror that hangs on the bathroom door, I watch my naked body turn, the breasts, the thighs glow. The body's beauty amazes. I stand here shameless, in ways he has never seen me. I am free, afloat, watching somebody else" (40), muses Panna to herself.

In the nakedness of her new found persona, Panna discovers a self that is shorn of the mantle of respectability as well as the facade of conformity, whether in response to the ingenuity of her Indian identity or the dictates of her grafted Americanisms, and which reaches out to a sense of wholeness that lies beyond the in-between world of a dual identity. Panna's state of mind the end of the story may be congruent with what has been called "the logic of identity" and "the ideal of community" which enables subjects to understand each other as they understand themselves. According to Iris Marion Young, "The desire for community relies on the same desire for social wholeness and identification that underlies racism and ethnic chauvinism on the one hand and political sectarianism on the other" (302).[3]

"The Tenant" is all about the transition in values and in perceptions that its female protagonist Maya Sanyal goes through in the course of her migration from Ballygange Park Road, Calcutta to different cities in America, forever on the move from one house to another, forever going through contraction and expansion, progression and regression in the pace of her response to the vicissitudes of her migrant life.[4] "Every place has something to give," believes Maya who stands for an open-minded and consciously evolved choice of relocation as the most tendentious avenue of self-fulfillment for an individual. Yet, her soul remains trapped in memory, memories of her childhood, howsoever banal, one of going to the circuses with her father in Calcutta, making her look at her past as that of "history in a net, the kind of safety net travelling trapeze artists of her childhood fell into when they were inattentive or clumsy" (98). Donna Haraway looks at sites of constant transition as unnatural boundaries and suggests that, "Boundaries are drawn by mapping practices; "objects" do not pre-exist as such. Objects are boundary projects. But boundaries shift from within; boundaries are very tricky.

What boundaries provisionally contain remains generative, productive of meanings and bodies." (201)[5]

Panna continues to feel alienated from the traditional mould of femininity that all Indian women are supposed to adhere to, whether it is in the nature of abhorrence for Indian wife-beating husbands or a distaste for elaborate Indian cooking styles. Yet, her American persona is akin to the survival of nothing more than a thin shell of utilitarian and practical responses to life, wherewith she is forever straddling her sense and sensibility into modes of content vis-à-vis frustration.

It is during the moments of her candid introspection that the author enables the reader to have a glimpse of the 'real' Maya in apposition to the illusory overlay of a modern go-getter woman that she appears to be much in keeping with the literal connotations of her name 'Maya' translatable as a mystical illusion. Maya's American room mate and friend Fran clubs her as a "headstrong adventurer," never really laying her hands on Maya's inner yearning for a steady and stable emotional anchorage in life which is disproportionate to her desperate worldly attempts to acclimatize herself to a culture of fickle-minded inconstancy. As per an authorial perception:

> Maya's taken some big risks, made a break with her parents' ways. She's done things a woman from Ballygunge Park Road doesn't do, even in fantasies. She's not yet shared stories with Fran, apart from the divorce. She's told her nothing of the men she picks up, the reputation she's gained before Cedar Falls, for "indiscretions." She has a job, equity, three friends she can count on for emergencies. She is an American citizen. But . . . (100)

In such respects, Maya comes across as a 'nomad,' who, like other nomads as per the opinion of Carole Davies, "are not necessarily migrants. Rather they often stay within a certain geographic range, continually evading the 'codes of settled people'." (45)

Maya's sensibility undergoes a tenuous tussle between rebellious non-conformity to the intrinsic 'Indianness' within her, versus an irrevocable emotional disenchantment at her own attempts to adjust herself to spurious Americanisms. As a woman she has undergone transconfiguration from the time when as a young student at Duke University, she was considered "too feminine," as someone who came from a world where women are "trained to speak softly, arrange flowers, sing, be pliant" (102). Revathy Krishnaswamy considers the concept of 'effeminacy' within a related context, when she asserts that the term emphasizes "the implied devaluation and disempowerment of women and femininity." (20)

Now, Maya is a naturalized American who does not mind sleeping around with men and who is entirely unsentimental in going out for a date with a gawky, awkward-looking Indian Dr. Rab Chaterjee. The prospect of sleeping with a married Indian man appears to her like an unpalatable challenge, as much of an inane "misadventure" (104) as her own divorce from an American husband. Acts of heroism for a woman like Maya, progeny to a grandmother who had been married at the age of five and a great aunt who had been burnt for dowry, now range from the possibility of seducing either her American landlord Ted Suminski or a date with a much married Indian man, Dr. Rab Chatterjee.

In Dr. Chatterjee's home, Maya comes across Poltoo, a young brilliant student from India who may be perceived as her 'alter ego,' a replica of her own thwarted yearnings as an outstanding student who has never been able to arrive at a fruition of her real academic caliber in the course of her transition from the uncomfortable and unsuitable moorings at Calcutta to a rootless and footloose existence in America. Poltoo epitomizes to Maya, the ghostly reverberation of her own restless rage against the rough deal that life has meted out to her. The "music of nostalgia" sounds to her as nothing but the "madness, self-hate" (105) of "the confused world of the immigrant—the lostness" (106).[6] Poltoo's curtailed desire to marry a Negro Muslim girl comes to his aunt Mrs. Chatterjee as a betrayal of his brahminical heritage, just as Maya recollects the brunt of her own anger over the betrayal suffered by her at the hands of her American husband John Hadwen. The same betrayal leads her to a retaliatory promiscuity wherewith "she lost her moral sense, her judgment, her power to distinguish" (107), even as she maintains an extraneous poise supposedly springing from her seemly brahminical breeding.[7]

The concept of love, for Maya, undergoes a sea change, as she perceives it to be a mere conduit resting on physical contact, an anarchy in the world that she lives in, rather than being a source of unchanging spiritual/emotional succor. So much so, that even the sedate and sober Dr. Chatterjee, trapped in a loveless marriage, appears to Maya as a hapless, discontented soul whose furtive attempts at masturbation fail to assuage the gnawing loneliness in his sensibility, which, as per his confession corrodes his sense of happiness in life. Maya's own longing to feel, palpably, the physical configuration of spiritual values is bound to feel outraged in the heartland of a 'new world' where a premium is placed on the aspects of physical, material life, even as the land that she has come from has subjected itself to aspects of failed idealism. Even now as Maya reads newspaper stories about the corruption, sloth, casteism prevalent in her motherland, she feels deeply shocked and unsettled, even as she chases the mirage of personal fulfillment through another relationship with a man.

An "immigrant courtship" (110) with a man who has inserted a made-to-order advertisement for a bride in the newspaper leads her to startling moments of self-discovery as she finds herself "stuck in dead space" (110) going through acute discomfiture over the prospect of a mechanized affair with a man, literally and figuratively in transit. A relationship with Ashoke Mehta who appears to her like a replica of her own self, caught as she is between the two worlds, appears to her as nothing more than "the sad parade of need and demand" (111), almost like a fated compulsive karmic duty to be loved and left out of real fulfillment. Maya's feelings, at this juncture, are in a state of tenuous conflict as an honest self-assessment makes her surmise a rock bottom level of self-esteem:

> She feels ugly and unworthy. Her adult life seems no longer miraculously rebellious; it is grim, it is perverse. She has accomplished nothing. She has changed her citizenship but she hasn't

> broken through into the light, the vigor, the bustle of the New World. (110)

The realization that she is living on a kind of temporary lease in the New World, even as she has all but severed her ties with her own motherland, assumes tangible enormity when her tenancy at Ted Suminski's house is terminated by her with immediate effect. Once again, it's time for Maya to move, this time, to take up inhabitation with Fred, a man who is considered a 'freak' because he does not have arms, someone who drives home to herself her own state of crippled dependence on the notion of a companion who could fill the void in her life. She realizes that she is no less handicapped than Fred in the zone of her emotional desolation and physical isolation amidst a life, where companionship, be it from any source, appears to her as the sole source of sustenance.

Maya settles into a relationship with Fred and feels an affinity with him, perceiving themselves as "two wounded people" (112) who needed the crutches of mutual support to arrive at the merest semblance of survival and happiness. However, stability is denied to Maya, almost by default, as she tethers once again at the edge of yet another foray into an experimental relationship with Ashoke who expects her to join him on the east coast of America, perhaps, knowing that a woman like Maya is forever destined to be on the move, never really having a fixed share in happiness or in rootedness, the typical migrant who forever straddles the world of her sense and sensibility under the duress of equally irrevocable modes of fragmentation and relocation.[8]

NOTES

1 Vijay Mishra dwells on the notion of cultural identity as one which is predicated on the inevitable mixing up of castes and peoples, on the remaking of ethnic identities and these are processes which never come to a standstill in diasporic life. In his own words, "Since cultural situation are not fixed but mobile, since cultures travel and become contaminated in the process . . . it is not simply a matter of re-articulating the past as though this is how it really

was—the danger here is that one begins to repeat racist or nativist discourses of cultural anteriority and superiority which emphasize lost glories (myths replacing history)—but a matter of radically re-interrogating the actual experience" (75).

2 Sunil Khilnani dissects the dichotomy inherent to the conceptualization of India as a 'great' nation versus the 'reality' of distorted ideologies, when he observes, "But the most imaginatively ambitious if also analytically elusive perspective on India since 1947 shows a rapid acceleration and intensification in the long-running encounter between a civilization intricately designed with the specific purpose of perpetuating itself as a society, a community with a shared moral order, one of the world's most sophisticated assemblages of 'great' and 'little' traditions, and, set against it, the imperatives of modern commercial society. . . . From this perspective one can focus on the question of whether a culture and its members can sustain their distinctive character once they entrust their destiny (as they must) to a modern state" (5).

3 Iris Marion Young further analyzes the relationship between community and individual Self thus, "Community usually appears as one side of a dichotomy in which individualism is the opposite pole, but as with any such opposition, each community exhibits a totalizing impulse and denies difference in two primary ways. First, it denies the difference within and between subjects. Second, in privileging face-to-face relations it seeks a model of social relations that are not mediated by space and time distancing" (305).

4 Carole Davies analyzes the split in human psyche as a kind of "borderline," which, in her own words, "is the space of transgressive or undefinable, the uncertain, the contradictory, a kind of catch-all reference for those people unable to deal with their worlds and social norms as they exist" (67).

5 As per another explication of Davies, "Borderlines . . . are physically present wherever two or more cultures edge each other, where people of two different races, sexualities, classes, genders, occupy same territory. One can also think of borderlines as places where multiple identities collide and/or negotiate space" (66).

6 The teleological concept of violence distinguishes between the literal violence of warfare and upheaval and that violence which always "involves frontiers, either 'literally' or in the sense which comes out more strongly in . . . 'frontier' confrontations between old systems or totalities and new." (Bennington 112)

7 With reference to hybridity, Carole Davies reaffirms the validity of the notion of "syncretism" which conceptualizes hybridity as a set of "relations which are animated by the partial presence of the other within the self." (48)

8 One could conclude with a reference to the succinct observation of Ania Loomba, "The point, then, is not to simply pit the themes of migrancy, exile and hybridity against rootlessness, nation, and authenticity, but to locate and evaluate their ideological, political and emotional valencies, as well as their intersections in the multiple histories of colonialism and postcoloniality." (183)

Works Cited

Bennigton, Geoffrey. "Inter." *Post-Theory: New Directions in Criticism*. Ed. Martin McQuillan, Graeme MacDonald et al. Edinburgh: Edinburgh University Press, 1999: 103-19.

Bhabha, Homi. "Signs Taken for Wonders: Questions of Ambivalence and Authority Under a Tree Outside Delhi, May 1817," *Critical Inquiry*, 12, No. 1 (Autumn): 144-65.

Davies, Carole B. *Black Women, Writing and Identity: Migrations of the Subject*. London: Routledge, 1994.

Haraway, Donna J. *Simians, Cyborgs and Women: The Reinvention of Nature*. New York: Routledge, 1991.

Khilnani, Sunil. *The Idea of India*. New Delhi: Penguin, 1998.

Krishnaswamy, Revathy. *Effeminism: The Economy of Colonial Desire*. Ann Arbor: The University of Michigan Press, 1998.

Loomba, Ania. *Colonialism/Postcolonialism*. London: Routledge, 1998.

Mills, Sara. "Post-Colonial Feminist Theory." *Contemporary Feminist Theories*. Ed. Stevie Jackson and Jackie Jones. Edinburgh: Edinburgh University Press, 1998: 98-112.

Mishra, Sudesh. *An Illustrated History of Indian Writers in English*. Ed. Arvind Krishna Mehrotra. New Delhi: Permanent Black, 2003.

Mishra, Vijay. "New Lamps for Old: Diasporas Migrancy Border." *Interrogating Post-Colonialism: Theory, Text and Context*. Ed. Harish Trivedi and Meenakshi Mukeherjee. Shimla: Indian Institute of Advanced Study, 1996: 67-85.

Mukherjee, Bharati. *Jasmine*. New York: Weidenfeld, 1989.

______. *The Middleman and Other Stories*. New Delhi: Prentice-Hall of India, 1989.

Rushdie, Salman. "The Indian Writer in England." *The Eye of the Beholder: Indian Writing in English.* Ed. M. Butcher. London: Commonwealth Institute, 1983: 75-83.

Safran, William. "Diasporas in Modern Societies: Myths of Homeland and Return." *Diaspora: A Journal of Transnational Studies.* I (Spring 1991): 83-99.

Young, Iris M. "The Ideal of Community and the Politics of Difference." *Feminism/Postmodernism.* Ed. Linda J. Nicholson. New York: Routledge, 1990: 300-23.

Tight Rope Walk: Relationships in Multiethnic Space

ILA RATHOR
Government P.G. College, Bilaspur, HP

An immigrant is caught in the vortex of decision-making because in a divided life the choices become more complex and the decisions more difficult. Hyphenated identities, fractured psyche, divided roles mark their existence. As such, marking boundaries, accepting or rejecting cultures become an essential part of their survival kit. Having crossed the borders they are more conscious of maintaining their ethnic identity, which besides marginalizing them also helps in marking a space. The ethnic and racial elements have to be stressed in order to maintain an individual 'self.' A crucial balance has to be struck between becoming an indistinguishable part of the new world, and maintaining a link with the old. In the process Bharati Mukherjee talks of two ways of looking at America, assimilation and rejection. Living as an immigrant or as an expatriate is reflected in the choices one makes. Shobha Narayan (2000) questions of the 'agonizing decisions' an immigrant has to make:

> Should I stick to the Indian community in the US, or should I make American friends, knowing that I could never be one of them?

Relationships are central to a society, a race, a culture. They mirror deeply embedded traditions, cultural attitudes and social mindsets. As we read the fictional and the non-fictional accounts of the immigrant experience in the multicultural United States we become conscious of the issues of racial, cultural and gender differences which are again and again reflected in the conflict within and without. The cultural shock, the racial prejudices and the struggle to maintain individual identity while consciously attempting to become an indistinct part of the alien culture leads to a duality in the lives of Indians in America. This duality, trauma and conflict are repeatedly presented in their fiction. To cover the larger social canvas we find that writers use relationships within the family or outside it as a metaphor for the entire range of emotions that an individual immigrant goes through.

As life in an alien culture is full of difficult choices, setbacks, dilemmas, and breakdowns, so is the fate of relationships, may it be man-woman, or parents-children, siblings, or even queer relationships. The immigrant writers have found a convenient metaphor to explore the diasporic experience. Relationships have become so crucial to it that rarely do we find any story situated outside the home. I don't agree with the view that in the North American-style Indian novel, the focus is on domestic family prattle while larger themes of migration, racism, caste and generational conflict are barely touched. The larger themes have in fact been strongly focused on as these issues are closely linked with the day-to-day existence of the people inhabiting lives there. Descriptions of mundane activities, food preferences, and social etiquette are in fact attempts to recreate the 'self' in a new environment. Moreover, the politics involved in the various power equations in a multicultural world are reflected in these social relations.

The eastern emphasis on social will and the western emphasis on individual freedom raise a clash which each writer tackles differently. We find that right from women writers like Chitra Banerjee Divakaruni, Bharati Mukherjee, Jhumpa Lahiri and Ginu Kamani to women filmmakers like Gurinder Chadha, Revathy Menon and Nisha Ganatra voices have been raised for individual will to choose. The choice can be any of the two cultures or the best of both the worlds, or even an attempt to break away from the strict code of conduct and the set patterns laid down by them.

Individual choices regarding human relations echo the socio-cultural trauma that a hyphenated individual has to go through. The day-to-day dilemma and the entire process of resolution mirror the life of the ethnic community in the US.

This is reflected in the writings of the diasporic women writers. Their stories centre around protagonists who are forced to make choices and the whole gamut of cultural upbringing, social conditioning and hyphenated existence goes into this process of decision making.

Here I would like to add that marriage serves as an important motif in the writings of these women writers. It could be due to the fact that marriage is one of the most important and crucial choices, and could be used to reflect the individual caught in the web of decision making; woman's role is central to the home and home still continues to mean a family with a marital harmony between the couple; and in the east-west dichotomy arranged marriage as a symbol for the East is sharply contrasted against the live-in relationships and the rising divorce rates of the West. The unsullied and heterosexual family is the space that the immigrant in its attempt to construct Indian-ness wishes to preserve. Marriage as a suitable motif is not just limited to the written text but has also overshadowed the entire diasporic experience on celluloid. Whether it is *Bend it Like Beckham, East is East, American Desi,* or *Mitr*, marital choices and relationships continue to serve as a perfect metaphor.

Marriage can be a suffocating one or a liberation. The man-woman relationship—with its trauma, joys, needs, desires, power equation, need for identity—remains an all-encompassing metaphor for the immigrant experience. It reflects the tensions and the problems internally and in relation to other communities. Jhumpa Lahiri's short story "A Temporary Matter" (*Interpreter* 1999) metaphorically presents the interracial relationships in a multiethnic world. The conflict and the crisis are mirrored in the crumbling relationship of the couple, Shobha and Shukumar. Their well-regulated life of stocked pantries and safe deposits receives a jolt at the death of their newborn baby. What follows is a series of misunderstandings, and complete breakdown of communication with each avoiding the other. This reflects the melting pot which turns sour when faced with a crisis, as was evident after 9/11. The mutual fear and distrust come to the fore. The hours of darkness help them in opening up and reaching out to each other. "Something happened when the house was dark. They were able to talk to each other again" (19). The invisibility helps in shadowing the differences. In the multiethnic space darkness neutralizes to a great extent the visible racial differences but daylight once again marks out their visible minority status. It calls for racial hatred and all pretence of amalgamation of cultures comes to an end. The conclusion of the story exposes the futility of communication as the temporary truce forced by the darkness comes to an end. It reveals the deliberate pain which they inflict on each other shattering their short-lived myth of a happy home. We are left feeling sorry for the couple for what they shared and lost, "for the things they now knew" (22). It reflects the intercultural miscommunication.

In "Sexy," Jhumpa Lahiri explores an adulterous situation and in the process brings out the cultural differences. It is one of the very few stories where we find people of two different cultures relating in more than a formal setting. The story links the experiences of an Indian woman trying to handle her husband's affair with an English girl, and the emotional see-sawing of an American woman, Miranda who suffers guilt pangs for her affair with a married Indian. A very innocent observation of the Indian woman's son that she is 'sexy' and that the word stands for "loving someone you don't know" (107) makes Miranda realize the outcome of her actions and re-examine her moral positioning as a home breaker. The story also comments on the need felt by the Indians to have a socially sanctioned marriage that provides a blanket of respectability and security while keeping another partner who can meet their emotional and physical needs. It gives Lahiri a chance to explore two world-views and give two different perspectives, and in an unusual instance the worlds coincide and as Narayan (2000) states, the East is able to give the West

> a sense of balance. They (immigrants—particularly from the East) bring Yin values to a very yang culture. They temper the swinging pendulum with spirituality. . . . Into a land of excess, they bring in

> values like contentment and letting go. To mix some metaphors they keep the melting pot from running over.

Lahiri creates a space to place her relationships. It is a deliberate attempt to borrow from the two worlds and what we have is a combination of rogan josh and rice, mortar and pestle, rice ceremonies, and ginger ale, vanilla cream cake, custard and spun sugar. She attempts to create a world with which one can identify. The isolation that is a part of being an immigrant combined with the stresses of coping with a foreign culture makes the characters in her stories crave for familiar sights and sounds. In a multiethnic world compartmentalizing thought and behavior to resolve the conflict between the opposing cultural influences preserve the 'self.' The 'home' and 'family' serves its purpose of creating the idea of a nation beyond a nation. The private space of the family is fundamental to national constructs. It all goes into creating an imagined nation beyond the geographical boundaries.

Sometimes the tensions in relationships arise due to these forced endeavors to preserve the nation in their homes. The culture of their native country is resuscitated from old cupboards and chests in the form of dresses, photos, paintings, music and other memorabilia. Culture is also revived by the reinforcement of fossilized customs. Frantz Fanon (1968: 224) has warned against this thoughtless appropriation of customs, divorced from their historical contexts:

> Culture has never the translucidity of custom; it abhors all simplification. In its essence it is opposed to custom, for custom is always the deterioration of culture. The desire to attach one self to tradition to bring abandoned traditions to life again does not only mean going against the current of history but also opposing one's own people.

This creates a distance between the immigrants and his country of origin as the idea vastly differs from the reality which has changed with the passing years, and the memory is also colored by nostalgia. It also creates a rift between the two generations. The parents force the customs on to their children who have no such feelings of longing or looking back. This conflict is reflected in the writings of most Asian American women writers. Lahiri's Shukumar prefers a "sailing camp or scooping ice cream during the summers to going to Calcutta" (13). Similarly Mukherjee's character Pam in "The Management of Grief" (*Middleman* 1989) prefers a trip to Wonderland than to India. Pam's mother is unable to relate to her and in their moment of grief the tensions are all the more pronounced with the daughter flying off to California and the mother totally withdrawing from her. For the daughter, India is a commodity she can sell—open yoga-cum-aerobic studio in Hollywood or give make-up tips to Indian and oriental girls. She is a far cry from her sister who epitomizes the ideal child, singing *bhajans* for Ethiopian relief and cherishing her Indian relations.

Generational divide is crucial to the immigrant life and Divakaruni presents a marriage between a first generation Indian immigrant, Deepak, and a second generation one, Preeti, in her story "Doors" (*Arranged* 1996). They tie the knot despite the warnings against marrying a man with "a set of prehistoric values" and an 'American' woman who would be 'always bossing you.' The husband brought up in a culture of social and familial openness is unable to understand his wife's need to lock doors and have her own space. Individual will is an idea strange to him. Moreover, they succumb to the pressures of the outside world which intrudes in the form of Raj. Preeti is virtually a stranger in her own house as she possibly cannot share their enthusiasm for Hindi movies, *samosas*, and Kishore Kumar's songs. The cultural divide created as a result of living between two worlds cannot be bridged by the skin color and the doors remain closed.

Such a situation leads to rebels. In Divakaruni's story "The Word Love" the narrator has a live-in relationship with an American man that is quite unacceptable to her mother in India. The American predictably fails to understand her dilemma and her feeling of having sinned. When forced to take a decision she rejects both the worlds to rejoice in her newfound freedom. It is this craving to escape the *trishanku* existence that we find a whole spurt of queer films made by Nisha Ganatra[2] and others. It is a rejection of the world order in which the immigrant finds himself crushed in an alien space, and the attempts to create a third space by merging the two prove to be quite futile. The two worlds cannot coexist in their original forms and each has to undergo changes before new cultural constructs can be created.

In the interracial relations sexuality and the different mind-sets towards it are sharply contrasted. The East remains associated with its suppressed sexual behavior, taboos and the mysticism so often attached to it; while West is linked with a total lack of sexual restraint and of inhibitions. The clash between the two, if not blatantly talked about, is an undercurrent in many of the stories written by these diasporic women writers. They deliberately shift the focus to the physical body to bring out the moral conflict in the life of an immigrant. Jasbir Jain feels that the foregrounding of the female body, its physical existence, procreativity or its absence, matrilineage, and consciousness of sexuality might be a strategy to create a space for construction or recovery of self (2002: 140). Women find themselves at crossroads to choose between the two sets of values—follow the *pativrata* tradition or to create a new space in a world in which they are doubly marginalized. Single women might enjoy the freedom to choose, but wives and daughters-in-law are expected to be the custodians of their national identities. The image of *Sita* in exile, prohibited to cross the *Lakshman-rekha* is reinforced. In an online article entitled "Sleeping Arrangements," Jaishree Abhichandani emphasizes that in America "we can dare to transgress, to exert autonomy over our sexual selves in ways we may be unable to do in India or Pakistan for fear of our reputations, our families, and even our lives." Ginu Kamani strongly believes that one's sexual control, or permissions, or dominations, or submissions, exert power over all the other areas of our lives and cites this as the reason she works constantly with the metaphors of sexuality. In dealing with sex, she is dealing with issues of intimacy, closeness, touching and physical contact, and through that accesses issues of power. Sexual politics reflects the racial, cultural and gender divides. The recent cases of honor killings in America to stop Asian women from having interracial marriages once again question individual freedom and bring out the gender bias evident in the multicultural society that burdens the woman with cultural baggage (*HT*). The desire to control is heightened when the threat to the idea of 'self' increases in an immigrant situation. Any challenge to the roles marked by the heterosexual patriarchal family is translated into a threat to the nation.

As we see, the familial and social relationships presented in the short stories of women writers explore the diasporic experience. Moreover, the relationships in a multicultural space are affected by the need to identify the 'self,' to mark a third space by marking boundaries, and to yield power, the need for which is more pronounced, and here again men enjoy a greater degree of freedom in charting their destinies than women. These stories also reveal a desire to recreate space by women in and on diaspora. Women as custodians of nation are at the centre of this repositioning of 'self' in the third space. Dislocation and relocation in a new culture gives them an opportunity to redefine their relationships vis-à-vis the family structure. Their concerns voiced in these writings cannot be dismissed as mere prattle as they echo the fears and problems faced in the multiethnic world. The world that these writers create imbibes the richness and complications of their hyphenated existence.

NOTES

1. Gurinder Chadha's *Bend it Like Beckham* is a story of an Indian girl in England, who wishes to play football instead of going in for an arranged marriage as desired by her family. *East is East* shows the attempts of a Pakistani, settled in London with an English wife, to have arranged marriages for his sons, one of whom exhibits homosexual tendencies. *Mitr* showcases an Indian family in US facing tensions due to the generation divide which causes the husband and wife to move away from each other.
2. Nisha Ganatra's first feature film, *Chutney Popcorn* received much acclaim, garnering several awards at different festivals. With Indian traditions on the one hand and '90s New York city values on

the other, it is a provocative new comedy that shows you can find family somewhere between the two. (*www.ChutneyPopcorn.com*). It centres on a lesbian who is willing to be a surrogate mother for her sister. Ganatra says that even *Bend it* was supposed to feature a lesbian relationship between Parminder Nagara and Keira Knightly but the makers were worried about the Indian audience (*HT*, Nov. 30, 2003).

Works Cited

Abhichandani, Jaishri. *Sleeping Arrangements*. Online. Internet.

Allison, Rebecca. "Death as an act of Dishonor." *Hindustan Times*. Oct. 5, 2003: 10.

Benderly, L.B., Gallagher, M.F., and Young, J.M. *Discovering Culture: An Introduction to Anthropology*. New York: D. Van Nostrand, 1977.

Divakaruni, Chitra Banerjee. *Arranged Marriage*. New York: Anchor Books, 1996.

Fanon, Frantz. 1968. *The Wretched of the Earth,* trans. Constance Farrington. New York: Grove/Black Cat.

Jain, Jasbir. *Writing Women across Cultures*. Jaipur: Rawat, 2002.

Kamani, Ginu. *To Sex or not to Sex: Junglees and Behenjis in South Asian America*. Online. Internet.

Lahiri, Jhumpa. *Interpreter of Maladies*. 1999. Delhi: Harper Collins, 2003.

Mukherjee, Bharati. *The Middleman and Other Stories*. New Delhi: Prentice Hall of India, 1989.

_____. "Two ways to belong in America." *New York Times*, September 22, 1996.

Narayan, Shobha. *Confessions of a Cross-Carrying Immigrant*. Online. Internet. http://www.rediff.com/news/2000/jan/04us4.htm.

Cultural Displacement in the Stories of Anjana Appachana and Shauna Singh Baldwin

ALKA SAXENA
D.A.V. College, Kanpur

Not long ago, writers living outside their country were known as expatriates or immigrants. Now this has been replaced by the term diaspora. Diaspora has been acknowledged as an umbrella term, which includes expatriates, immigrants and writers of the exile. The migrant diasporas experience displacement, cultural crisis, rootlessness and marginalization. The South Asian diaspora at present exceeds eleven million people. Several South Asians have written about their diasporic experience. The focus of my paper will be on the short stories of two women writers of the Indian diaspora, Anjana Appachana and Shauna Singh Baldwin who have made significant contribution to diaspora literature. For these writers, settled in the United States, fiction becomes a means to convey their diasporic experiences.

Anjana Appachana lives and works in Arizona, USA. She is the recipient of several awards including two Hawthorne Fellowships, an O. Henry Award and a National Endowment for the Arts fellowship. She made her debut as a writer of fiction in 1991 with *Incantations and Other Stories*, a collection of evocative mostly women-centered narratives. Her first novel, *Listening Now* was published in 1999. Completing her studies from Delhi University and Jawaharlal Nehru University, she left India in 1984 to live in the United States. Her stories have been widely published in journals and magazines in India and the USA.

Although Appachana has lived in the USA for over two decades, her writing is firmly based in India. In an interview published in *The Times of India* (1999: 14) she says, "When I write,

I live there again. . . . I hear the voices of my family and friends all of whom are so far away from me physically." She also states that all her main characters had to be women: "I write about women because I'm very close to the women of my life. Women matter deeply to me and their stories, those told, ring endlessly in my ears. I can't write from a man's point of view. I don't understand how their minds work. I wrote what came to me and what came to me were the voices of these women. I could barely hear the men's voices." Despite living in the United States she has not made any concession to the western audience in her use of language or in the narration of her stories claiming that, "The women in my book are India women . . . the question of restraining their voices or actions in order to feed a western audience didn't even occur to me."

Incantations and Other Stories (1992) portrays the tragedy of those caught in the whirlpool of modern India. One of the stories "Sharmaji" was included by Salman Rushdie in the collection *Mirrorwork: 50 years of Indian Writing*. Appachana traces the genealogy of her novel *Listening Now* to the short story entitled "Her Mother." This story is closest to the novel in terms of theme and structure. Although Appachana's stories came in 1991, almost after two decades of her stay in Arizona, there is little in them to suggest that the author has ever been away from India.

With all the cultural and social freedom available in the U.S.A., it is astonishing to find that in her short stories Appachana seems to be deeply rooted in Indian myths and traditions. In stories like "My Own Gods," "Bahu," "Sharmaji," and "Incantations," there are references to the great Indian epical stories that give a true and vivid account of middle-class values and problems. The stories highlight the problems faced by girls in India—issues like the problem of finding a suitable match, of the tradition of the *bahu* to adjust in the husband's family, the sanctity of marriage versus the Americans who divorce at the drop of a hat, have been tactfully handled.

"Bahu" is the story of a young wife, who, after two years of marriage has failed to conform to the traditional expectations of a good wife. She remembers her pre-marital days when she was independent and pursued her interests keenly, including her passion for music. But after marriage, her own sitar gathered dust as she heard her sister-in-law talking of liberty and life, her mother-in-law discussing the negative influence of the western culture on Indian women. When she conceives, the discussion shifts to the desire of a son and to the custom of getting gifts from the bride's parents. The *bahu* is disturbed and has a miscarriage. This marks the end of her endurance. She finally decides to leave and tells her husband, Siddharth of her decision.

Her husband tries to sort out things and tells her that this is the way things are and she will have to accept them as he has done. He feels that abdicating responsibilities is not the answer. But she has made her decision and starts packing. As the taxi leaves, her husband says he will wait for her, but she had already made up her mind. The summer season is over, the rains have just begun and as the taxi moves on she at last smells the wet earth.

The Srivastava's search for a tenant and the 'haunted barsati' form the theme of the story "When Anklets Tinkle." Several neighbors of the Srivastavas make an appearance in the story. Srivastava's daughter Namita, is of marriageable age. They discuss with the neighbors that India is no place to live in. There is too much of red tape-ism and bureaucracy in India. Perhaps, Namita should look for a doctor or engineer in England or America. She should go abroad and make money. And if she has a baby, the child will have foreign citizenship and so many more opportunities than in India. As chance would have it the Singh's son, Surinder, arrives from England. He is a doctor there. The Srivastavas ask him how the English feel about Indians and how they treat them. Surinder sadly replies: "sometimes it is alright. And sometimes they are discriminating. . . . British calling us Indians and Paki pigs" (*Incantations*: 79).

Mr. Rao, the tenant, has also lived in England for some time. He shares his experiences saying that the British still believe that the sun hasn't set over the British Raj. Either they are writing of maharajas and tigers and snake charmers or else they are writing of slums and people shitting in the open. The British are either glorifying India or they are going to the other extreme.

"Sharmaji" is the story of a disgruntled clerk who philosophizes gloomily about his place in the scheme of things. "The Prophecy" narrates the story of a hapless college student who gets gaited a few days before an abortion appointment. A critical study of Appachana's stories reveals that distance has not distanced her from the emotional, cultural and social ties with India. Referring to *Listening Now*, an American woman journalist interviewed her and said she could not stand Padma because Padma weeps in front of her child. The interviewer said that in America we don't cry in front of our children. Appachana remarks: "How do you answer such people? . . . . What some people including this interviewer see as melodrama, is to me the way things are in the India I know and to me this is not melodramatic but very, very normal." (*The Times of India* 1999: 14)

Appachana gives voice to the lives and concerns of middle-class Indian women with an immediacy that has seldom been accomplished before. The stories in *Incantations* are about Indian men and women, where no comparison has been made with American life and culture. But in the penultimate story, "Her Mother," Appachana subtly comments on the issue of cultural displacement. Having said everything about the contemporary Indian values and traditions she makes a comparison between the Indian and American ways of life in this story.

The story "Her Mother" captures the anxiety of a mother whose daughter has left for America two months back. When the mother reads the first letter from her daughter in America she has a good cry. She reads the letter several times and examines her daughter's handwriting to see if there are any traces of loneliness, discomfort or insecurity. The story continues in the form of the mother's reply to her daughter. She keeps comparing the Indian way of life with the American and advises her daughter, "Eat properly. Have plenty of milk cheese and cereal . . . so don't start stupid western dieting fads," (*Incantations* 131) which tend to make one haggard and faded. She muses on the questions of bride burning, corruption and religious fanaticism and caste division in India. The mother feels that the daughter has gone to a more civilized country, but the mother's views are very thought-provoking and pungent. She reminds her husband that in America wives are abused and beaten up. American fathers molest their children. She also adds that the Americans are as foolish about religion as Indians. As for discrimination against untouchables in India—it happened among the uneducated, whereas discrimination against blacks was rampant even among educated Americans. "Blacks were the American untouchables" (*Incantations*: 138). The mother asks her daughter to give a more balanced picture of American society. She advises her daughter to keep distance from American men, for there kissing is as casual as holding hands. She is worried she might have to accept an American son-in-law. In order to maintain her Indianness the mother asks her daughter to join an Indian Association in the university.

Written with a raw and vibrant energy Appachana's stories capture the poignant, unexpected and optimistic moment. Every story is a social encounter fiercely accurate in tone and attentive to the minutest details. Her characters try to reach out to a place beyond the traditionally prescribed boundaries for the middle-class in urban India.

Shauna Singh Baldwin was born in Montreal, grew up in India, and now lives in Milwaukee. Stories from *English Lessons and Other Stories*, her first collection, have appeared in magazines in Canada, USA and India. "Jassie" won the 1995 Writers Union of Canadian Short Prose Competition for Developing Writers. Baldwin considers herself to be the third generation of Indian writers in English. The first generation writers were R.K. Narayan and Kamala Markandaya, who were writing from India. Next came writers who migrated to the west like Salman Rushdie, Vikram Seth, Bharati Mukherjee. New writers like Jhumpa Lahiri and Baldwin who are Indians but born elsewhere are truly diasporic writers as they had a spell of schooling in India but never held an Indian passport. Baldwin states that she had strong links with India, the country of her origin. She has a good understanding of the emotional impact of her country's history. Though the characters in her book are not people she has necessarily met, she approaches these characters with emotional empathy. What she lacks by way of personal experience she makes up with research through talking to the elders and through the trips to the native country. At the same time she writes about people in Canada and America. Her comment in *The Times of India* of April 17, 2002: "My first book *English Lessons and Other Stories* is set in three countries. I'm equally comfortable in all three countries" thus becomes very significant.

English Lessons and Other Stories (1999) is a collection of short stories ranging from 1919 to the present. The stories interweave the experience of women in North America and India. The common thread lies in tying together the countries. Boundaries don't bother her. She feels indebted to all three countries. The background of her stories is the diverse cultural displacement experienced by the fictional characters. The collection begins with "Rawalpindi 1919," a simple narrative about a mother's fears for her foreign returned son. "Toronto 1984" revolves around three characters, Bibiji, Priya and Priya's brother. Priya represents the younger generation. She is twenty-four and works in a computer company in Canada. Bibiji represents the older generation, who still values Indian culture and traditions. She does not approve of the way Priya works day and night. She wonders if it is right for an unmarried girl to go travelling all over Canada. She wants Priya's brother to find a suitable match for her from India, preferably some Jat-Sikh. She stays at home and prepares typical Indian food—*baigan, dal, basmati kheer* etc.—for the children. Bibiji prepared hot milk for Priya, forgetting that she has developed a flavor for cold, sugarless, Canadian milk. According to Bibiji, Priya is "Typical Canadian, got a new car, you think you can give answers back patak-patak like a firework. Too much freedom, that's what I told your Bhaiya." (*English Lessons* 54)

Priya's feelings for her homeland are stirred when she refuses to stand for toast to the queen of Canada, at a business party. She tells her boss, "Maybe she's your Queen but she isn't my Queen" (*EL*: 85). Memories of the Queen of England, the symbol of the empire her grandfathers fought against for independence and got imprisoned, flash before her. At the end of the story Priya and Bibiji are ready to leave for India where a suitable match has been found. But at the last minute they get the news of Indira Gandhi's assassination. Bibiji asks the son to cancel the tickets. She finally compromises to stay back in Canada. On second thoughts she seems to approve the Sikh boy settled in Canada for Priya. Since the boy has not been in Canada for many years, not much freedom has gone to his head and he has not become a Canadian.

The cultural displacement is strongly emphasized in "Devika." On a cold June morning in Canada, Devika has just washed her waist length hair, cooked 'mutter paneer,' inserted a Kishore Kumar cassette and remembers it would be 46°C in Delhi. It must be sunrise and her mother would be bowed in prayer chanting the *arti*. She reads a letter from her friend Asha. Devika had come to Canada after a year of marriage, waiting for the visa for a long time. Her apartment in Canada had bare white walls. "Terror hit her low in the stomach, she could see no people in other apartments, there were no people walking along the side of the road, no people sitting on the scraps of green between the expressways. No people. A country with more acres of land than people" (*EL*: 154).

Devika's husband Ratan was busy most of the time. His mother's description of Devika as a convent educated homely girl, made him smile. In Indian English homely meant domestic but in Canadian English homely meant ugly. Ratan observed that Devika's face was too round to be considered beautiful in Canada. She had a good figure but was a bit plump for Canadian standards. He thought that Devika should take a few changes, her clothes for example. He tried to imagine Devika in black velvet skirt and white silk jacard blouse, like his Canadian boss's wife. He wanted her to wear a dress and no nose-ring. Devika develops a split personality. She imagines herself to be Asha. In Asha's role she admires a western outfit in a store. She buys cowboy jeans, jacket and boots but on returning home she locks them away in the closet. Ratan also finds cigarette stubs left behind by Asha in the ashtray. Asha's tastes were getting more expensive. She indulged in cocoa, bokchoy and marmite and marinated artichoke hearts (*EL*: 160).

Towards the end of the story Devika and Ratan drive down to a relative's house. Devika looked so much like a convent girl, Indian, constantly adjusting that impractical marigold yellow silk *dupatta*. On the highway Devika observes that her *dupatta* was caught in the car door. In a fraction of a second she pulled at the handle and was thrown out of the speeding car. Ratan got out to attend to her. He held her small and shivering in the cold grey foreignness until the ambulance came. A policeman came to make enquiries. Devika found it difficult to make him understand that it was her *dupatta* and not scarf that got caught. Devika's strong ties with Indian values and culture are reflected when she thinks:

> A *dupatta* is more, so much more than a scarf. It is a woman's modesty, her goodness, to be protected, cherished by her husband. She wanted her mother, her father and at least twenty solicitous relatives telling her what to do with it, how to live, how to be good, how to be loved. But there was only Ratan, sitting in sterile whiteness . . . there was only Ratan, and Canada, and herself. No one else. . . . She tells Ratan, "I'm Asha, . . . Devika was afraid of living here, so she just . . . flew away." (*EL*: 170-71)

Then Asha closed her swollen eyes and felt Devika drift away as though she had never been.

The mental agony of a Sikh wife is the subject matter of "Montreal, 1962." The woman is sensitive to her husband's humiliation as the Canadian authorities have told him that he could have a job if he could take off his turban and cut his hair short. She remembers how emigration was made to look so attractive earlier. Then no one had said, "You must be reborn white skinned—and clean shaven to show it—to survive" (*EL*: 14). The woman's feelings are once again hurt when the dry cleaner held her wedding sari like a dishrag and asked her if it was a curtain or a bedsheet. Overwhelmed she returns home and spreads her sari and her husband's colorful turbans in the room. She washes them gently. She holds them carefully as one would lift children. She remembers the fondness and care her mother and grandmother had towards the turban which was a sign of a Sikh's pride and glory. She admires the glorious turbans that refused to accept the drabness and obscurity and instead wielded the curtain rod like the strut of a defending champion. She dries the turban and folds it deftly and places it over her head. She is determined to be worthy of it. By the end of the story she says:

> And so, my love, I will not let you cut your strong rope of hair and go without a turban into this land of strangers. The knot my father tied between my chunni and your turban is still strong between us, and it shall not fail you now. My hands will tie a turban everyday upon your head and work so we can keep it here. (*EL*: 7)

Thus, Baldwin proves that she has the ability to lift everyday dilemmas and narrate them in an effective and touching manner.

A critical analysis of the short stories of Anjana Appachana and Shauna Singh Baldwin shows that the migrant's initial fascination with the glamorous country wanes with time. The protagonists soon realize that to live in the west and be at peace, one must, to a considerable extent, become western and adopt western attitudes, beliefs, habits, and assume if possible, a western personality. Although diaspora literature is marked by a sense of nostalgia and pain, yet by trying to adopt a new homeland the writers promote multiculturalism, making diaspora a positive act.

Works Cited

Appachana, Anjana. *Incantations and Other Stories.* New Delhi: Penguin, 1992.

Baldwin, Shauna Singh. *English Lessons and Other Stories.* New Delhi: Harper Collins, 1999.

The Times of India. New Delhi, March 26, 1999.

Strictly Male Voice: A Study of Prem N. Chopra's *Salaam New York*

EAMI MATHEW
Government College, Madappally, Kerala

Salaam New York is a novel purely based on the actions of a male character, called Rajesh. He links the 'homosocial' society of Indian and other ethnic communities who dwell in America. The characterization of Rajesh partly fulfills the male identity as defined by Marc Feigen Fasteau in his discussion of 'Male-Machine.' He is "functional, designed mainly for work. He is programmed to tackle jobs, override obstacles, attack problems, over-come difficulties and always seize the offensive" (Fasteau 1). He, at the same time misses the "competitive framework." And his most important positive reinforcement is not 'victory' but 'love.' Social and enterprising by nature, he establishes himself as insurance underwriter of Metropolitan Insurance Company.

Rajesh, soon after his arrival in New York, realizes the vast difference between his Indian and American space. As a science graduate at Delhi University, he was cherishing a private dream of going to the "land of opportunity." Right from the beginning of the novel, the reader is guided through a series of 'motion images' like the 'train,' the 'elevator,' 'the car' and so on; suggesting his inner urge to travel and go forward in life. The 'pen factory' arrives as an image of stagnation to his masculine identity that thrives upon an onward journey. The punching system and time schedule try to limit this identity but he overcomes it with the most mobile profession of an insurance agent. The Metropolitan Insurance Company is the most powerful and original of all images that remind one of his financial limitations and financial powers.

Apart from the images and narration of the surface structure, *Salaam New York* unveils a true love story. The attempts of Rajesh to woo and win Christina are Indian in style and human in essence. His effort to 'Indianize' her was a great success. The visit to "Bombay Palace" to taste Indian food and to the "India Saree Shop" to teach her how one can wear a saree, are but nothing when compared to the way she decorated herself as an Indian bride for their 'Indian Wedding.' She even "followed him and completed the seven rounds, thereby binding herself to him in wedlock" (140). His mode of 'Indianizing' the girl was a great success as it is proved by his mother's comments: "I like the girl, she looks so charming and Indian in a saree" and "perhaps you did the right thing" (155). She later added: "Well, you did what you had to do, we bless your marriage" (156).

Rajesh and Christina's romance blooms and withers like a flower. The writer makes use of the food imagery to suggest youthfulness, health and love for life. Christina, like other women characters, is reduced to the status of a shadow at times. Her urge to 'Indianize' herself makes her go away from her familiar social circle, her professional companions and keeps her busy with private chats with Rajesh. Before making love with Christina, Rajesh had set up a male society around him both for his personal comforts and professional benefit.

This study concentrates upon the masculine world of twin identity that is Indian as well as American. Through a close observation of the novel it is possible to refute Mary Jacobus' argument that "gender is constructed through language" (Jacobus 1030). Masculinity is used in the novel as the most forceful agency to establish 'the fear, the anxiety, the threat, the violence that underlie' the male world of American culture. Almost all the male characters Rajesh makes acquaintances with, narrate to him of their past and present. The language they used is the language of the heart, not strictly that of a male world. Rajesh too had a supreme sense of understanding of their narration and had fully recognized his role in the particular situations of the human drama he is enacting himself.

American or Indian, human society is based upon the age-old patriarchal setup. The fathers and sons carry on the male dynasty and the role of a mother or a daughter is just complementary to their efforts. When the sons challenge the authority of fathers, the father-son relationship is cracked. Thus the masculine identity of the society is uprooted. *Salaam New York* deals with a series of fathers and sons and falls into the group of 'Paternal fiction,' a name given by Joseph A. Boone in his study of Faulkner's *Absalom, Absalom!* (Boone 1070).

The first of the male series in the novel is Richard, 'A six-footer' who is in his 'mid-fifties.' He was a Jew, born in Egypt. He came over to America as a student about thirty five years ago. He says that he had "become a widower, went in for a second marriage and got separated." His two sons "studying in London" are estranged from him. The reason for this was shocking that when he remarried, his sixteen-year old girl felt neglected and took to drugs. She ended her life by jumping from the window. Intoxicated with drink, he realizes how easily he himself had broken the ties of father-son relationship. Therefore he regretted: "I wish I had not married the second time. The second marriage took my children away" (110). Rajesh feels the impulses of a father figure while he consoles Richard. He visualizes that "there was no second marriage in this world. It is a fake, a fraud, and hard on the children of the first marriage" (111). Richard committed himself to lust and not love. So he lost his daughter. Richard's desire to combine the paternal and maternal roles within himself and like a father he wishes to establish his long lost authority over his sons and like a mother, tries to unite them with love and concern.

The story of Mr. Khanna is different from Richard's. To him, his son Victor turns out to be a problem child. When transplanted from the familiar Indian scenario, Victor felt a stranger amongst his friends. Santiago, his classmate gave him company. Victor's problem was to find a space in an alien country and Santiago helped him much. He was totally unaware of the situation of the American society and took everything for the best until Mr. Khanna got a letter from his school saying that he didn't attend any classes.

Khanna's evaluation of his son in the Indian scenario was ideal. He says, "He was so submissive and respectful. He has changed so much and so fast." In the changed situation he retorts to his father, "It was his life and he would do as he pleased." (80) Such male arrogance had collided with Khanna's male domination. As Susan Jeffords suggests, as a general rule for rending the historical stability of the father/son dynamic and the patriarchal structure it enacts, masculinity of two generations engage in single combat. If the father is the loser, the son will be the winner or vice versa.

Mr. Khanna lived in a modern world but with traditional beliefs. He had not sensed the challenges his progeny would face in a new situation. Therefore, Victor's being late creates a problem to his parents and he replies: "I had gone to Philadelphia with my girlfriend." Also, the comment, "I am no longer a child, I am grown up" (107) made him lose his temper. His male identity was fully matured as he threatens that "if my parents push me around too hard, I may start living with my girlfriend" (108). He is what Rajesh observes, "a victim of a new environment. He is finding it hard to adjust." The difficulties of adjusting to the westernized American society affected him. Children, once they overcome social/community inhibitions, will go their own ways. Victor's actions forced Khanna to retire from life. There too the hero witnesses how sons outgrow their fathers and cause anxieties as well as threats to them.

Victor provides an excellent example of children who are misused by elders for drug trafficking. Excess amount of pocket money allured the child to taste things prohibited. Lack of social and domestic responsibility and a source of easy money led him to the world of marijuana, girlfriends and holidaying. In order to save him from Mrs. Santiago, Rajesh had to threaten her a bit. He said, "I think you have exploited the child. You've used him to deliver drugs" (82). She retorts, "In fact, I like Victor and since you people are new to this country, I want to help. Also I know how difficult it is to settle down in a new country with a different culture and environment." (84)

Victor's case reveals Mr. Khanna's lack of understanding his own child. Being a disciplinarian by nature and economical by practice, he had charted out the life of his son. This great mistake had intensified the misunderstanding deeper than ever. For each and every thing Victor did, Mr. Khanna questioned him, put limits to his freedom and compelled him to burst out, "My parents hardly find time to talk to me" (85) and expresses his wish to get separated from them. Parents in a busy lifestyle fail to keep contact with their children. Janice Joseph observes that "those who are strongly attached to their parents are less likely to be involved in delinquent behavior" (1995: 479). She further says, "Youths who associate with delinquent friends are more likely than those who do not have such associations to engage in delinquent behavior." Mr. Khanna was too late to realize that his son is neither a child nor a grown-up and is facing the problems of adolescence. The Victor-Santiago friendship blossoms as a result of Victor's belief that his future opportunities are blocked or limited by his father. Surprisingly, nowhere in the novel are we given a description of Mrs. and Mr. Khanna taking their children for holidaying or any sort of entertainment outside their home. At that phase of life when he was urgently in need of guidance and friendship, Victor found it hard to live his lonely life.

The fathers who brought their children to the new social environment could not cope with their sons' 'acculturization' with the western ways. It seems paradoxical, yet significant. They feared that the patriarchal authority and the continuation of parental dignity of the Indian tradition would be broken. Razvi, another client of Rajesh, who was a Pakistani by birth, had been in the United States for the last fifteen years, also complained of his sons: "My sons are young and spendthrifts. These plans [insurance] suit them and give them the habit of saving." He also said that he told them further to meet Rajesh but "they are young and they don't listen" (90). Mr. Khanna lacks Razvi's power of observation and conclusion that young men act beyond one's expectations. They can possibly be spendthrifts and disobedient. These hallmarks of youth that he noticed helped him to avoid the kind of open combats that Mr. Khanna had with his sons.

Mr. Sharma openly admits his failure in Indianizing his sons. He says, "They came to this country when they were kids. . . . They have assimilated all the characteristics of the life here despite my efforts to teach them about our culture back home." Everything seems good back at home according to these fathers who simply wished to control their sons. His sons' efforts to identify themselves with the western tradition are approached with a self-analysis. "Maybe I'm not realistic and rational," Sharma observes. But "when I see my daughter going out with someone, despite his objections, I feel like killing myself." He adds, "It's nothing that serious. A clash between eastern and western values is natural. . . . I've got to find a middle path for my children." (50)

Rajesh, who walks along the middle path, does not forget his loyalties. Unconsciously he imbibed the paternal influences on him by sharing his father's burdens. His father, who always believed that Rajesh would not challenge his father's decisions, feels hurt at the announcement of his wedding with Christina. He took enough time to get it digested. Rajesh had one but firm answer to his father's enquiries: "I love Christina deeply. I married her before leaving for India" (155). His father took sometime to realize that his only son is now a grown-up man to whom the freedom to love and marry a girl is natural. When his mother recognized her son's role as a loyal lover and husband, she congratulated him without hesitation: "You did the right thing," she said (155). Thus his father was compelled to accept the truth of his son's acculturation. This is the middle path as Sharma suggested.

In her critical study of films, Susan Jeffords raises a pertinent question and seeks to answer it as well:

> Is the apparent resurgence of cultural violence . . . an indication that the father/son dynamic has suffered from challenges to its sufficiency and means to be reaffirmed?

These narratives indicate how the father/son dynamic is able to respond to local historical conditions while maintaining its determination of its structure of social relations and, at the same time, reformulating those structures to adapt to different social circumstances (1064).

Under the light of Jeffords' evaluation, it is easy to categorize fathers and sons of *Salaam New York*. Fathers who believe in the old definition of masculine subject and the significance of Indian culture are threatened by the way in which their sons challenged and altered the stability of that culture in new social circumstances. In that sense, the novel is a narration of Rajesh. Yet, at another level, the novel uplifts the construction of masculine subjects and has been restabilized in relation to those challenges raised by sons; it is the narration of the fathers. Rajesh belongs neither to the 'father' category nor the 'son' category. He belongs to the mid-way group of Razvi, not dismissing the Indian culture and father dynamic altogether but listening to the guiding inner voice of son dynamic. As the title suggests, Rajesh fails to adjust thoroughly to the conditions of the new environment due to his personal tragedy, which, if happened in an Indian city, he would have reacted in the same way. His return suggests that the 'son' of the new environment would naturally turn to the 'father' of the old situation.

Works Cited

Boone, Joseph A. "Creation by Paternal Narrative, Sexual Anxiety and the Reauthorizing Designs of *Absalom, Absalom!*," *Feminisms: An Anthology of Literary Theory and Criticism*. Robyn R. Warhol and Diane Price Herndel ed. 1977. Hampshire: Macmillan,1068-86.

Chopra, Prem N. *Salaam, New York*. New Delhi: Sterling, 1993.

Fasteau, Marc Feign. *The Male Machine*. New York: Dell, 1975.

Jacobus, Marry. "Reading Women." *Feminisms: An Anthology of Literary Theory and Criticism*.1029-45.

Jeffords, Susan. "Masculinity as Excess in Vietnam Films: The Father/Son Dynamic of American Culture and Criticism" in *Feminisms: An Anthology of Literary Theory and Criticism*. 1046-67.

Joseph, Janice. "Juvenile Delinquency among African Americans." *Journal of Black Studies* 25: 4 March 1995: 475-88.

Warboys, Loren M. and Carrole B. Shauffer. "Protecting Youth Rights." *Understanding Troubled and Troubling Youth.* Peter E. Leone. California: Sage, 1990.

"The Ignored Americans, Speak": Critiquing Native American Female Voices

MUKUL SENGUPTA
Principal, Maharani Kasiswari College, Kolkata

Contexts of multiethnic literatures in the Americas, is a complicated, vast space of study of variegated issues—cultural, historical, economic and political. As Edward Said tells us (1978: 32), there are two indivisible foundations of imperial authority—'knowledge' and 'power.' 'Knowing' is basic source of imperial dominance of Europe over the world, the New World. The process of knowing is the most effective tool of suppression of a vast wealth of indigenous cultures and exportation of European language, literature and learning as part of a so-called civilizing mission of the dominant hegemony. Gradually, this European, more specifically British imperial power would begin to be dismantled by the effects of two world wars and the rise of independence movements all over the world. This process is part of the process of decolonization. It asserts a rejuvenation of creative activity in postcolonial societies. Decolonization is an attempt, a systematic effort of resistance and representation, rejection and subversion of all literary, cultural and political activities. 'The empire' writes back in the process of re-inscription, re-appropriation, subversion of the heterogeneous issues of the imperial culture. This rewriting and rejuvenation is not a one-way process, a monistic approach. While destructuring the canonized, entering into the centre from the margin, the margin itself becomes essential and canonized. Questions of gender, class, race, ethnicity, also are vital aspects of this cultural process. The concept of otherness resists the existing power structure and struggles for empowerment. Contexts of multiethnic literature and culture therefore involve different issues: migration, slavery, suppression, resistance, representation, difference, race, gender, place and space. It also involves different discourses of imperial Europe, history, philosophy and linguistics, as well as experiences of speaking and writing.

These heterogeneous contexts are important factors of creativity for the multiethnic people, whose voices are submerged, bruised and eroded. In this paper, I intend to focus on the complicity of the hidden spaces of survival of the multiethnic people, the Native American people, specifically the struggle of their women, for registering their voice. My intention is to include the suppression and restructuring of the voices of the Native American women and thus highlight the extremely creative context of these women's survival, struggle, resistance and representation as published in different anthologies.

While introducing Native American women, their history, culture and politics, I have to enter into the vast area of a series of incidents, pre-Columbian history, Columbus's victory of the so-called New World, the history of colonization by European settlers from Britain, Spain, France, and Denmark, the gradual degeneration, the drying out of the sap of existence of these indigenous people, the so-called 'savages' who are multi-faceted and multilingual. I stress on the multilingual aspect of these ancient people of the Americas, their multi-culture, multi-technology, multi-strategies of survival. I also focus on the process of their pre-colonial, pre-Columbus existence; the period of colonial domination, usurpation of their land, their multi-tribal culture, the intermixture and cohesion among their own cultures, the dispossession of their own land and loss of sovereignty. It is a painful, yet interesting history of bloodshed, resistance, war, frailty, of being threatened and doomed into the farthest corner of the country, into the darkness of 'reservations' like driven animals. I also intend to offer a critique of the essentialist position of the indigenous, tribal, aboriginal existence and culture of Native-Americans.

History is thus a very vital and fundamental aspect of this critique of Native American survival strategy. The brutal force of colonization affected as well as eroded a vast, multi-faceted, multi-ethnic civilization and culture. I propose to highlight representations of this resistance history by focusing on two primary texts, namely Laura Coltelli's edited venture published in 1990 entitled *Winged Words: American Indian Writers Speak* that contains different interviews with Native American women writers, and an anthology of memoirs, poetry and fiction, *Reinventing the Enemy's Language: Contemporary Native Women's Writings of North America* (1997), edited by Joy Harjo and Gloria Bird.

The writings of the Native Indian women are in constant search of expressive language beyond the lost, silent and terrible history of their existence. Dispossessed of their homelands by series of successive invasions of Europeans, the first, real Americans have been hidden within myths and legends. These women's writings attempt to locate the actualities, histories, richness and diversity of American Indian culture. If we look into the archaeological history of the Native people of the Americas, we find that it goes back more than thirty thousand years. When Columbus landed in this "New" World, it was already a very old world having diverse civilizations rise and fall through the centuries. In their writings, the women offer a fresh look at the Americas, that in other words are the perspectives of the original inhabitants of the Americas. It is the history of struggle, adaptability, rebellion in the face of 'removal' or extinction of these Native people's existence in the past five hundred years. Also, when the heinous predators came in the garb of the White European invaders, they were forced to cope with the intrusion into their lands.

One significant aspect to be noted in the critique of these Native women's writings is the complicated relationship between the oral and the written language. Writing is still suspected in Native American tribal communities. It goes back to the bitter, hidden history and belief that it was through writing in the colonizer's language that their lands had been stolen, their children taken away. To speak and write the language of the occupier of their lands is even sometimes regarded as betrayal. This is an interlocking dichotomy of Native American culture, since these cultures are primarily constructed out of oral tradition, oral literature. As I analyze one of the anthologies of Native women's writings, *Reinventing the Enemy's Language*, I gradually comprehend the collective voice from the women of this indigenous community. The objective of publication of this anthology is also to exert the survival of the Native women who are already facing the onslaught of destruction. They spoke of the ills of colonization in its many forms of hatred, including self-doubt, poverty, alcoholism, depression and violence against them. They also spoke of their coming out of wars, for one or two centuries.

One of the significant problematic issues is their use of the "enemy language." Language is a fundamental site of struggle for postcolonial discourse, because the colonial process itself begins in language. Language, through the function of naming, exerts power over the colonized people. Some of the Native people speak native languages as well as English or Spanish or French. The use of tribal languages is prohibited in schools, as is the use of adoptive names. Native languages were thus suppressed to near extinction. Shame thus outlines the loss of their own language.

The women insist to speak. For them, it is empowerment rather than being victimized by destruction. In their responses to imperialist dominance of language, the Native-Americans, and especially their women, started a decolonizing process of rejection and when that was not possible, subversion. Colonizer's languages, which often usurped Native American tribal languages, sometimes diminished them, now carry emblems of Native American cultures, designs, bead work, quills etc. Thus reinvention of their history and language is also a transformative process for the Native Americans.

For Native-American women writers, the politics of publishing is also a neo-colonial domination. Their words are edited and legitimized by the male authority. Very often, the voice of tribal, land-based women writers with ties to community, history and language has been marginalized and also silenced by the dominating, publication agency. When these women speak, they reinvent the colonizer's language, they turn the images of the colonizer into their own. The process is transformation and politicization of their experience. The images of the colonized are thus mirrored in the opposite direction.

An examination of the above-mentioned anthology of contemporary Native women's writing reveals the multifarious nature of their origins. It includes eighty-seven writers from many varied tribes and backgrounds, from the Tohono O'dham people born near the Southern border of the United States, to the Athabascans living near the Arctic Circle. They represent approximately fifty tribal nations and come from traditional, rural homelands as well as from the cities that sprang up around these original lands. The issues are interlocking in their writings—the issues of being Indian and female under subjection. The issues of independence and sovereignty of tribal nations, their relationship with intruder nations, the imposed borders around their 'reservations,' and tribal identifications are crucial in their writings.

Women are involved in 'reinventing' their existence as individual human beings struggling towards knowledge, as persons born into families, tribes, nations, as literary artists involved in the creative act. Survival is the final unifying theme. As Native women, they have confronted institutionalized attacks on gender and forced sterilizations. As custodians of their tribes, nations and culture, these women are aware of the growing influence of the Aryan nations, of the neo-Nazi race-hating movements, of the White women's struggle to assert their voice in a patriarchal, hierarchical system. In their tribal society, 'Indian' women were heard, relied upon, and they have even controlled the politics of their tribal groups. Female subjection took place when colonization and war broke out, when women were possessed as commodities, as slaves. Patriarchy intervened along with colonialism and imperialism. Tribal culture upheld women's role as worker, farmer, participant in production, nurturer. The Native American women also reacted against damaging stereotypes of Native culture. Writing for them is a continuous process of resistance and creation, identification against non-entity. As a female, the Native woman writer focuses on her ties with her community, her self, her history and her culture. Her subjectivity as a colonized subject is highly significant.

A writer like Emma LaRocque, plains cree, Metis criticizes the misrepresentation of her Native culture: "This gross misrepresentation and brutal objectification of aboriginal peoples in mainstream culture made me a writer and a scholar. . . . Writing is a process of confronting what is human in oneself as well as in others." (Harjo and Bird: 360-61)

For Linda Hogan, a Chickasaw, the act of writing comes out of her deepest wanting of justice and survival. She states:

> I feel committed to the telling of Indian story, culling the lies out of history to find what is beneath them and then speaking those found truths. . . . I am still hopeful enough to think the world might be changed by the words and the telling.

Hogan also expresses her critique of the men folk in her poem, 'Skin':

> The men wore human skins
> but removed them at night
> and fell to the bottom of darkness
> like crows without wings. (Harjo and Bird: 321)

Scott Kayla Morrison, "Kela Humma" (Red Hawk), CHOCTAW expresses her different experience as a Native woman. She speaks of White men's rewriting of Native history with a deliberate objective of distortion and erosion of the original history and struggle. She focuses on the collective memory of the Native Americans in contrast to the "educated" academics who miswrote and misrepresented their origin legend.

Senses of place, a deep-rooted link with the natural world, ties with environment and the animal world are the sources of the creative writings of Elizabeth Woody, warm springs, Wasco, Navajo. In her own words, "In the panorama of language and the land that makes the language, in my mother's plateau—Wasco River oratory and my father's Dine' movement, words heal others or bring strength." Words are thus the source of power for these women in their position of subjectivity.

Native American women very often refer to land and its significance in their life and writing. In their struggle of resistance, when they refer to land and its relation with human being, these writers speak of the intertwined, interwoven struggle, beginning with dispossession of land caused by the white invaders, usurpation of their space, earth, language and culture. Leslie Marmon Silko, Laguna, a noted Native woman writer thinks, in her own language, "Human identity, imagination and story telling were inextricably linked to the land, to Mother Earth, just as strands of the spider's web radiate from the center of the web." She further states that from the spoken word or story telling comes the written word as well as the visual image.

Paula Gunn Allen, Laguna Sioux, analyzes the reasons for her community's empowerment after the terrible past of usurpation, brutality and war. She focuses on the need of contextualizing Native writers' works and feels that the Native writers must get control of definitions, contexts and images, represented in terms of dominant White culture. Katsi Cook, Mohawk, sought after the expression of her hidden, terrible struggle. It is part of the significant history of Native people being reconstructed. She refers to the deliberate process of denigration of Indian women since colonial times. The history of the distortion of native word, "Squaw" is an interesting critique of colonization, not only of land, place, environment, geography, but also of culture, the language itself. "Squaw" is a Mohawk word that means "it's slippery," describing the vagina. In its native context, "squaw" is an excellent and empowering word to describe the clear, abundant, thready mucus the cervix produces when a woman is fertile. But the colonizer used it to hint at the sexual denigration of these women.

Katsi Cook in her story, "The Coming of Anontak" creates a unique female experience in terms of labor pain. The female body in this story is highlighted as a space of empowerment. Giving birth to a child is a creative experience. This courageous and creative act of birth soon follows another complication when the State of New York police displace the mother and her community to the farthest corner of the reservation. Referring to the

American Indian movement, Mary Brave Bird spoke of the fight of the Indian women and hailed their rights on their own land, which has been usurped.

> After five hundred years of being held in subjection, we are finally standing up on our hind legs. Together with my sisters from many tribes, I am a birth-giver, a rebirth giver, fighting to ensure a life for unborn generations. I am a Sioux woman!

In a series of interviews with American Indian writers, which also include women writers, Laura Coltelli in her book, *Winged Words, American Indian Writers Speak*, focuses on various critical issues related to their writings and existence. In mainstream American literature and culture, sincere anthropologists on the one hand and Hollywood stereotyping on the other interpreted Indians in radically different manners. Both failed to highlight the reality and history of their survival in America. But since the late 1960s, a generation of highly articulate and talented Native American writers has begun to reinterpret and re-orient the existing stereotyped images of Indian American people. A rich literary tradition has emerged out of their ongoing self-definition, a sense of the past and sting of the present.

Laura Coltelli has interviewed Paula Gunn Allen, Michael Dorris, Louise Erdrich, Joy Harjo, Linda Hogan, N. Scott Momaday, Simon Ortiz, Wendy Rose, Leslie Marmon Silko, Gerald Vizenor and James Welch. These writers candidly analyze each of the major issues confronting current Indian writers: the debt to old and the creation of new traditions, the proprieties of age and gender, the interrelations between Indian writers and non-Indian readers and critics, differences between writers and anthropologists and historians. These writers explore a wide range of topics. Erdritch and Dorris, husband and wife together speak of their unique literary collaboration, Allen analyses her Feminist perspective, Joy Harjo regards her writing as empowerment to overcome "a terrible silence," Momaday speaks of the immense power of naming, Silko of her developing "Almanac of the Dead," Ortiz of the coyote figure, Vizenor of a benevolent trickster, and Welch of his use of imagery and humor.

Coltelli also highlights their voice of protest, of resistance, of literary creativity. The most significant aspect of their writing is their declaration of cultural independence. It is their own story, their history, existence and struggle. Memory, language and storytelling are intertwined in their writing. Their personal and historical recollections overlap each other and are conveyed through a powerful language. For all these writers, words are not mere referents, they are life-giving. For them, to use language is literally to create: "We imagine ourselves, we create ourselves, we touch ourselves into being with words." For them, "Language is a way of life . . . by language we create knowledge." As Momaday points out, the ethics of the word born of an oral tradition, for all Native American writers, is a means of knowledge and experience. It stands at the core of community life. To quote Momaday again:

> It seems to me that in a certain sense we are all made of words, that our most essential being consists in language. It is the element in which we think and dream and act, in which we live our daily lives. There is no way in which we can exist apart from the morality of a verbal dimension. (Collelli: 1990)

In their writings, imagination shapes new dimensions from the old. Momaday believes that "the writer, like the storyteller . . . is concerned to create himself and his audience in language."

One of the interesting aspects of Native American writing, as Paula Gunn Allen points out, is their geographic origin. It explains differences in personalities and is source of multiethnic dimension of Native American writing. Wendy Rose explains:

> To be tribal and to be Pan-Indian exist side by side and in fact Pan-Indianism is intended to protect those tribal identities, not to replace them.

Another significant issue of Native American writing, as Coltelli analyses, is the issue of mixed blood. To quote Wendy Rose once again, mixed bloods are not mere "a biological thing" but "a condition of history, a condition of context, a condition of circumstance . . . a political fact." Mixed-bloods have been able to re-establish their relationship with the land, their roots and tribes, this "appropriation" of the North American continent is a significant step toward the acquisition of a new identity.

Women play a unique role in current Native American literature. They have been transmitters of culture in creation myths and in the storytelling tradition. The contemporary Native American women maintain vital connections from one generation to the other in spite of the devastating effect of loss of their tradition and imposed pressures towards acculturation. Linda Hogan focuses on this point, "It's almost as if we have to reeducate ourselves to be families again, to be mothers." American Indian women's writing originates from a whole gamut of experiential and emotional landscapes: it is the interrelation between traditional values and new lifestyles, the development of the artist, the difficult and complicated relationship with feminism and white women's organizations. The recurring images of wholeness represented by women in Native American myths symbolize continuity, self-definition and universal cosmologies as opposed to cultural disintegration.

To conclude it must be mentioned that Native American writings offer a significant critique of anthropologists who misinterpret Native American culture and are dominated by western colonialism, its bias and myths. While interviewing different authors, Laura Coltelli attempts to locate these unified voices of protest, resistance and creativity within Native American existence in spite of differences of language, tribe, environment and space.

Works Cited

Ballantine, Betty, Ian Ballantine, ed. *The Native Americans—An Illustrated History.* Atlanta: Turner, 1993.

Coltelli, Laura. ed. *Winged Words, American Indian Writers Speak.* The U of Nebraska P, 1990.

Harjo, Joy and Gloria Bird. ed. *Reinventing the Enemy's Language, Contemporary Native Women's Writings of North America.* New York: W.W. Norton, 1997.

Kopper, Philip et al. ed. *The Smithsonian Book of North American Indians*. (Before the Coming of the Europeans). New York: Harry N. Abrams. 1986.

Robin White's Works: A Reverse Navigation

I.H-Shihan
Deshbandu College for Girls, Kolkata

Among the twentieth century major human concerns *migration* is one key area where human drive is easily discernible on a global scale. The major transmission curve manifestly moves from the so-called underdeveloped countries to the so-called developed countries, or, in other words, from the East to the West, from the colonized to the colonizers, and so on. A great body of the twentieth century fiction receptively accommodates this new historical and human phenomenon. Here again fact and fiction merge together—the diasporic literature seems to dominate the field now. However, Robin White,[1] as an author of cultural interface, has a complicated designation.[2] Born in India to an American missionary family, White, at sixteen, relocated himself to the mainstream American life for good. To his credit he has a few novels and short stories that illustrate some Americans' cultural navigation to India. The navigation in his works interestingly exemplifies a perspective in reverse to the popular trend—i.e. from the US to India, and not the other way round. As against the vast popular westward wave of migration, this *reverse navigation* looks rather thin in its volume; but even then the phenomenon reflects at least a minority group of American 'Huck Finns' firmly negotiating an alternative mode of living in a so-called 'backward place.' In any case whatsoever, White's works are more than they just confirm America's literary interest in India.

It is worthwhile, in this respect, to make a reminder of the observation Robin White himself makes in the "Preface" to his collection of stories, *Foreign Soil:* "Indeed, there *are* no more unexplored geographic rivers for our Huck Finns to travel down, there are only the cultural ones." This is, of course, a crucial observation. Historical evidences amply certify that attempts at negotiating other cultures have often been prompted by intentions other than purely cultural. For example, Warren Hastings' era evinces a keen interest in Indian and Indo-Persian cultures in general. Political motivation behind the so-called Orientalism was evident. Otherwise, as Hastings argued, "the British would be treated as aliens, rapport between ruler and ruled would break down, and the empire would ultimately collapse." (Kopf 18) And in recent times when *globalization* has become the latest maxim for the so-called advanced countries, the stress is again on the need for knowing others culturally as a precondition for successful business relationship. In both the cases the main drive behind the interests in other cultures is either overtly political or economic, and in both the cases the onlookers apparently see India (or the Third World for that matter) from a supposedly elevated position. It will, however, be difficult to bracket White in the same category. In his case, when we speak of *reverse navigation*, the question of 'superiority' is absolutely redundant, and his mission is neither political nor is it economic.

In White's case a spirit for experimentation with an alternative structure of culture motivates this *reverse* routing. The present paper investigates into this particular aspect and appreciates how a few 'Huck Finns' from the so-called 'superior culture' attempt at relocating themselves to the so-called 'inferior culture' and recognizing merits in an otherwise alien approach to life. The portrayal of the encounter between the dictates of the parent and the host cultures highlights certain marginal areas where traditional American image of India loses its popular implications, and at the same time the validity of the US culture as the 'premier' form itself is put to severe tests. The big question of the universality of western culture itself appears to be facing opposition from a western author. These individual responses, however feeble it might appear side by side the mainstream popular responses, are no doubt significant as they recognize new trends during the postcolonial era. This, in a way, reflects at least one of the US perspectives on India as well.

Many of White's people, thus, clarify the relationship between the two cultures, and also between Americans and the US culture. *The Christian Science Monitor*, while commenting on *Elephant Hill*, remarks that White may not always equal the intricacies of E.M. Forster in explaining philosophically the 'mysterious' East, but no doubt his novels are well worth reading for the sheer humanity they portray." (*BRD,* 1959: 1056) What is omitted in this observation is the way White predicts the absurdity of cultural domination or classification of culture in terms of gradations is glaringly absent in Forster's treatment. Relatively less 'outsider' than Forster, White finds India less intricate and less 'mysterious.' He is in a theoretical position to portray India from an altogether different perspective as he can doctrinally recognize that the "whole idea of separateness had no basis in human reality to begin with." (Letter, 4 Oct. 1994) Naturally, his portrayal is highlighted by a deep empathy for the human beings and it is displayed in a style that makes cultural interaction meaningful and aesthetically graceful.

House of Many Rooms is a story of American missionary family, the Fishers, in Meigudy, south India. The basic framework of the novel is determined by an in-depth study of the varying degree of the US integration with India. The "book's theme might broadly be summarized as the breakdown of Western values when subjected to the equivocal moral climate of Hinduism." (*TLS*: 18 March 1960, 173) However, as a micro study of the clash and compromise between the two dominant religions, it deserves attention. Both Hinduism and Christianity imbibe from each other to such an extent as would be firmly disapproved of by puritans on either side. The mission of the missionaries profits and fails; the mass transforms religions as religions too transform the mass.

However, in *Elephant Hill*, Beth Sumner essays in a purely social and secular territory. The main outline of the story details how a chance meeting between Beth Sumner, an American tourist, and Alargarsami, an Indian businessman, although through a series of misunderstandings, blossoms into a far-reaching relationship in a very short period of time. The death of Beth's father, her frustration with Fred and her uncertainties with the school board created in her a vacuum, feelings of emptiness, loneliness, despair, and that might be an indirect drive leading her to visit her sister, Agnes, in India. To her sister she confesses: "'I'm not going back,' Beth said fiercely, 'not to Old Fordham, not there at any rate.'" (65) Agnes also tries to understand sympathetically Beth's vulnerable position in homeland: "You grew up with the comfortable assurance that the older generation would always be there, between you and the end, as sort of shield. And then, one by one, the front-runners dropped away, and you found yourself out there alone, the shield now, with nothing beyond." (67) However, through her smart handling of the complications between the Alargarsamis and the Westmores, Beth is able to set everything right for her sister's family and for herself as well. She finds her Mr. Right in Alagarsami and a support system she has apparently lost in the US. The *Kirkus* observes that while there is "no immense philosophical problem posed or solved, one feels that there is a lesson in communication, an area in which international relationships have suffered so much." (*BRD*, 1959: 1056)

It is, however, not much comprehensible as to why Beth chooses India for migration except that the only near and dear one now she has, Agnes, lives in India. Identity of a person, therefore, is not just a question of physical psychological attachment to his/her birthplace alone; it has something to do with a metaphysical sense of belonging and security, meaningful interaction and real human bond with people around. Robert Ezra Park thinks that in the western hemisphere the individual is emancipated and society is automated and this has, in a way, affected adversely "the individual's sense of inner security, upon which the control and direction of his personal life finally rests." (Park 12) Martin Luther King seems to have come to a similar conclusion about modern western civilization based more on science and technology and less on human grounds: "scientific power has outrun our spiritual power. We have guided missiles and misguided man." (Qtd. *Times of India*, 1) Once the axis of faith in her homeland lost, Beth launches her search for an alternative central human support system for subsistence. In the US, a lost self in an otherwise known world, Beth cannot spiritually negotiate her surroundings. She, therefore, needs a relocation to establish a kind of human relationship and thereby reactivate herself. For Beth, it is not a question of comparison in terms of inherent merits or demerits in the two cultures involved; it is a question of just suitability in her own context, a simple question of security and emotional stability. For her it is a very postmodern question—one of just *being.* Being an American or Indian is just irrelevant.

The same question of *being* and *belonging* is again the central issue in White's another novel, *Men and Angel.* Luke Baber, who happens to have been born in India, after a long period of Americanization, revisits India with a view to investigating a report of his father's mysterious death. His parentage, his long exposures to the States, his education and experience there have made him a thorough American. His birthplace, India, has become at present a dim past—"the spirit it had given to and nourished had fled. The interval of time had somehow invalidated it. I could not claim this as my origin." (40) Once he locates himself with the Chellappas, he begins to appreciate the meaning of an integrated Indian family life. Initially not very comfortable with the Chellapa tradition, Luke gradually discovers a sense of *being* and *belonging* there:

> It had been a long time since I had felt so much at ease, so much a sense of belonging. I had been accepted and treated, I thought, not with the formal courtesies extended to a guest but with the casual intimacy of another member of the family. . . . I had been here a little over two weeks, and already I felt as if I were by some strange process of osmosis being slowly absorbed, and that the day was not far off when not only they would think me as related, I would think of them as family. (123-24)

Many western commentators on India have often spoken highly of this *in-group feeling* and *togetherness* in the traditional Indian family structure. Noted German filmmaker Zoltan Paul, although not commenting on the Indian style, is acutely conscious of lack of it in the western world. His observation lends strength to the

Indian position: "I can't deny that the mechanized lives in big metros, with no one to care for you, and so much of emotional vacuum, takes a toll." (*Times of India* 12 Oct 2003, 2) This explains why Ruth Jhabvala's Judy in *A Backward Place* and the narrator in *Heat and Dust* too find this family cocoon a safe and guaranteed destination to retreat into. While commenting on Jhabvala, Jacquelin Singh, a European expatriate in India, backs this aspect unconditionally. She observes that some people may be sleeping in the streets, "but they are whole families together, not fragmented," and like the westerners "not frantically trying to put back the pieces of meaningful human relationships by means of fads like communes or experimental sex." She even philosophizes that the "spiritual pains of alienation and the agony that have made so many Europeans and Americans robots at best, monsters at worst, have not ravaged India's wretched ones." (Singh 22) However, despite the initial tension and stress, through a process of osmosis, Luke Baber proves himself an "American son" to the Chellappas. He refuses the *dhoti*[3] initially, but without conviction. The coherent Indian family structure is a dream in the western hemisphere. Luke Baber has seen and experienced an altogether different kind of life in the States. He fluctuates between two worlds in time and space:

> And there the memory breaks, with nothing to tie it to my first impression of America: riding in enormous trains and buses, sitting endlessly in gloomy, stream-heated waiting rooms, sleeping in strange and transient beds, passing dull hours with prescribed amusements, eating unpalatable institutional food, living out of suitcases, breathing dump, polluted air that left an acid taste in my mouth, walking up streets over which only a narrow strip of gray sky was visible. (34)

Secretly, he and Sarojini, the educated Chellappa daughter, get emotionally involved and think in terms of marriage and fulfillment thereby. Although initially opposed, he finally gets the nod of the family for the relationship. In the same novel, another American, Joan, married to an Indian doctor, too finds everything satisfactory in India: "We have got a wonderful thing going. . . . Oh, I'm used to things all right. I have learned the language and customs and manners, and I am accepted, and our kids play with the neighbours' kids and I couldn't ask for better." (216) Joan, in fact, has the guts to reduce the entire East-West dialectic to a dispute between the uses of water and 'toilet paper,' (221) making an interesting antithesis to the oft-quoted Kipling adage, "the twine shall never meet."

All the three, Beth, Luke and Joan, thus testify to successful experimentations with an alien culture under an alien sky. That way many of White's people agree with Brislin's observation and act as independent individuals not regulated by preconceived images: "people are active processors of information and do not simply surrender themselves to the situation they encounter. Rather, they modify their behavior to cope with the sorts of new problems they will invariably encounter as part of their cross-cultural experience." (Brislin 15) White, therefore, confirms the Brislin theory more than many Anglo-Indian, Indo-Anglian and British novelists can do. Either strong racial or political prejudices make up their orientation and the mind-set. Never can they get out of the locked mind they inherit from their culture that defines India too. They do not seem to negotiate India themselves on their own terms and the question of subjective adjustment remains illusive. Kipling advocates a philosophy of distance and E.M. Forster comes close to a 'not yet' sort of hyphenated position. White rejects them all.

Compared with the British observers on India, the American writers write with a more unlocked mind. That Americans do not have an unpleasant past affair with India and that the Americans are used to a kind of collage culture may account for such attitude. Pearl S. Buck has incidentally tried her hand at depicting India and Indo-US interactions in her two major novels. In *Come My Beloved* (1953) she covers almost four generations of the MacArds and registers gradual shift in American attitudes toward India. David Hardworth MacArd's opinion of India is very similar to what Miss Mayo portrays in her tirade of abuses, *Mother India*. (1927) Naturally, MacArd's India too is a 'continent of circe,' or 'an area of darkness' sort of human habitation—full of snakes, heat, beggars, filth, naked men strutting around pretending to be saints. But the later generations seem to redefine the western image of India and shift away from the conformist position. They appreciate certain demonstrable features of India and its culture, which are not as awful as the western cultural tutelage about India caters them. *Mandala* (1970) further strengthens the position through Jagat-Brooke relationship. Despite the unsatisfactory outcome the attempt itself, is no doubt, a step forward. Other American works—Carl Bartholomew's *My Heart Has Seventeen Rooms* (1959), Carl Pope's *Sahib* (1972), Lillian Carter's *Away from Home* (1977), Jean Bothwell's *White Fawn of Phalera* (1963) etc. too add to the Americans' social and literary experiments with India. However, what is special about White's people is that in the process of acculturation, in place of rigid resistance, they assert their capability under an altogether different cultural environment and discover their potentiality. Never do they seem to seek to revise history like many Asian Americans. Rather they transfigure their ethnicity; the point is not to return to the original with a sense of supremacy but to stimulate a possibility under a different context and objectify an attempt to negotiate a ground on which they can establish their new identity. "Shower of Ashes," a short story of White, thus comments on the integration of the Traverses: "And in a way I sensed an implied threat in it all as if the Traverses had succeeded in drawing a line between East and West and has rejected us for the other side." (*Foreign Soil* 65) The "implied threat" is understandable—the Traverses overtly destabilize the age-old western discourse on India and thereby restructure West's own image itself. Given the fact that it is very difficult for a person to achieve self-actualization without first identifying his/her affiliation with his/her own cultural heritage, White's novels and many American novels can surely be an interesting field for scholarly investigations. In many cases home culture is simply defied and the host culture accepted as a refuge. Some facts also substantiate this trend of American state of affairs. During the 1960s and onward, the hippie influx to India, or *turning east*, as Harvey Cox terms it, has often been seen as a counter reaction to America's own cultural scenario. White's people too are navigating India for a replacement of culture and thereby renew inner resources. Both the types can be regarded as reactions to a pressurized environment at home. The participants attempt to discover a kind of human gravitational force, a bond in the alien culture, and rescue themselves—another kind of a *pilgrim's progress*—from LSD to spirituality, confusion to clarity, or homelessness to home.

White's robust optimism has often been sternly criticized. For example, while commenting on *Elephant Hill* in a *New York Times* column, Peggy Durdin goes on to suggest "that next time, beside pumping a little vitamin B into his Americans, Mr. White, the novelist, would shake off the do-good, hands-across-the-sea instincts of Mr. White, the missionary's son." (*BRD*, 1959: 1057) This is, of course, an unpleasant proposition. Be it Robin White, the missionary's son, or be it George Bush, the politician's son, anybody may have a 'mission' either "pioneering the universality of the human spirit" or promoting "a new world order" of this or that kind. And if Peggy wants to do away with any mission whatsoever, the attempt itself becomes a mission and ultimately that may help guide missiles and misguide man, or vice versa. It is very obvious that White has a definite doctrinal position, which has given him the fame of "the sannyasi of South Pasadena." (Letter, 13 Sep 1997) He strongly believes that the "planet is essentially a spaceship, and no one will survive if its life-support systems are irreparably damaged. So it is urgent that people start working together instead of wasting time, energy and resources in mindless hatred, corruption and greed." (Letter, 9 May 1993) Science and technology may immensely help us achieving our goals; but here again a strong 'mission' is necessary to guide missiles and man together.

NOTES

1. Born on 12 July 1928 in Kodaikanal and raised in Manamaduarai, of an American missionary family posted in south India, Robin stayed in India for the first 15 years of his life. Later relocated to the United States for education and settlement. His major literary

works, mostly novels, include such works as *House of Many Rooms*, *Elephant Hill*, *Men and Angels*, *Be Not Afraid*, *All in Favor say No,* and a collection of short stories, *Foreign Soil: Tales of South India.* His later work, *The Winning Writer: Studies in the Art of Self-Expression,* is a college textbook. He has been widely reviewed in *New York Times, London Times, Chicago Tribune, Time Magazines, Washington Post, Sun Francisco Chronicle, Los Angeles Times*, etc. Finally settled at Pasadena, he has served as a faculty member of UCLA and California State Polytechnic University. He is listed in *Who's Who in the World, Who's Who in America, Who's Who in the West* and also *International Authors and Writers' Who's Who, Burke's Peerage, Contemporary Authors,* etc. White has also been elected to the American Academy of Poets in 1998. All his manuscripts and correspondences are archived at the Special Collections Department, Boston University Libraries.

2. Robin White himself, in a letter, admits: "When my first four books on India were published, pioneering the universality of the human spirit, the American literary establishment looked on me as a 'foreign' writer, and UK rather naturally considered me a displaced provincial . . . " (Letter to the author, 19 May/1991) However the problem of being an American or Indian author does not seem to have bothered him much. In the "Preface" to *Foreign Soil* he makes his stand quite clear in this regard: "In this age of rapid communication and fading national boundaries, it would seem to me deeply important that we accept that our literature must be less concerned with the problem of being American, per se, than with the problem of just *being,* and that this composite notion recognize the validity in the experience of any of its members, coloured or colour less, in *any* locale."
3. *Dhoti* (also *dhooti*) is the traditional Indian dress for men worn from the waist down. It's a long one-piece cotton fabric without stitches used in many parts of the country, especially by the Hindus.

Works Cited

Brislin, Richard W. *Cross-cultural Encounters: Face to Face Interaction.* New York: Pergamon Press, 1981.

Cox, Harvey. *Turning East: The Promise and Peril of New Orientalism*. New York: Simon and Schuster, 1977.

Dorothy, P. Devison, ed. *Book Review Digest,* 1959. New York: H.W. Wilson and Co., 1960.

Kopf, David. *British Orientalism and the Bengal Renaissance*. Berkeley: University of California Press, 1969.

Park, Robert Ezra. *Race and Culture*. Glencoe: The Free Press, 1950.

Singh, Jacquelin. "Dear Mrs. Jhabvala," *The Illustrated Weekly of India*, Vol. XCIII. 3 September 1972.

The Times of India. Kolkata: 17 October 2003.

The Times of India. Kolkata: 12 November 2003.

Times Literary Supplement. 18 March 1960.

White, Robin. *Elephant Hill*. New York: Harper, 1959.

_____. *Foreign Soil: Tales of South India.* London: Bodley Head, 1962.

_____. *House of Many Rooms.* New York: Harper, 1956.

_____. *Men and Angels.* London: Bodley Head, 1961.

_____. Letters to present author, 19 May 1991; 9 May 1993; 4 Oct 1994; 13 Sep 1997.

Past the 'Shadow' and the 'Silence': Interpreting Arab American Women's Poetry

INDRANI DATTA (CHAUDHURI)
Krishnanagar Government College, West Bengal

"If a literature's life and energy are determined by the activity surrounding it, the Arab-American literature is experiencing a renaissance," writes poet Elmaz Abinader (35). Presently, with the United States celebrating the emergence and development of ethnic and immigrant literature, many feel that the Arab American voice is a recent discovery and that it has just sprouted. They either forget or are not responsive to the fact that this immigrant community, from the last quarters of the nineteenth century, has been silently contributing to and enriching both the original and the American literatures and cultures. This fact was sufficient enough to stimulate me to steal a look into Arab American literature, particularly poetry, because of a traditional Arabic saying: *al-shi'r diwan al-arab* (the true register and history of the Arabs is to be found in their poetry).

The heterogeneity of the Middle East, coupled with a century long history of deterritorialization (and reterritorialization), has made this community enormously assorted. Countless complexities vis-à-vis their homes include twenty-two different countries with further divisions along religious and sectarian lines. The Arab world has censorship issues, vestiges of colonial mentalities and endless peace processes: all these producing a miscellaneous network of cultural multiplicity that thwarts any prospect of a national self-consciousness based on religious, cultural, economic or political similitude. It becomes difficult for the inhabitants to interlace their sense of identity with the forces of art. The immigrants, obviously, carry these boundaries and classifications.

The 'Arab' identity has become an immensely political and complex term for these immigrants to tackle. 'Middle East' is actually a geo-political term fashioned by the Western/European colonizers and meaningful only to those who suppose their existence, and fatherlands, are the centre of everything. 'Middle East' gradually distorts into a stereotype, a deliberate demonization synonymous to sheikhs, camel rides, harems, polygamy, belly dancers and whores. It carries an aura of the 'exotic': feminine, mystical and naturally inferior.

It is difficult to contextualize the Arab-American writers within the prevailing paradigms of cultural discourse. Any integrationist approach is not adequate because it fails to unveil the complex dynamics that outlines our knowledge of the Middle East. If we include these authors within the rubrics of minority literature we deny them cultural translation. Contrary to the conventional predicaments that figure out postcolonial protest literatures, these Arab American immigrants produce a different variety of text that are unique in their own way.

Few contemporary poets, all women, have dared to challenge the patriarchal society and also the idea that the Arab world is exotic. In their works we find the first accent of remonstration against any kind of coercion. Amidst their society-imposed restrictions these Arab-American poets have converted their verses into weapons. As I read the book, *The Poetry of Arab Women: A Contemporary Anthology*, edited by Nathalie Handal, I realized that there lies a complex and heartrending ocean of tumults that can stir every human heart. These poems generate multidimensional meanings of culture, identity and existence, a fact Amal al-Jubburi writes about: "Poetry is a surprise; . . . Poems recreate interpretation, develop meanings, and unsettle convictions . . . poetry is a rebellious creature, violating every law and challenging all authorities. . . . The logic of poetry should not fall in the jurisdiction of any authority except poetry."[1]

Mainstream or peripheral, poetry has always provided an accent to the dissatisfaction and angst arising out of inequality and coercion. This is also true in the case of Arab American women's poetry. Tradition has imposed restriction, but these poets have fought against it. Al-Jubburi informs: "Writing in the Arab world remains a masculine realm in which it is difficult to accept women transferring the traditional fertility of their bellies to their minds."[2] Yet they remain bold and unbeaten in their quest. Al-Jubburi's concluding words are relevant here:

> My response is that poetry itself is a great loss. It is enough to present wounds, memories, regret, and importantly, your inner feelings, either sweet or bitter, to others on a plate. My consolation is that this is my only loss, my gamble in life because it makes me renew, grow, and overcome myself. Death does not threaten me in my steps toward the world of poetry, but rather life. Poetry will forever open my eyes.[3]

These poems emphasize issues involving race, ethnicity, gender and, therefore, the otherness. They also travel beyond the temporary problems of survival by propagating ideas of assimilation and acculturation in a world tormented with intolerance and separatism. They remind us that this immigrant culture can look back to those principles that have given the world the three monotheistic religions: Judaism, Christianity and Islam.

In any male-dominated society oppression, obviously, makes women the silent sufferers. But a time comes when women begin to resist and fight back; they gather courage enough to ignore obstacles and torture. Today, the Arab-American women are not afraid of exploring adventurous areas and uncharted territories of identity and knowledge despite the fact that they do not enjoy more freedom in USA and the natural trend is to enforce greater censorship to counter the American sense of freedom and liberty. Etel Adnan discusses this crisis:

> I think that men who are devoid of social and political powers will have the temptation to make women submit, the only people left on whom they can exercise power. Humiliated by dictatorial systems in their minds and bodies, they look for a victim, to reach a balance so to speak. Possessing little or nothing they feel they can 'possess

> women,' make them obey, hide them as one hides a treasure or a simple spoon. They think, "If I can hide you, erase you from the eyes of others, then you will be exclusively mine." Going further in this line of reasoning, they seem to say, "Of course, by veiling you, my wife and daughter, I too possess the veil, and *I too hide behind it*. Behind the veils worn by my women, I hide my own shame, my own weakness, my own *corruption*. (1)

The Arab woman's veil, therefore, becomes a symbol of the subjugation and distress they face even at the onset of the present century. But it fails to throttle the emergence of their powerful voice. These poets persistently write against three predominant predicaments haunting their lives both inside their society and outside it. First, they assert themselves as human beings and not merely as sex objects in a social order that hurls them into painful and silent torture. Second, as women and as Arabs, they search for a suitable identity in the diasporas. And last, they resist the stereotyping of the Eastern—the Arab—female by the West. It is "one's claim and sentiment that creates one's identity" (iii), explains Nathalie Handal in her introduction to *The Poetry of Arab Women: A Contemporary Anthology*.

In almost all the cultures of the world there are matters of pride, honor and family loyalty. There are imaginary lines and unspoken boundaries of self-disclosure and representation. To cross over the threshold of community values is to be forever estranged from it. This fear of alienation paralyses almost every writer of this group when they engage in such subjects as patriarchal torture, gender inequities, homophobia, *et al*. Their community feels besieged and ostracized. Any work created out of this self-censored atmosphere is hard-pressed with severe constraints and also lacks the authentic tones of resounding truth. Palestinian-American poet Naomi Shihab Nye states: "There is a tension between Arab communal values and the individualism and freedom America is seen to offer. It is a tension not resolved as much as honoured."[4]

Amidst this kind of repression, literatures about and by women seem to open up to the world the otherwise hidden image of the oppressed Arab female. These authors simultaneously struggle to break free of the traditional barriers and yet remain attached to their roots: an ambiguous standpoint indeed. The process of assimilation and acculturation, however, help them tackle the hurdles. They dissent their community-imposed isolation and highlight their own agonies and ecstasies. In *Bint Arab*, Evelyn Shakir says:

> the Arab woman not only faces . . . discrimination in the mainstream culture, but the very ground to seek refuge, the family, has issues of another flavour, with patriarchy and tradition holding sway. This double bind impacts the Arab woman writer, who might feel that any criticism she might direct at her own culture will only feed on such material to degrade the entire culture. (14)

She further explains how women's literature, at present, moves beyond the troubles of genital mutilation and patriarchal families and tells much more. They reveal the rich cultural heritage of the Arab and Arab American women, where before the commencement of liberation movements in the west, females were regarded as human beings equal to men. For example, the seventh century poetess, Tumadir bint Amru, better known as Al-Khansa, had remarkable eloquence and courage. Walladah hint al-Mustakfi, famed beauty and princess of Cordova, serves a paradigm for the status of women in her contemporary society. As early as the eleventh century, she could write:

> Forsooth, I allow my lover to
> Touch my cheek,
> And bestow my kiss on him who
> Craves it. (77)

During the twentieth century too, women in the Middle East have mirrored the multiplicity of political, intellectual and religious beliefs and their own revolt against patriarchy. Fadwa Touqan speaks of resisting the cruelty thrust upon her:

> Freedom
> My freedom
> I shall carve the words in the
> Earth.
> Chisel their sounds

on every door in the Levant. . . .
below the slope at every street
corner inside the prison
within the torture chamber. (12)

The legacy continues with the Arab-American women poets as well. The Syrian American Hamid al-Iryani writes:

Tear it
This veil
Discard it
Tatter it . . .
Destroy
Destroy fears with violence. (89)

Fifteen year old Nizzar Qabbani says:

I fear to say what I have to say
I fear if I do
The skies will burn out your east. (23)

But in "Of Woman Torn" Suhair Hammad is fearless:

Her father lit the match, brothers poured the flammable
The women they watched the women they tucked
        their sex way under
        skirts under secrets . . .
        Family pride laid
between her thighs,
honour in her panties
And no Oslo accord
or Camp David signing
could free her sex
from its binding. (96)

These poets have assiduously investigated the long unresolved, often tenuous, relationship between the male and the female. Through the portrayal of dreams and their shattering, amidst a world of conflicting realities and morals, they have touched every human heart irrespective of culture, as in Hammad's concluding lines, in her poem "Of Woman Torn":

Where was he when they found the swelling
of your belly proof of humanity?

> Where was he when they stuck fists up
> inside you to prove you loose? (98)

Literature is frequently subversive in its probing into the deepest stratum of the human psyche. Imagination, here, remains unanswerable even to governments. The Arab American women poets challenge convention in order to explore their authentic selves. Theirs is a constant endeavour to understand manifold realities and, more crucially, to redefine their 'otherness.' Their marginalization becomes a kind of double burden—one of fighting against their own society as women and the other of resisting the mainstream as Arabs. The responsibility to represent a 'coloured' minority, mixed with the essence of womanhood, has forced them to contribute significantly to Arab-American literature.

Moreover, this community—both men and women—has been thrown into decades of racism, discrimination, negative stereotyping, and hostility in the Americas. And the women have an additional pressure, imposed by their people, of embodying both their families and culture. Their ability to communicate the challenge they face everyday, within and without, has to be frequently reconciled. This crisis hinders the real and perceived need for unity among a beleaguered minority and an honest discourse of such controversial topics as honour killings, arranged marriages, incest, queer relationships, and mental health problems. The women poets, however, have attempted to walk ahead of such obstacles. They express their experiences with an incredible directness. They also explain that theirs is not a unique problem but alleged throughout the world. Etel Adnan writes in "Shabra and Shatila Refugee Camps": "This story I've heard whispered in all languages,/ all accents" (17). These poets also protest against the United States politics of exclusion. Nathalie Handal makes an excellent remark in her introduction: "I can't say politics aside, the poetry here is fantastic—putting politics aside would negate many poems in the book, and would be unfair to their authors" (ix). The poets, thus, try to seek a common bond—an alternative—that can harmonize different cultures and all of humanity, as in Mohja Kahf's "The First World":

> I left the world of Abraham
> jugs sealed with cork,
> cooking-grease fires
> Sarah's careful kitchen fires
> I moved over, severing
> slates of earth,
> sediment of ancient seas. (103)

This kind of search is not without the dilemma of a marginalized identity. Nathalie Handal asserts: "I know what my identity is" (xi), and, then, she asks: And where was the real Bethlehem—the one my grandfather came from? (5). Dima Shehabi expounds, in "The Cemetery at Petit Saconnex; For my Father": "I wonder if you think of exile/ and how this land now fills our blood/ with roots of belonging." (*The Poetry of Arab Women* 171)

There is another predominant issue these woman writers are extremely critical about: it is the West constructed picture of the oppressed Eastern—particularly the Arab—female. Razing individuals and groups by pigeonholing them is not a new phenomenon. It is difficult to imagine a society or a period in history completely devoid of this brutal method of robbing people of their humanity, and to envision a person who has lived a life without being either a victim or villain in the process. The western dearth of being aware and informed has compelled the Arab and Arab American women to become helpless sufferers in this kind of stereotyping. The mainstream has fashioned their image as imprisoned behind the veil of powerlessness and subjugation. This is a major concern the poets have to grapple with. But they are determined to eradicate such typecast.

The injury, inflicted by this stereotype, is magnified by the added assumption that the Arab woman is just beginning her struggle and protest against suppression, as if they are being born anew, after discarding their age-old veil of an uncivilized non-entity. The truth is otherwise. Like Evelyn Shakir, these poets too assert that the Arab female was emancipated long before western women could unite themselves, let alone organizing themselves as a group deprived of human rights. When the Roman Catholic Church was debating the existence of a woman's soul, the Middle Eastern female already knew she had one. The decline of the Arab civilization into the drudgery of colonialism, despondency and decadence was perhaps to blame for the conversion of women into veiled commodities. Dima Hilal illustrates the point in her poem "*Ghaflah*—The Sin of Forgetfulness":

> We come to America where they call our land the East
> meaning different/ dark/ dirty.
> We soon forget
> our grandmothers combed hair like ours.
> We wish our hair blonde our eyes and skin light. . . .
>   We think French makes us sophisticated so
>   we greet each other with *bonjour* instead of *salaam*,
>   proud of our colonizer's tongue. (90)

This misconception devalues women's struggle to achieve equality after centuries of effort and resistance. My intention, however, is not to undermine the western image of the free-thinking woman, for we all—Eastern and Western—can understand the battle too well.

In their effort to liberate themselves from this label, the Arab-American women poets contradict the supposition that the western feminist model is quintessential, inspiring females the entire world over to achieve freedom. Liza Suheir Majaj observes, "the biggest problem for the Arab American writers is the Arab Woman stereotype. It silences us, it shadows us" (5). Mona Fayyad feels "haunted by the constant companion called the Arab Woman—the Faceless, Veiled Woman, silent, passive, helpless, waiting to be rescued by the West. . . . As a construct invented by the West, this two-in-one Arab woman is completely overwhelming. Her voice drowns mine" (18). This anxiety forces the poets to present a multi-faceted icon. It is because of this Nathalie Handal enquires in "West Bank":

> What are we to do without the light of shadows
> And the devil in the shadows we've repainted in our history? (61)

And she also asks:

> What are we to do, continue to listen? . . .
> Or sing our songs? . . .
> Cry?
> Scream?
> Cry?
> Death after Death? (62)

In order to defy the stereotype, these poets have also constructed multidimensional pictures of the Arab female. They portray their women in three moulds: the Sultan's Wife, subdued, "whose ambition has been killed/ so that their greatest remaining hope is to get pedicure" (36), the Reckless Woman who, connecting sexual repression to political oppression, can bravely proclaim: "Before me a thousand and one executioners/ Behind me a thousand and one bitchers/ Dear Lord, is there no shame in my nakedness?/ Dear Lord, does this East have no work/ but fussing over my hemline?" (55), and the Rebellious Lady in Exile to whom all sensitive human beings must surrender at will: "I sense that the arts wear thin with you/ And that eloquence pants/ and poetry and prose and speech/ race around your waist, not catching up" (57). (All these poems are originally written by Kabbani in Arabic, and translated by Mohja Kahf).

These characteristics may, however, lead us to believe that Arab-American women's poetry is propagandist in nature. This is, however, a misconception. For, they mean much more. Being the products of a culture that has nurtured such visionaries as Omar Khayyam, Abul alal al-Ma'ari, and even Ameen Rihani and Kahlil Gibran, the same quest for global fraternity and cultural harmony can be recognized in these poems too. They transcend the ordinary concepts of identity, ethnicity, race, gender and injustice—as in Nathalie Handal's "Hesitate," "the songs of resistance, myths, . . ./ Jailed screams in our heart" (11)—and translate them into prayers of sublime imagination and prophecy. Thus, in "Ephratha," Nathalie Handal asks:

> Are our memories filled with pale notebooks, fading paint, falling walls.

To understand this place must we understand its howls, to understand
its howls must we understand its verses, to understand its verses
must we understand agony? (123)

and, finally, concludes:

You stand between the dream of two questions
awaiting the day you will unfold yourself,
like prayers unfold themselves
from our tongues. (124)

Spatio-temporal dislocation facilitates this kind of poetry to signify universal joys and sorrows, struggle and salvation. A reading of so diverse a literary variety compels me to put forward a forceful question: is the general impression, as Nada Elia elucidates that the Arab-Americans are the "enemy, other, fanatical terrorist, crazy Muslim" justified? (32). We, as women belonging to the third world, must acknowledge these powerful voices trying to bring hope to suffering millions. What mother, daughter, sister and friend, irrespective of nationality, language and culture, would not warm up to the following lines in "Two Little Girls" by Fawziyya Abu Khalid?

In the late afternoon we jump from one world to another;
We play in the wind
like sparrows that opened the door to the cage. . . .
We share one apple and innumerable dreams,
We paint a paradise of questions on the face of the desert,
We spray each other with the water of the mirage
Accompany a fleeting doe. (101)

Works Cited

Abinader, Elmaz. "Children of Al-Mahjar: Arab American Literature Spans a Century," *Journal of Contemporary U.S. Literature*, Annual vol. New York: State Govt. Press, 2000: 35-47.

Adnan, Etel. "Shabra and Shatila Refugee Camps," *The Poetry of Arab Women: A Contemporary Anthology*, ed. Nathalie Handal. New York: Interlink, 2001: 17-18.

_____. "Who is Being Veiled," *Al Jadid Magazine*, Vol. 2, No. 13. Los Angeles: Al Jadid Press, 1996: 1-5.

Al-Jubburi, Amal. "Reflections: A Personal Vision of Poetry," *Al Jadid Magazine*, Vol. 6, No. 31.Los Angeles: Al Jadid Press, 2000: 1-4.

Elia, Nada. "A Woman's Place is in the Struggle," *Food for Our Grandmothers: Writings by Arab-American and Arab-Canadian Feminists*, ed. Joanna Cadi. Parkside: University of Wisconsin Press, 1994: 29-32.

Fayyad, Mona. "The Arab Woman and I," *Food for Our Grandmothers: Writings by Arab-American and Arab-Canadian Feminists.* ed. Joanna Cadi. 18-25.

Hammad, Suheir. "Of Woman Torn," *The Poetry of Arab Women: A Contemporary Anthology*, ed. Nathalie Handal. 96-98.

Handal, Nathalie. "Bethlehem," *The Poetry of Arab Women: A Contemporary Anthology*, ed. Nathalie Handal. 5.

_____. "Ephratha," *The Poetry of Arab Women: A Contemporary Anthology*, ed. Nathalie Handal. 123-24.

_____. "Hesitate," *The Poetry of Arab Women: A Contemporary Anthology*. ed. Nathalie Handal. 11.

_____. Introduction, *The Poetry of Arab Women: A Contemporary Anthology*. i-xx.

_____. "West Bank," *The Poetry of Arab Women: A Contemporary Anthology*, ed. Nathalie Handal. 61-62.

Hilal, Dima. "*Ghaflah*—The Sin of Forgetfulness," *The Poetry of Arab Women: A Contemporary Anthology*, ed. Nathalie Handal. 90-91.

Iryani, Hamid al-. "This Veil," *The Poetry of Arab Women: A Contemporary Anthology*, ed. Nathalie Handal. 89.

Kabbani, H.M. "Lady Friend." Trans. from Arabic Mohja Kahf, *The Poetry of Arab Women: A Contemporary Anthology*, ed. Nathalie Handal. 57-58.

_____. "Reckless Woman." Trans. from Arabic Mohja Kahf, *The Poetry of Arab Women: A Contemporary Anthology*, ed. Nathalie Handal. 54-55.

_____. "Sultan's Wife." Trans. from Arabic Mohja Kahf, *The Poetry of Arab Women: A Contemporary Anthology*, ed. Nathalie Handal. 36.

Kahf, Mohja. "The First World," *The Poetry of Arab Women: A Contemporary Anthology*. ed. Nathalie Handal. 103-4.

Khalid, Fawziyya Abu-. "Two Little Girls," *The Poetry of Arab Women: A Contemporary Anthology*. ed. Nathalie Handal. 100-1.

Majaj, Liza Suheir. "The Hyphenated Author: Emerging Genre of 'Arab-American Literature' Poses Questions of Definition, Ethnicity and Art," *Al Jadid Magazine*, Vol. 5 No. 26. Los Angeles: Al Jadid Press, 1999: 5-12.

Mustakfi, Walladah hint. "Kiss." Trans. from Arabic Etel Adnan, *The Poetry of Arab Women: A Contemporary Anthology*. ed. Nathalie Handal. 77.

Nye, Naomi Shihab. Quoted by Judith Gabriel. "Emergence of a Genre: Reviewing Arab American Writers," *Al Jadid Magazine*, Vol. 7 No. 34. Los Angeles: Al Jadid Press, 2001: 2-7.

Qabbani, Nizzar. "I Fear to Say," *The Poetry of Arab Women: A Contemporary Anthology*, ed. Nathalie Handal, 23.

Shakir, Evelyn. "Arab and Arab Women Writers in the United States," *Bint Arab*. London and New York: Oneworld, 1997: 1-18.

Shehabi, Dima. "The Cemetery at Petit Syconnex; for my Father," *The Poetry of Arab Women: A Contemporary Anthology*. ed. Nathalie Handal. 171.

Touqan, Fadwa. "Freedom," *The Poetry of Arab Women: A Contemporary Anthology*, ed. Nathalie Handal. 11-12.

Self and the Southern Heritage: A Reappraisal of the Short Fiction of Katherine Anne Porter and Eudora Welty

PRATIBHA NAGPAL
Punjab University, Chandigarh

The focus of this paper is to examine the influence of the distinctiveness of the South in the writings of Katherine Anne Porter and Eudora Welty, highlighting how their radically different attitudes towards the region closely tie each author's formulation of the concept of self. It also seeks to analyze the effect of both the author's conception of identity upon their process of writing.

Conservatism of religion, prominence of Blacks, the rural nature of the region, dependence on agriculture, persistence of violence—all due to the presence of plantation slavery—laid the foundation for the unique characteristic of the South. The challenging situation in 1860s led to a new awareness of values by which men had been living and the social upheaval that followed the Civil War evoked an emotional response that expressed itself through literature. Later the war shook the personal values of both the soldier and those manning the homefront, as a result of which there was a new movement towards a better industrially organized South. When Southern youth returned home from the battlefield, their old-fashioned provincial prejudices had been challenged by new associations and the widespread unease of a 'lost generation.' The home situation did not allow settling into the old grooves that led to desire for exploration and expression.

Katherine Anne Porter's birth into a Southern family that shook off code and agrarian tradition in the changing milieu led her to scrupulously examining her present situation as an American and her apprehensions for the future of her heritage in an unpredictable world. Porter seemed to share a problematic relationship with the South, which in very unexpected ways shaped her writing process. Porter often oscillated between adopting or rejecting the image of the Southern belle in her fiction and consistently buried her distinctly non-aristocratic upbringing characterized by poverty, minimal education and nominal exposure to culture, supplanting these old terrible times with a fictional history, replete with wealth, culture, education and social distinction—all the trappings of the mythological plantation South and its symbol, the Southern lady. Her biographer Joan Givner, commenting on Porter's relationship with the South says:

> she produced simultaneously with her stories another work of art. She transformed herself and her own personal history. In the place of Callie Porter, raised in poverty and obscurity, she created Katherine Anne Porter, an aristocratic daughter of the Old South and the descendant of a long line of distinguished statesmen. In this reincarnation she became one of the most celebrated personalities of the American literary scene. . . . With her magnolia skin, her velvety voice and white hair, she presented the perfect image of a southern belle, a member, as she styled herself, of the "guilt-ridden white pillar crowd."

Yet Porter did not fully claim this fictional world that she created at the cost of rejecting reality and many a times complained that the reporters often wanted to make a Southern lady of her. If on the one hand Porter scrupulously structured an alternate history for herself, and guarded that history against revelation of the real during her lifetime, she on the other hand carefully preserved and accumulated the regalia of her lifetime. Paradoxically, her biography reveals "what her life was" while some of her interviews portray her life as "it should have been" and this contradiction is best stated in this quote:

> Porter was torn between wishing to be an accomplished, independent woman, speaking out authoritatively on literature and world events, and wishing to be a charming capricious belle, sought after for her beauty and arousing chivalrous thoughts in every male breast.

Clearly Porter's memory of the past was painful and her constructed history, not merely what she *wished* were true, but what she felt *should* have been true. This sense of confusion, disquiet and fragmentation that Porter experienced in her childhood and early youth prompted her to create an alternate history which she hoped would provide her with wholeness, integration and solid definition which she as well as her fictional characters sought.

Porter left the South at the age of twenty-nine to lead a nomadic life in several states and foreign cities. Living in the South was a constant reminder of the fractured past that she had known, both personally and socially. The writing process that would most provide her with wholeness and integration would be restricted in the South and she felt she "had to leave the South because I didn't want to be regarded as a freak. That was how they regarded a woman who wanted to write." Porter objected to being called a regional writer because she felt that region restricted the process of writing, stating that there is no, "first rate person who is a regional writer. . . . I think we ought to drop two words: Americanism and regionalism. They are coins with the designs rubbed off. They are cramping people with perfectly good instinct." Porter also felt that the region could be considered redeeming only when the regional, the particular is used in such a way that the meaning is universal.

Therefore, the South does not figure in Porter's short fiction but when it does, it is usually the South of Porter's fictionalized history, a southern background that allows her to imagine a direct and unwavering line from the past to present or future, a South whose culture and advantages could produce a successful writer, even if she was a woman. It is this South that Porter refers to when she speaks of the intense sense of location, of background and tradition and locale that exist for her. However, Porter herself has a different explanation for the infrequency of southern setting in her fiction and expresses the need for distance from the real South that disturbed her sense of the writing process. In one of her interviews she talks of writing about a country may be ten years after she has been there. Thus Porter sets some of her stories like "Maria Conception," "Virgin Violeta," "Flowering Judas," "That Tree" in Mexico and some like "Theft," "The Cracked-Looking Glass," "Pale Horse, Pale Rider" in parts of the United States other than the South. Significantly her novel *Ship of Fools* is set on no man's land but on a ship crossing the waters between Orleans and Germany, serving as an appropriate metaphor for various efforts of Porter to escape from her chaotic Southern past. The writing process for Porter is like a single, steady, unbroken, and continual thread which leads to the essence of her short fiction. Writing was the *core* of her existence as suggested by some of her interviewers and the function of writing afforded a continuity of self to Porter. If one of the significant concerns of Porter's short fiction is the expression of the self against annihilation then it is also her most compelling motive for writing. Porter imagined annihilation as fragmentation, a disruption of integration and order, and writing for her was a means of establishing unity and coherence for herself and the world.

This influences the manner in which Porter attended to the question of self. Towards the end of one of her stories, "Pale Horse, Pale Rider" Porter's heroine Miranda has a vision as she draws near death of a "hard unwinking angry point of light" which she acknowledges as her still surviving sense of the self—a single, focused "fiercely burning particle of being that knew itself alone, that relied upon nothing beyond itself for its strength." This image, which also appears in "The Jilting of Granny Weatherall" and "Holiday," defines Porter's conception of self. She often uses the image of the solitary point of light with its hardness and unwinking quality to indicate the quality of the essential self which, alone, strives for integration, wholeness and order on one hand and resists change on the other. The stories mentioned above depict Porter's viewing of self as unified and static conforming to ordered roles or choosing passivity, both of which provide stability and predictability, though often at the expense of independence and voice. All Porter's women protagonists, therefore, are driven by a need for order and totality, a need to unify the fractioned aspects of life, to shape a stable, singular and coherent sense of self that resists change and rejects all experience, relationship and possibility which threaten to disrupt the self's struggle for continuity and integration. This impulse constitutes and is itself the sense of *core* that Porter spoke of in her interviews and through her short stories. This is however, not to suggest that Porter's perception of self is dismal because in some Miranda stories, she allows her protagonists heightened subjectivity, independent voice and positive rationality, which her protagonists achieve only imperfectly, if at all.

Eudora Welty's fictional world is hardly ever set outside the South and the inclusion of Southerners in Welty's fiction suggests a certain comfortableness with her region and easy assimilation of place in her writing process. Welty has frequently spoken of the role of place in her understanding of her self and her characters. Welty's view of the South rejects its more common portrayal as circumscriptive and she seems unencumbered by the South's racism, sexism or class struggles. She views the South as adding on to her writing process with its ever-expanding chain of connections, and giving her access to a continually widening range of perception and interpretation. Welty speaks of the region as the realm, basis and foundation which expedites a growth that transcends place, and blooms into multiple possibilities. Welty regards place as an "openness to otherness" which does not seek to limit or define the profound and the mysterious both within and without. Pertinent here is Welty's comment that place "never really stops informing us, for it is forever astir, alive, changing, reflecting, like the mind of man itself." Thus place for Welty is not just a social and geographical location but also includes in its ambit sensitivity to the physical environment. Welty's sense of place determines her attitude towards the act of writing and informs her writing with repletion and expansiveness. Language becomes for Welty a way of possessing more of life, of expressing the many different aspects of the world and of her own self. She is able to create endless possibilities in her short fiction through a passion so strong that it gives the stories a depth and extension and encourages a variety of interpretations. A work of art is seen by Welty as a complex unit of contradictions that does not seek reconciliation but delights in the possibility of being all: a text coming out of life yet returning to it; solid yet transparent, visible when embodied, through which all life can be seen or imagined. Speaking of the influence of region on her writing process Welty felt:

> Your characters' growth out of place, and that's the way you test them as to their validity and their propriety in your work. . . . It's the fountainhead of [their] knowledge and experience. I think, of course, we learn to grow further than that [background], but if we don't have that base I don't know that we can test further knowledge by.

The acceptance of place as other, as outside of self and yet to assimilate it also as a part of the self, allowing it to expand one's sense of self and of others is what formulates the writing process for Welty. Therefore, the writing process is like a fabric of life for Welty, where multiple threads weave, tangle, and connect to create beautiful patterns and textures. This connection is not limited to the attachment we feel towards a text, or even to the relationships which exist between characters in a work, but also suggests Welty's interaction with her own texts as she is in the process of creating it. By acknowledging the independent voices of her characters and of herself, Welty allows her protagonists reality, not to be wholly dependent on her creation. Using dialogue as an ultimate form of communication, she grants her characters a subjectivity and a reciprocal voice.

This suggests Welty's different conception of the self as infinitely variable, uncontained and wide-ranging. Such conception allows a fullness and variety to the self that will allow contradictions and the co-existence of apparent incompatibilities like individuality, relationality or the otherness of others. Welty perceives the reason for experiencing dissatisfaction or lack of fulfillment of the self to be the refusal or inability of an individual to relate to, acknowledge and accept the full range of identity available to them. In her short stories Welty often uses boundaryless expanses with her women protagonists indicating the possibility of limitless expanse and avenues available to them. Her women's space is nearly always uncluttered by signs of possession or hierarchy and that enables them to experience change, self-assertion and limitlessness. The lake and the night sky in "Moon Lake," the image of the ocean in "The Winds," the open fields and endless woods in "Livvie" are examples of how Welty allows endless possibilities to the self in her short fiction. Her greatest accomplishment lies in her ability to dissolve the oppositional positioning—though not the positions themselves—usually associated with subject/object to demonstrate that independence can survive within relations, that need and dependence are not in opposition to independence but can, in fact, strengthen personal independent self. Welty endows her characters with a mutual gaze that enables them to participate in both positions in an energy of exchange. Snowdie Maclaine in "Shower of Gold," for example, is able to maintain her subjectivity, taking pleasure in her husband's absence and developing a life independent of his "visits" despite the fact that she is little more than a sexual object to her husband King Maclaine.

Critics have often recognized and praised the multiplicity present in Welty's short fiction in general and in her women protagonists in particular. Robert Penn Warren commented on the great variety and multiple layers found in Welty's first collection of short stories *A Curtain of Green and Other Stories* (1941). This plural sense of self allows Welty and her women characters change and unrestricted sense of being, and a fluidity which resists boundaries and definitions. As a result Welty's short fiction provides her women the freedom to affirm their subjectivity through questioning or rejecting convention. Acting autonomously, and exercising a strong sense of voice that is rarely objectified, it survives and grows and shows a full range of possibility. The value Welty places on keeping text and character full and multiple is depicted through one image that she uses in the short story "The Wanderers." The woman protagonist Virgie Rainey, in her search for self through unconventionality and vitality, becomes an outcast in the story set in the Southern society which has a history of basing a woman's virtue almost exclusively upon her sexual purity. Virgie as an unmarried sexual being, understandably does not fit in. Music, that provides fullest expression to Virgie's self, while not offensive to the citizens of Morgana, is nevertheless certainly as foreign. In a telling moment in the story, Virgie struggling to cut out a dress from some real hard plaid material, faces the challenges of preserving and maintaining the intricate and complex pattern of the cloth while shaping that pattern into new creations and newer possibilities. Using the sewing metaphor, Welty focuses on the multi-dimensional possibilities for Virgie's self and also the challenge of literary creation. Like a seamstress managing the intricate motifs without separating or breaking the clear thread in the fabric from the thick of the tangle, Welty too understands and reiterates that the essential 'core' in the story survives best where it can connect and be a part of the pattern and where it would not be solitary and simply linear.

To conclude, it would be essential to point out that the writing process for Porter is like a single, steady, unfragmented and continual thread that leads to the core of her short fiction and subsequently Porter's conception of self is about maintaining an intact, unwavering sense of self through all confusion and disorder of life that threaten to destroy an integrated self. The desire to formulate an immutable, singular and coherent sense of self that resists change and rejects all experience, relationship and possibility which threaten to disrupt self's continuity and integration forms the essence and core of Porter's short fiction and that of her women characters. By contrast, Welty sees plurality centered in self and in feminine consciousness that allows the coexistence of opposites within each character. Differences are not viewed as opposition by Welty, but as expansive possibilities that allows the inclusion of disparate elements and experiences without leading to confusion and chaos.

Works Cited

Brinkmeyer, Robert H., Jr. "An Openness to Otherness: The Imaginative Vision of Eudora Welty," *Southern Literary Journal* 22.2 (Spring 1988): 69-80.

Bryant, J.A, Jr. *Eudora Welty*. Minneapolis: U of Minnesota P, 1968.

Givner, Joan. *Katherine Anne Porter: Conversations*. ed. Joan Givner. Jackson: UP of Mississippi, 1987.

_____. *Katherine Anne Porter: A Life.* New York: Simon and Schuster, 1982.

Porter, Katherine Anne. *The Collected Stories of Katherine Anne Porter*. New York: Harcourt Brace Jovanovich, 1979.

Welty, Eudora. *The Collected Stories of Eudora Welty*. New York: Harcourt Brace Jovanovich, 1970.

_____. *One Writer's Beginnings*. New York: Warner Books, 1984.

Ethnic Tribulations in Ralph Ellison's *Invisible Man* and William Styron's *Sophie's Choice*

K.B. RAZDAN
University of Jammu

At the outset, one cannot resist quoting William Shakespeare's immortal lines from one of his sonnets: "The summer's flower is to the summer sweet / Though for itself it only live and die." These words, pregnant with a feast of philosophical reflection, paradoxically apply to the creatively subtle nuances by which ideology operates as canonicity in ethnically-loaded texts of black American modernist and postmodernist fiction. As an introductory prelude to the infallible expertise with which certain African American writers transcreate text as the end-product of a given culture, a discerning and creative reader finds it pretty hard to avoid a challenging reflection over the trials, tribulations and oddities of fractured human existence. The question that haunts the inquisitive mind is, do we evaluate the protagonists in the novels of Ralph Ellison and William Styron as the architects of "a process of meaning-creation," participants in an odyssey of existential reconstruction, or else, do we at best consider Ellison's unnamed anonymous hero in *Invisible Man* (1952) and Styron's Peyton Loftis in *Sophie's Choice* (1979) as alazonic figures who are irresistible specimens provoking and posing fundamental issues related to class, race, and ethnicity?

The final choice is simple and self-explanatory. Both Ellison and Styron use the novel as an infallible instrument for treating the historical experience of their race, besides representing in their own characteristic way, how the ethnic people in America can best achieve an optimal human existence—cultural, social, material and moral—in modernist and postmodernist America. The respective protagonists of *Invisible Man* and *Sophie's Choice* undertake an intense struggle to find existential moorings in an ethnically hostile environment. A dire do-or-die necessity to reconstruct, reorganize, as well as reorder the very architecture of living, willing, and desiring, becomes the only viable option available. Yet the ethnically loaded American novel poses a basic question—does the entire exercise of individual reconstruction vis-à-vis the exigencies of a mass-society and a demonic decadent ethos become a venture in Kafkaesque absurdity or existential reaffirmation? A separate look at Ellison's *Invisible Man* and Styron's *Sophie's Choice*, followed by a cumulatively concluding analysis, could possibly be the better way to arrive at certain revelatory definitions and explanations.

As we know, the Harlem Renaissance brought about resurgence and a radical awakening of ethnic conscience within the Black American self which earlier seemed to be disappearing, lost, or non-existent. It is against this kind of formulation that Ralph Ellison's *Invisible Man* has to be assessed as a classic of twentieth century American fiction, a work in which the problems of an awakened individual gets intrinsically linked to a perennial problem confronting the American novelistic hero, the encroachment of society upon the self. The very title of Ellison's novel symbolizes an existential odyssey of the ethnic psyche, the ethnically super-sensitive and super-conscious human being who wages a grim battle in a world of bondage, pain, and confusion. Ellison invests his hero with an armor of invisibility, the term 'invisible' becoming a paradigm of a socially, ethnically ostracized, and persecuted self. After its publication in 1952, *Invisible Man* came to be acclaimed as a furthering force on the path of Black revolt and ecstasy. As Noel Schroufnagel (1973: 78) states:

> The publication of *Invisible Man* (1952) is the climax of the revolt against the Wrightian protest novel. . . . In triumphing over this fictional problem the author demonstrates his concept of the basic unity of human experience. Racial elements are merely a part of

> the more universal questions associated with a chaotic world such as moral responsibility, identity and revolt.

The preceding words reveal that Ellison's anonymous hero, who presents himself to the reader in an incognito form, is bestowed an almost universal status vis-à-vis the fundamental issues of existence which have constantly been afflicting mankind in contemporary times. The voice of the anonymous hero-narrator becomes a pragmatic subtle voice, expressing certain deep and challenging philosophic truths, facts which qualify and give an ironic essence to the contemporary human condition. As Esther Merle Jackson (1984: 135) states: "*Invisible Man* recapitulates the odyssey of the philosophic 'I,' the journey of the fragmentary self through experience to knowledge and ultimately to being." A young Negro's baffling experience on the road to self-discovery becomes a philosophic saga. Besides indicating the ironic dissolution of black identity in a white dominated social order, 'invisibility' gets explained as Ellison's existential metaphor for the loss of self, 'the theft of the self,' as the ultimate ethnic horror in a white dominated sociological order.

The Prologue introduces the narrator in his underground hole, the gutter, reflecting over the events of his life, while listening to Louis Armstrong's recording: "What did I do/ to be so black / and blue?" Paradoxically, this refrain follows each major episode of the novel as Ellison's protagonist tries to play the various dehumanizing roles that the white community assigns to him. Every time the hero discovers that his attempt to play the game according to the white rules has left him more 'bruised' than before. The following twenty-five chapters of the narrative become first-person singular flashbacks, covering nearly twenty earlier years of the unnamed hero's life. At the end of the novel, the modern-day ethnic Sisyphus descends back into his underground retreat. The concluding epilogue picks up the thematic threads of the Prologue in the manner of a *bildungsroman,* where the reader witnesses the hero metamorphosing from an innocent victim to a straightforward narrator and observer of himself and his earlier life. Like the titanic hero of Albert Camus, Ellison's incognito *alazon* on the verge of being 'thrown' into the abyss of 'eironic' dismantling, eventually realizes the utter futility of ironic detotalised-totalizing, from the status of a rebel to that of a rebel-victim. After experiencing a tribulatory existence for a number of years, the anonymous hero understands that he was like a pawn in the hands of white hegemonies, that he has been 'invisible' not only to others, but to himself as well.

Being recognized as a Negro-stereotype, an aimless and purposeless victim of biological forces over which he has no control, the hero's ethnically apostatic and tribulatory plight gets reflected in the Prologue:

> I AM AN invisible man. No, I am not a spook like those who haunted Edgar Allan Poe, nor am I one of your Hollywood movie ectoplasms. I am a man of substance of flesh and bone, fiber and liquids—and I might even be said to possess a mind. I am invisible, understand, simply because people refuse to see me when they approach me they see only my surroundings, themselves or figments of their imagination—indeed everything and anything except me.

Right from the beginning of the narrative, the hero makes it amply clear that on the existential plane he simply does not exist and labels himself as a "figure in a nightmare which the sleeper tries with all his strength to destroy" (3). The implication is clear—the sleeper is the white man, the arrogant individual operating in a biased, prejudiced and cloistered society. The constant ache and obsessive antipathy, two poles of the colored hero's existential axis, forces him to reflect:

> You ache with the need to convince yourself that you do exist in the real world, that you're a part of the sound and anguish, and you strike out with your fists, you curse and you swear to make them recognize you. And, alas! It's seldom successful. (3)

The hole, which becomes the hero's home, is described in these words:

> a hole in the ground . . . damp and cold like a grave, there are cold holes and warm holes. Mine is a warm hole. . . . I say all this to assure that it is incorrect to assume that, because I'm invisible and

> live in a hole, I am dead. I am neither dead nor in a state of suspended animation. Call me Jack-the-Bear, for I am in a state of hibernation. (5)

The 'hole' of the hero which "is full of light," is the underground gutter lighted by powerful electric bulbs, gives the protagonist at least a bare modicum of identity and existence:

> I have been boomeranged across my head so much that now I can see the darkness of lightness. And I live light. Perhaps you'll think it strange that an invisible man should need light, desire light, love light. But maybe it is exactly because I am invisible. Light confirms my reality, gives birth to my form. . . . Without light I am not only invisible, but formless as well; and to be unaware of one's form is to live a death. I myself, after existing some twenty years, did not become alive until I discovered my invisibility. (6-7)

For the unnamed hero, existence and essence become ironic entities. Above ground, the hero is 'invisible,' inside the hole, the gutter, he attains visibility of his self, thanks to the light emanating from the electric bulbs.

After getting injured while working as a labor in a white man's factory, through an explosion, the black hero suffers from a bout of amnesia and loses his memory for a while. This temporary loss of memory adds insult to injury and the result is an apostatic picture of human identity—the hero becomes a modern-day *pharmakos,* ready to be sacrificed on the despotic altar of deculture and satanic opportunism:

> WHAT IS YOUR NAME?
>
> A tremor shook me. . . . I realized that I no longer knew my own name. I shut my eyes and shook my head with sorrow. . . . I tried again, plunging into the blackness of my mind. It was no use. I found nothing but pain. (182)

The treatment given to a black man, either way, implies an attempt in terms of the white hegemonic social appropriation, to render the Negro a physical and mental wreck, dismantle and fracture his identity, thereby rendering him "invisible," making him a living cabbage, a vegetable, a formless entity condemned by the nature of his protagonistic situation to wallow chronically in a mire of despondency, anomie, and enervating *angst.*

In existential vocabulary of need, the quest of the African American hero for meaning, affirmation and identity, becomes in terms of the novel an attempt to illustrate and define that "human possibility is to be found and the possibility of a meaningless life to be explored" (Greengbery 1972: 182). The hero's invisibility becomes a universal and permanent metaphor for all those humans who constantly engage themselves in the task of "willing," and "existing." The hero in *Invisible Man* appears as more of a voice than an identity and thanks to his 'invisibility' in relation to the black racial aesthetic, Ellison's anonymous narrator assumes the status of a human being "who is an assumed identity, a persona" (Paulson 1973: 197). As a secular Sisyphus, the 'invisible' protagonist is still grappling with his 'boulder,' trying to combat the engulfing absurdity all around him.

Sophie's Choice can be defined as William Styron's experimental and innovative narrative in which the reader is presented with a tripartite existential axis in which a Polish lady, Sophie, occupies the central focal point around two men, the Jewish Nathan (her lover), and the white American individual named Stingo. In trying to coalesce the problems of these characters, we get an existential compendium of ethnically diverse individuals, one white, the other Jewish, and the third, a Polish Catholic. Styron thus expands the zones of American consciousness. The narrative itself, operating through the consciousness of Stingo, becomes a collage of diverse types of existentially unfortunate and upsetting events and relationships. As Michiko Kakutani (1982: 6) summarizes:

> *Sophie's Choice* concerns the friendship that develops between Stingo and a couple he meets one summer in New York: Sophie a beautiful but haunted survivor of Auschwitz, and Nathan, her darkly charming lover. It is a complicated story about innocence and evil, memory and desire—a story about the way in which the past intrudes relentlessly upon the present.

Sophie's Choice, obviously, becomes a narrative medley of past and present in which the novelist interweaves a tapestry of sufferings and chaos, dismembered relationships and violence. This demonic spectacle of ethnic tribulation gets further complicated by the incidence of frenzied sex, death, guilt, and suicide. A web of existential predicaments gets woven into the very texture of the narrative through Styron's use of a metalanguage of the self in which the past operates as equally as the present. In fact the past becomes an absolute entity constantly encroaching upon the present, something reminiscent of Quentin Compson in William Faulkner's *The Sound and the Fury*. For Sophie, the central protagonist, the past, the present, as well as the future, form three essential dyschronic polarities of existential experience in which the passage of time itself becomes a barometer of the heroine's psyche, measuring all the parameters regarding the final choice. Scene, space, and scenario form an existential past for Sophie in which "the present is something transitory, it is flow, it is an eternal continuation without beginning or end, it is denied an authentic conclusiveness and consequently lacks an essence as well" (Bakhtin 1982: 20)..

The eventual fate of Sophie represents a total lack of essence, a kind of an ethnic apostasy and tribulation. The very title, *Sophie's Choice,* becomes an emblem of a destructive and catastrophic culmination of living time in which the idealization of the past constitutes a generic upliftment on the part of Styron. The novelist valorizes all the images of the heroine Sophie's life. A "sense of time and the hierarchy of times" (Bakhtin: 20) becomes an irresistible force in which language about something which is gone becomes the external expression of a dominant force. The scene and scenario and a sense of space, make the language in *Sophie's Choice* stylistically quite different, particularly when the ironic existence of modern humans is taken as a kind of an inconclusive present as the novelist himself confesses to Kakutani (1982: 7):

> but it seems to me that human beings are a hair's breath away from catastrophe at all times . . . both personally and on a larger historical level. I was never a slave nor was I at Auschwitz but somehow

> these two modes of existence sort of grabbed me and became a kind of metaphor for what I believe a great deal of life is all about.

These words make it clear that the gamut of generalized human suffering and the attendant predicaments, render existence as an open challenge not only to the American ethnic self, but to the self of any aware and sensitive human being.

The backdrop to the action in *Sophie's Choice* is the genocide of the Jews by the Nazis during the Second World War. Adopting a dyschronic narrative, what the reader gets from Styron is the inner spectacle of the minds and psyches of the central protagonists, along with the complexities of psychological ramifications. In the self of Sophie, Styron presents a single human entity, a person in whose mind are interwoven multiple and dyschronic narratives. Such narratives eventually become the channels of pain implicit in Sophie's existential self. Styron's ethnic feminine protagonist narrates six tales of revelation, each stamped with the 'choices' she has made or refused to make. In each of Sophie's befuddling and gripping tales, a choice is made or avoided as a kind of desperation, created by the unsavory nature of her existence. The first tale portrays a highly civilized life in Cracow, a life enmeshed in certain fatalistic events. In the second tale, Sophie is presented as having stolen a ham to take to her mother, who is suffering from consumption and is apprehended by the Nazis. In the third tale, Sophie tries to seduce Rudolph Hoss in order to escape from the labor camp for Jews at Auschwitz and also to try to save her son Jan. In her fourth revelation, Sophie refuses to join the resistance movement led by Wanda, because she feels inundated by an overpowering maternal instinct of nurturing and supporting her children. In the fifth disclosure of her past to Stingo, Sophie chooses Auschwitz to try to steal a radio for Wanda and the resistance movement. Towards the final and concluding spectrum of Styron's labyrinthine narrative, the reader learns about Sophie's monstrous revelation of having surrendered her daughter, Eva, to the gas oven of Birkenau, the locale for the extermination of the Jews.

Sophie presents her civilized life in Cracow as ideal. Her father was a nice human being and both she and her husband, Kazik, were professors at the university, and her mother was a pianist:

> Oh, there are so many memories of Cracow so many I can't begin to describe them. They were wonderful times, those years between those wars. . . . We lived in a wonderful civilized way, the best kind of life you can imagine, really. (Styron 85)

Sophie reveals to Stingo that she became a civilized innocent in a world where the Nazis were the brutal aggressors. By murdering her father and her husband, the Nazis had destroyed Sophie's idyllic past and ravaged her innocence. A sense of guilt enveloped Sophie because she had been unable to bid farewell to her father and her husband before they were killed. Sophie's own lucky survival became a curse and virtually agonized her conscience, besides the guilt which all the time was there:

> You can perhaps think that it is little thing, Stingo, but to permit someone to die without a farewell, an adieu, a single word of comfort or understanding that is so terrible to bear. . . . So Stingo, I have lived long with this very very strong guilt which I can't lose, even though I know it has no reason. (93)

The second tale underlies Sophie's self-image as a victim after her arrival at Auschwitz:

> I got caught for a reason which may seem to you very absurd. I got caught smuggling meat into Warsaw, from a place that belonged to a friend in the country just outside the city. It was completely forbidden to possess meat, which was all commanded to go to the German army. But I risked this anyway, and tried to smuggle the meat so as to help make well my mother. My mother was very sick. (156)

Sophie spends twenty months, incarcerated, Auschwitz being the labor camp and Birkenau the place for the extermination of Jews. Her involvement with Rudolph Hoss, the station officer of the Nazi camp, is encapsulated in her portrayal of herself as a victim of the Nazi horror. An accomplice-victim combination determines Sophie's self vis-à-vis her father, and on the verge of her third tale, reveals the father as an anti-Semite proclaiming the necessity of exterminating the Jews. In spite of realizing the tyrannical nature of her father, Sophie's subservience to him is total and her surrendering to his wishes, something inevitable. The meek surrender of Sophie to her tyrannical father's work and personality in all probability, was due to her Polish Catholicism. All the same, her subservience also reveals her weakness for an attraction towards Nazism as a kind of patriarchal worship.

In the fourth and fifth tales of Sophie, the reader is treated to the problems of ethnically complex relationships based upon·the fractured essence of man-woman relationship. In the fourth tale besides showing that she is a mother and daughter with two children and her own mother to provide for, Sophie attempts to pull herself back together and also to life herself from the quagmire of guilt, revealed by her true relationship with her father and Hoss. To atone for her father's views, Sophie attempts to keep herself away from all political tangles, as she tells Wanda: "I've told you and I'll tell you again. My dear, I can't, I won't. . . . I can't risk it, with children" (403). But fate intervenes and has something else in store for Sophie. She is imprisoned along with members of the resistance, including Wanda, on the way to Auschwitz. The fifth tale's main relationship is between Sophie and a German industrialist, Walter Durrfield, one more patriarchal figure. Sophie met Durrfield for the first time in Cracow in 1937, when the latter turned up at Auschwitz to see Hoss and demand more Jewish workers for the cause:

> During the spring afternoon's jaunt in the company of Poland's most influential anti-Semite, her admirer Walter Durrfield . . . uttered not a word about Jews. Six years later almost all that she heard from Durrfield's lips concerned Jews and their consignment to oblivion. (423)

In this manner, Sophie's first "spasm of adulterous guilt" (422) for Walter Durrfield in 1937 blossomed into blasphemy and eventual suicide in the climactic sequence of the heroine's tale. As a consequence of the ethnic self getting dismantled through a series of tribulatory happenings and relationships, Sophie's guilt becomes a total existential "eclipse," darkening her identity and her psyche and making her a coward who has been "turned to stone" (450).

A final self-image foreshadows Sophie's own death. After fleeing with Stingo, Sophie returns to die with Nathan, leaving a note for Stingo: "I love Nathan but now I feel this Hate of life and God. FUCK God and all his handwork. And life too. And even what remains of Love" (545). Losing all faith in the redemptive power of divinity or in an organized form of religion can only be a symptom of a bleak and unsettling scenario. Sophie's ethnically problematized, protagonistic situation gets defined and qualified in terms of a cynical, almost nihilistic assertion of choices in a turbulent and anarchic world where "self and world are thrown out of joint and self-transcendence sought though all the gods may be defunct" (Hassan 327). Alienation of humans from one another reigns supreme, and Sophie becomes alienated not only from her lover Nathan, but from herself as well essentially because the love life in which she takes refuge turns to ashes for her.

As the epicentric personage of the novel, Sophie's ecstatic rebellion against unsavory developments and forces finally produces an agonized and painful climax in which the modern ethnic self becomes consummated in an act of self-annihilation. The rebel becomes the rebel-victim: an alazonic-eironic-cum absurdist configuration forms the sum-total of Styron's fictionalized quest in *Sophie's Choice.* To use Northrop Frye's 1973 phrase, a "catastrophe of defective intelligence," (Frye uses this expression to delineate the existential predicaments of middle-class married women, entangled in the labyrinthine contexts of man-woman relationships) seems to act as a virus in dismantling Sophie's self, and like Ellison's unnamed hero, Styron's named heroine finally allows herself to be swallowed by the decadent and demonic ethos of a mass society.

In concluding the observations on these two ethnically gripping and revelatory texts of modernist and postmodernist American fiction, it would be quite pertinent to point out a few cardinal issues that emerge as a consequence of a powerful sociological-cum-ethnic syndrome. In Ellison's *Invisible Man*, the anonymous black hero-narrator launches himself on a voyage of self-discovery by coming out of his underground retreat, only at the end to retreat to the 'womb' of the mother earth, his self-esteem badly bruised and mauled by the apostatic elements of racial discrimination, let loose in a contemporary society in the form of masquerading secular satans. In *Sophie's Choice,* the ethnic scene, space, and cultural construct become even more problematized. Both the Black American and the Jewish American protagonists encounter the ethos of a mass society, and like Mark Twain's immortal hero Huck Finn, the only choice, as an act of existential affirmation, even though ironic, remains to "light out for the territory."

Both Ellison and Styron reincarnate in their respective individual protagonists and protagonistic situations, the resurrected persona of Huck. The nameless hero of *Invisible Man* and the disturbingly beautiful heroine of *Sophie's Choice* become inveterate and itinerant rebels, committed to the task of fulfilling a quest as the products of a culture given, the architects of "a process of meaning-creation." In both these novels, ideology powerfully operates as canonicity, and *Invisible Man* as well as *Sophie's Choice* become ethnically loaded texts in which textuality, in terms of the narrative, operates as a revelatory mechanism. Alienation, contradiction, and disorder followed by irony, profundity and rapidity, form the role-playing matrix on the spectrum of ethnic diversity and existential angst.

Works Cited

Bakhtin, M.M., Michael Holquist et al. ed. *The Dialogic Imagination: Four Essays.* Austin: U of Texas P, 1982.

Ellison, Ralph. *Invisible Man.* Penguin Modern Classics, 1952. rpt. Bombay: Allied.

Frye, Northrop. "Theory of Modes," *Anatomy of Criticism.* Princeton, N.J.: Princeton UP, 1973.

Greengbery, Alwin. "Choice-Ironic Alternatives in the World of the Contemporary Novel," *American Dreams, American Nightmares.* Ed. David Madden. Carbondale: Southern Illinois UP, 1970.

Hassan, Ihab. "The Pattern of Fictional Experience," *Modern American Fiction: Essays in Criticism*, ed. A Walton Litz. New York and Oxford: Princeton UP, 1963.

Jackson, Esther Merele. "The American Negro and the Image of the Absurd," *Richard Wright: A Collection of Critical Essays*, ed. Richard Macsey and Frank E. Moorer. Englewood Cliffs, NJ: Prentice Hall, 1984.

Kakutani, Michiko. *International Herald Tribune.* 11-12 December 1982.

Paulson, Ronald, ed. "Satire." *Modern Essays in Criticism.* Englewood Cliffs, NJ: Prentice Hall, 1973.

Schraufnagel, Noel. *From Apology to Protest: The Black American Novel.* Delamd, Florida: Everett/Edwards, 1973.

Styron, William. *Sophie's Choice.* New York: Vintage Books, 1979.

Ideology and Attitude towards Nature: A Comparative Study of Claude MacKay and Bharathidasan

S.S. KUMAR
Presidency College, Chennai

The relevance of cross-cultural and multi-ethnic studies has gained recognition for the involvement of tolerance, excitement, multiple perspectives and values. Comparative literature, however, does not involve pronouncements of ethical and cultural judgements on national and international literatures. The focus of this paper is on the comparative study of the poems of Claude McKay (1889-1948), the Jamaican-born African American poet of the Harlem Renaissance and Bharathidasan (1891-1964), the revolutionary poet of the Tamil Renaissance with reference to their ideologies and attitudes towards nature. Both the poets were fascinated by the ideology of communism in the early stages of their literary careers though they were disillusioned with it later.

"The business of art," according to D.H. Lawrence, "is to reveal the relation between man and his circumambient universe, at the living moment" (127). The poems of McKay and Bharathidasan are compared in this study to reveal such a relation between man and nature, vis-à-vis the concept of *utile (*utility) and *dulci* (pleasure). Although poems on nature are found scattered in the entire oeuvre of these poets, special attention has been paid to Bharathidasan's *Azhagin Sirippu* (The Smile of Beauty) and McKay's *Songs of Jamaica* which are entirely devoted to the celebration of nature.

France and the ideologies of the French Revolution influenced the poets under study, directly or indirectly. McKay was directly influenced by France since he stayed there during his sojourns in Europe and wrote his novels *Home to Harlem* and *Banjo*. Bharathidasan, on the other hand, was a citizen of French India and its ideologies ever since his perceptive age liberty, equality and fraternity permeated his body and soul.

The two-race theory in America and the *Varnasrama* concept in India have common elements; servility, segregation in public places and untouchability. Ideology here refers to "a set of beliefs underlying the customs, habits, and practices common to a given social group" (Martin and Ray 164). In a multi-ethnic society such beliefs may appear to be universally applicable to a particular group but may seem false to another. In a pluralist society, multiple ideologies may coexist, out of which one or more may become dominant, leading to a revolution, discrimination or exploitation.

Although McKay's father was a senior deacon of the local church in Jamaica, he began his career as a heretic peasant bard but died a virulent Catholic pamphleteer. Bharathidasan, on the other hand, was in his early life an ardent devotee of Lord Murugan, a typical Tamil deity unalloyed with any non-Tamil culture. Later, he became a follower of Periyar E.V. Ramasamy and became an atheist. Affinity to communism varied according to the poets' affiliation with certain related socio-political movements. McKay refused to be a tool for political parties and declined to propagate in Russia that the American revolution was just around the corner. But he participated in non-political pleasures of the moment. Bharathidasan, on the other hand, notwithstanding his support for the universal proletarian ideologies of communism, refused to have truce with the Indian communists since they were hostile towards his avowed ideologies of relationalism and love for mother tongue.

Rampersad considers McKay as "the first of the seminal artists of the Renaissance" (189). Linking Marxism with the poet, Geta Leseur observes that among "the literary triumvirate" of the Harlem Renaissance—McKay, Hughes, and Toomer, McKay was "the most controversial" because of his own brand of Marxism (219). McKay's affinity to the communist ideology took him to Russia where he addressed the Fourth International Communist Conference as an unofficial observer. To the Russian criticism that his poems were not proletarian, he replied that he wrote poetry to express his feelings.

Nature, according to Thaninayagam, is "the outer world of sense perception which is not man, nor the immediate work of man" (22). Several African American poets of the Harlem Renaissance have expressed a variety of views on nature colored by segregation. Nature, especially rivers, reminds them of their ancient harmony with it, in sharp contrast to their present condition. Langston Hughes, for instance, while crossing the Mississippi thought of its association with the slave market, and Abraham Lincoln (Barksdale and Kinnamen 523). Arna Bontemps expresses his desire to return to Africa after death (Chapman 423). Jean Toomer strikes a universal note when she calls the Mississippi "sister of the Ganges" (379). The inability of the Blacks in Harlem to enjoy nature is well symbolized in Paul Laurence Dunbar's "Sympathy" (350).

Bharathiar, Bharathidasan's mentor, has written poems on several aspects of nature, such as phenomenal, anthromorphic, cosmic, vedantic, divine, etc. Bharathidasan's poems, in contrast, reveal his proletarian, secular and democratic slant in his attitude towards nature. The relation between man and nature acquires a new dimension in Bharathidasan's poems. In "*Kili*" (Parrot), for instance, the kingdom of a parrot is described thus: Coconut palm is the swing; sky the street. The world is its sacred country it seems (439). The parrot is the right sovereign for a world state with food for all but sans boundaries. Political propaganda is employed in this poem to emphasize the idea of mankind's unity. Using the parrot as a symbol, the poet has made nature and universal love his subject. Turning to social consciousness even while singing of nature has not diminished the artistic character of the poem, comments C. Kanagasabapathi (261-62). Obviously, the smile of beauty in nature as observed by the poet is not for its own sake, but for the welfare of society.

The smile of beauty was appreciated by McKay and Bharathidasan in nature as well as artificial objects. McKay, for instance, admired the smile in the following objects in nature:

"And swarthy children in the fields at play,/ Look upward, laughing at the smiling skies" (20). He asks the city-moon to go and spill its "beauty on the laughing faces/ of happy flowers that bloom in a thousand hues" (69). He described "the morning joy . . . Golden-lipped/ The laughing grasses heaven sweet wine slipped/ The sun rose smiling by the river's breast" (70). Referring to the smile of Night Jasmine, McKay observes: "Your face was in the mirror. I could see/ You smile and vanish suddenly away" (103). While admiring the beauty of architecture in Moscow, he says: "All colors laughing richly their delight/And reigning over all the color red" (83). His love for the Sukee river is expressed thus: "Wavelet laughin' hound me" (2: 79). In these lines, the laughter of things artificial and natural indicates the poet's love of nature along with his personal attachment. But Bharathidasan observes the smile of beauty in unusual things from different angles:

> She's there as the vision of the child's eye,
> She smiles in the temple's lighted lamp,
> She dances in the finger movements
> Of the maid that fastens flowers scented with a cord,
> She rejoiced in the spirited walk of the peasant
> Who went with a plough on his sturdy shoulders.
> She held my eyes in the wet lands with ripened corns
> She filled my heart with ecstasy inhabiting it. (Murugan 104)

In these lines, the Tamil poet gives equal importance to aesthetic delight and utilitarian value in the smile of beauty, without personal attachment. Unlike McKay, the Tamil Poet links mother-tongue with nature and believes that sweet Tamil is responsible for the origin of human life on this planet and includes ten stanzas on it in his *Azhagin Sirippu*. To him, Tamil is not a mere language, but a leader who gives a clarion call to the Tamils to take up the sword to proclaim that there is no caste or religion (448).

Both the poets under study hint at the co-existence of nature with man. When Bharathidasan, for instance, admires the beauty of doves gathered in a circle, he derives the lesson of equality from their behavior (435). McKay, on the other hand describes the life of a hermit who wants to build his house by the woodland to lead "a peaceful life of solitude" (1: 41). The admiration of nature is linked with its aesthetic appeal in the poems of McKay, whereas it leads to a utilitarian function in the works of Bharathidasan. In the description of an Easter flower, McKay observes that many thought that it was a "sacred sign" and some called it "the resurrection flower" but he in wonder "worshipped at its shrine yielding his heart unto its perfumed power" (14). But Bharathidasan, while describing a host of red lotuses which give honey to the bees, compares them to Tamil "bards of ages past" who infused Tamil feelings in the hearts of all and "went unwearied yet" (Murugan 126).

Unlike McKay, Bharathidasan observes and portrays humorous scenes in nature. He differs from McKay in his satirical description of natural phenomena also as evidenced in "*Mayil*" (Peacock). The narrator who compares its long neck with the short ones of women appreciates the dance of the peacock. Mother Nature has endowed women with short necks to prevent them from peeping into their neighbor's rooms. The peacock, on the other hand, gets a long neck for an upright posture since it is a blotless bird with beautiful feathers. The poem ends with this emphatic message: The narrow minds of women have not broadened since the men folk have been misdirecting them (Bharathidasan 157-58). This poem is an amalgamation of art and propaganda since an aesthetic appreciation of beauty in nature leads to social criticism. The poet concludes the poem like a preacher: "I would like to convey this to the world" (157-58). This kind of satire and preaching is not found in the nature poems of the Jamaican poet.

The relationship between nature and divinity has been portrayed by poets in different cultures and a few comparative studies have been attempted from this angle. In a comparative study of Wordsworth and Bharathidasan, A.A.Manavalan observes that the English poet realizes the divine reality in the objects of nature while the Tamil poet admires it as a "scenic tonic against man-made human ills" (156). P.T. Nazimudin opines that Bharathidasan has used nature as an abode of aesthetic feelings and a platform to proclaim his revolutionary principles (71).

In conclusion it can be stated that both McKay and Bharathidasan view nature as a source of personal pleasure as well as social utility. The former considers it a nostalgic balm for his troubled soul, while the latter links it with his mother tongue. Bharathidasan pays more attention to nature's link with socio-economic aspects than McKay. In the poems of Bharathidasan and McKay cited above, the derivations of pleasure cannot be separated from the utilitarian aspect. Hence one can concur with the observations of Houston A. Baker Jr: "There has always been a host of ideologies competing, combining and conflicting in an attempt to gain the ear of art, but there never has been and never will be an essential distinction between *utile* and *dulce*" (6).

Universality and the discovery of the uniqueness of each culture are the historic motivations of comparative literature. Universality according to the *Dictionary of World Literature* is "that quality of work of art whereby its significance is made to exceed the limits of the particular (incident, situation, place, time, person) and to extend itself throughout the universe." Priscilla P. Clerk expands the scope of comparative literature and observes: "Comparing texts in some sense implies comparison of societies that speak to and draw upon those texts" (86). This reveals that the boundary line between literature and sociology is vanishing slowly.

Discussing the relevance of inter-cultural studies, Ayyappa Paniker observes, "The wider the application, the greater the universality. It is of course the particular that should demonstrate the universality of the theory" (64). Comparing the concepts of the West and the East, K. Chellappan avers that the Western notion gives importance to "the individual becoming universal but still remaining an individual." In the Indian view, on the other hand, "the drama is enacted simultaneously in the theatre of the cosmos and the mind of man as signified in the dance of Siva" (304). Comparative literature does not limit itself with the search for universals and unity. It also studies the divergences as well as the silences. Cultural differences can be more essential than the commonplace "essence" (Fokkema 20). In the opinion of Levi Strauss, "It is only through differences that progress has been made" (18). Although the basic colors in pictures by writers all over the world are the same, the shades and perspectives are totally different. The multiplicity of languages, races, and languages, in our sub-continent offers a fertile field for Indian comparative literature. Commentaries on classical works in such ancient languages as Tamil and Sanskrit have elements of comparative literature like textual criticism, indication of parallels, provincial traits, discussion of embellishments, style and the *rasa*. If a historical perspective is added to them, Indian Comparative Literature, an antidote to the narrow provincialism of regional languages, will yield fruits fit for export.

While referring to "*Vishva Sahitya*" (World literature) Tagore observes:

> Just as this earth is not the sum of patches of land belonging to different people . . . so literature is not the mere total of works composed by different hands . . . we must strive to see the work of each author as a whole, that whole as a part of man's universal creativity and that universal spirit in its manifestations through world literature. (qtd. Pathak 20, 21)

The future of comparative literature is bright since it creates an awareness for the social justification of literature. Multiethnic studies linked with comparative literature will be a significant factor in international relations vis-à-vis the admiration of the social and the spiritual mores of all societies in the world.

Works Cited

Babbitt, Irving. *Literature and the American College*, Cliffton: Augustus M. Kelley, 1972.

Bharathidasan Kavithaigal (complete works of Bharathidasan in Tamil) Comp. A. Thiruvasakan and Suradha Kalladan. Chennai. Arul Sudar, 1993.

Chellappan K. "Comparative Literary Theory: An Indian Perspective." *Comparative Literature*. ed. Amiya Dev and Sisir Kumar Das. Simla: Indian Institute of Advanced Studies, 1989: 293-306.

Clark, Priscilla P. "Literature and Society: A Comparative Perspective." *Year Book of Comparative and General Literature* 32 (1983): 35-92.

Dictionary of World Literature, ed. Joseph T. Shipley, New York: Philosophical Library, 1943.

Fokemma, Douwe W. *Issues in General and Comparative Literature*. Calcutta: Papyrus, 1987.

Lawrence, D.H. "Morality and the Novel." *Twentieth Century Literary Criticism*, ed. David Lodge. 1972; London: Longman, 1983: 127-31.

Leseur, Geta "Claude McKay's Marxism." *The Harlem Renaissance Revaluations*. Ed. Singh et al. 219-31.

Manavalan, A.A. "Wordsworth and Bharathidasan as Poets of Nature," ed. Kadigachalam, *Bharathidasan*, Chennai: International Institute of Tamil Studies, 1991.

Manikar, T.G. "Comparative Literature for India," *Jadavpur Journal of Comparative Literature*, 14 (1986): 50-59.

Martin Ross, and Supriya M. Ray. *The Bedford Glossary of Critical and Literary Terms*. New York: Bedford, 1997.

McKay, Claude. *Selected Poems of Claude McKay*. New York: Harcourt, 1953.

Murugan, V., trans. *Selected Poems of Bharathidasan*. Chennai: International Institute of Tamil Studies, 1994.

Nazimudin, P.T. *Bharathidasan Patalkalil Iyarkai* (Tamil). Madurai: Meenakshi, 1973.

Paniker, Ayyappa: "Hardy's Wessex and Tinai Poetics." *Littcrit*, 19 1-2 (1993): 63-72.

Pathak, R.S. "Comparative Literature and Aesthetics: The Search for a Significant Order," R.K. Dhawan, ed., *Comparative Literature*. New Delhi: Bahri, 1987.

Rampersad Arnold. *The Art and Imagination of W.E.B. DuBois*. Massachusetts: Harvard University Press, 1976.

Singh, Amritjit, et al., ed. *The Harlem Renaissance: Revaluations*. New York: Garland, 1989.

Strauss, Levi. *Myth and Meaning*. London: Routledge, 1978.

Thani Nayagam, Xavier S. *Landscape and Poetry: A Study of Nature in Classical Tamil Poetry*. Mumbai: Asia, 1966.

Wellek, Rene. "Literary Theory, Criticism and History," *Concepts and Criticism*. ed. Stephen G. Nicholas, Jr. London: Yale University Press, 1963.

Wellek, Rene. *Discriminations*. Delhi: Vikas, 1970

Politics of Complexity: Mapping the Space of Multiethnic 'Herstories'

DEEPSHIKHA KOTWAL
University of Jammu

This paper grew out of my dissatisfaction with the perception of gender as outside or counter to the canon. Feminine writing can be co-opted or subsumed into the canon, if they meet existing standards of aesthetic excellence. Nina Baym and Annette Kolodny wanted expansion of the canon to accommodate a large number of female voices. Sandra Gilbert and Susan Gubar created a counter-canon of women's texts rejecting androcentric values for gynocentric ones. "Feminist critics have found it easier to write about their resistance to traditional canons of taste than to articulate what a radical feminist politics of literary judgment would look like."

Lillian Robinson, Christine Froula and Jane Tompkins contend that challenge to the canon must be rooted in interrogation of the traditional aesthetic and cultural values that create the canon (1983). Why should irony and complexity be valued over sentimentality and simplicity? Why should football be better than sewing, why should Dickens be better than Jane Austen? Women writers must interrogate the process through which the values of the canon are produced to understand the relationship of feminist criticism to traditional theories of value and to the political agenda of feminism. The canon is forged in the classrooms, in seminars, syllabi, textbooks, in what is taught, written and published. Richard Ohmann says this process is "saturated with class values and interests, inseparable from the broader struggle for position in our society, from the institutions that mediate that struggle, as well as from legitimation of and challenge to that social order" (201).

What is required is a dialogical theory that ceases to take for granted the values of the canon as homogeneous and timeless but sees it as a continuous interaction and debate, a field of intersecting and often conflicting interests. Feminism is not just an occasional academic exercise that we air at seminars or a fashionable foible at drawing rooms soirees. It is the raised eyebrow in academic circles on a project about lesbian politics that makes you want to expose the political violence that inheres in institutions of literary studies, under the guise of neutral and objective scholarship. It is the endless juggling of myriad commitments as teaching schedules, parenting a teenage son, maintaining a long-distance marital affair, and exuding an impeccable façade of the woman in control that makes you want to effectively implement strategies of political resistance to sexual oppression. The dilemma for women writers and scholars is how to proclaim new politically progressive truths.

Simone de Beauvoir's celebrated manifesto in 1952: "One is not born but rather becomes a woman" (301), has committed most feminists to a belief that male/female are specific forms of mediation and not fixed ontological essences. Yet feminists are also committed to social construction of gender because our oppression has been fobbed of us "natural" and the result of universal and immutable "differences" between the sexes. What do feminists do? Look for a progressive feminist politics that perceives gender and indeed reality as social constructs that can be dismantled and reconstructed in new and more egalitarian ways. Donna Haraway puts the problem confronting feminist theorist succinctly as:

> How to have simultaneously an account of radical historical contingency for all knowledge claims and knowing subjects, a critical practice for recognizing our own semiotic technologies for making meanings, and a no-nonsense commitment to faithful accounts of a "real" world, one that can be partially shared and that is friendly to earth wide projects of finite freedom, adequate material abundance, modest meaning in suffering, and limited happiness. (519)

The Haraway model enables women a way out of the impasse by enabling them to recognize the historical contingency of the social relations of gender while allowing them to claim their own truths, however partial or contingent.

Laurie A. Finke in *Women's Writing* has used the term "politics of complexity" which, I think, answers the feminist need for a label that best sums up the myriad and difficult questions thrown up by feminist theory. Complexity allows us to move away from totalizing systems and the "maze of dualisms" that makes us view reality in binary terms, and focus on collecting the difficult questions posed by contemporary feminism about theory, language, history, culture under the rubric of complexity. The complexity of women's experience can best be expressed by a politics of complexity. The feminist project is not only how science or literature might be changed by feminism but how we might appropriate aspects of dominant discourse to seek a way out of the maze of dualisms by which we have traditionally defined ourselves and our politics of male/female, nature/culture, mind/body, reason/imagination, order/disorder.

Order is coercive because it is achieved through exclusion and marginalization of what lies outside the norm, even scientists are challenging totalizing beliefs about theory. Stephen Hawking says, "Quantum mechanics is essentially a theory of what we do not know and cannot predict" (138). Postmodernism in the 70s and 80s has broken away from totalizing and universalizing perspectives towards local fractured systems and modes of analysis. It has allowed the celebration of difference and the presence of multiple and changing subjectivities, in other words, towards theories of complexity. Women's voices ('herstories') are the noise which complexity seeks to restore, a noise which was previously marginalized and which seeks now to expose the ficticity (constructed nature of facts) of dominant discourse.

Disorder is not absence of order just as women is not lack or want of a penis or phallus. Complexity insists on local applications rather than global laws or principles. There are no universal roles, no eternal feminine or masculine principles, only networks of differential relations that construct men and women, masculine and feminine in culturally and historically specific ways. Foucault uses the term "disposatif" or "grid of intelligibility"

(194) to establish links "among such disparate practices as discourses institutions, laws, morality, scientific statements, philanthropy" as a means to demonstrate how societies, organize and control their constituent subjects. Michel de Certeau uses the term "poaching" to describe those strategies that undermine hegemonic cultural practices and enable the disempowered to manipulate the conditions of their existence. "Everyday life invents itself by poaching in countless ways on the property of others" (xii). Poaching is neither straightforward conformity, nor rebellion, but a dialogic encounter between conflicting cultural codes.

Bakhtin argues all discourse is dialogic and double voiced (not in the sense that it is structured around binary oppositions)—"it involves intense interaction and struggle between one's own and another's word" (354). He sees language as a struggle among competing codes and reconstruction of meaning. He does not see the oppressed or marginalized as passive victims and gives them the power to participate in defining their struggle, in turning the oppressor's words against him. Language can never be the sole property of any group or individual, both sexes contest the same language:

> If patriarchy has created the illusion of monologic utterance monopolized by men, then feminists can dispel that illusion by appropriating the notion of heteroglossia, highlighting the dialogic nature of all discourse, insisting that these contested voices be heard. (14)

E'criture feminine/common women's language is as Haraway said, a "powerful infidel heteroglossia" (101). "The female contains the male not monologically as the universal masculine is said to contain the female but dialogically, as the possibility of politically refracting the utterance of the other. Politics of complexity is dialogic because it partakes of half ours, half someone else's, centripetal forces that impel societies towards monologic, and centrifugal forces that impel it towards chaos, heteroglossia and change. Michel Serres' "noise" sees history as competing discourses. He describes "noise" as anything that survives as part of the message, but that which was not part of the message when sent" (42). Alice Jardine says the noise of western history has often been troped as the feminine "alterity" or noise:

> "The space outside of" conscious subject has always been connoted the feminine in the history of Western thought and every movement into alterity is a movement into that female space; any attempt to give a place to that alterity within discourse involves a putting into discourse of "woman." (114-15)

The presence of multiple and changing subjectivities has enabled ethnic women writers of African and Indian descent to shed their invisibility and articulate a voice and occupy a visible space in the American society. A progressive feminist politics depends upon perceiving gender and indeed reality as social constructs that can be dismissed and reconstructed in new and perhaps more egalitarian ways. Ethnic women writers like Toni Morrison, Gloria Naylor, Maya Angleou, Jhumpa Lahiri and Chitra Banerjee Divakaruni are practicing "poaching" i.e using the text to wrest their own meaning from the patriarchal cultural practices designed to keep them in their place. This paper focuses on Toni Morrison and Chitra Divakaruni as representatives of each genre and foregrounds the "noise" of their texts to see whether they are to go beyond suppression of women by various institutions to a "powerful infidel heteroglossia" aimed at restructuring larger cultural institutions.

From her first novel *Bluest Eye* to *Paradise* (her latest is *Love*), Morrison has used her stories as the "noise" which "complexity" seeks to restore, a noise that was previously marginalized and which seeks now to expose the ficticity of facts. *Paradise,* the title of the novel, raises several ironical questions about the nature of paradise, and those who inhabit it. Is it a closed, sexist institution that stifles liberty and change or an open democratic society that interrogates all forms of suppression and encourages growth? Ruby is an all black town founded by nine families who faced persecution from whites as well as light skinned blacks. Except for two people no one in Ruby had ever died, so the town prided itself on being blessed with immortality.

In the center of the town was the community oven inscribed with the stern admonition "Beware the Furrow of his Brow." For Ruby, the town was an exclusive paradise meant only for the members of the nine families, and violation of the bloodline was severely dealt with.

For most of the women folk in the town and for the four women Mavls, Grace, Pallas, and Seneca, who are battered and traumatized by patriarchal society, paradise is an old convent outside the town inhabited by the ailing Mother Magna and her protégée, Consolate alias Connie. The inmates of the convent offer a stark contrast to the townsfolk at Ruby: the women are an odd bunch: "They pilled out of the car looking like go-go; pink shorts, skimpy tops, see-through skirts; painted eyes, no lipstick; obviously no underwear, no stockings. 'Jezebel's Storehouse' raided to decorate arms, earlobes, necks, anklets and even a nostril" (157). Everything in Ruby was orderly and in place, there was no deviation from the norm. Ruby had "white and yellow houses, full of industry, and in them were elegant black women at useful tasks, orderly cupboards minus surfeit or miseries, linen laundered and ironed to perfection; good meat seasoned and ready for roasting."

Inbreeding among the nine families had led to sterility and icy suspicion of outsiders which was soon directed at each other. They lived in the past talking about the heroism of their ancestors, "but why were there no stories to tell of themselves? About their own lives they shut up. Had nothing to say, pass on. As though past heroism was enough of a future to live by. As though, rather than children, they wanted duplicates" (161). Just as Mother Magna had guided Connie, after her death, Connie took over her job and became an ideal friend, companion and parent to the inmates of the convent. Beautiful imagery from cooking is used to convey Consolata's loving humane nature:

> Six yellow apples, wrinkled from winter storage, are cored and floating in water. Raisins are heating in a saucepan of wine. Consolata fills the hollow of each apple with a creamy mixture of egg yolks, honey, pecans and butter, to which she adds, one by one, the

> wine swollen raisins. She pours the flavored wine into a pan and plops the apples down in. The sweet, warm fluid moves. (260)

Connie weaves a sensuous magic with her cooking as well as with human beings. No one who comes into contact with her can remain unaffected by her overwhelming sensual presence. As a result the inmates of the convent who were free to go and come as they pleased always returned to Connie who "was the perfect landlord who changed nothing and welcomed anybody" while the younger generation of Ruby were "roosting everywhere except at home, eager to get away from the peace they found dull, the industry they found tedious, and the heat they found insulting." (13)

The narrative is worked through a dialogic encounter between the conflicting codes of the masculine and the feminine worlds and the result is destabilizing of the phallocentric order and the visibility of feminine space. Both sexes contest the same world/language—the women's voice retracts the male voice to create a counter discourse. Antithesis threads the narrative creating a dialogic discourse that confronts the ficticity of the dominant voice. The town that prides itself on immortality was ironically a town of death because isolation kills generations. It has no future, when Grace comes to town she finds no motel, no restaurant no public place to sit or eat but at the convent she sees a huge kitchen loaded with food. The convent is like an exotic paradise worth an abundance of colorful peppers, luscious melons and golden fields of corn. The nine chapters of the novel correspond to the nine families who founded Ruby but each chapter is named for the convent women or the town women. If Connie leads the convent by love and humanity, Steward Morgan leads Ruby by hate and violence. He leads an assault on the convent and kills the inmates but the bodies miraculously disappear. Even in death, Consolata weaves her magic as Ruby opens its windows under parson Misner to the outside world. The redemption of the town begins with the funeral service of a little girl, Save Marie. Like a master craftsman, Morrison weaves a tapestry that is half them and half us, but makes no bones about which is more colorful. The feminine paradise prevails.

Sister of My Heart, set in India and America, weaves a poignant tale of two women Sudha and Anju, who bond together in a sisterhood of hearts. The narrative has a circular structure and begins with three women—Gouri Ma, Nalini and Pishi—raising the two girls under the benign shadow of a father figure Singhji and ends with Anju and Sudha raising Sudha's daughter under the protective presence of Sunil, Anju's husband. The "landscape of loss" follows the narrative as the lack of a father looms large:

> We moved in a world of women, at home and outside small muted sounds, the tinkling of bangles, female laughter. Because we had no fathers, that other worlds sweat and sunlight, male cologne, a man's voice raised in a command-seemed distant, full of mystery like the dim roar of an ocean seen through a telescope. (51)

Even the presence of three mothers cannot compensate for the lack of a father. The first part of the novel is entitled "The Prince in the Palace of Snakes." The princess is Sudha and the snakes refer to guilt she feels at her father's betrayal of Anju's family. The snakes creep into Anju's palace as well because she is guilty of marrying a man who loves someone else. After marriage both women deceive themselves by defining happiness as usefulness. The second part of the novel is the "Queen of Swords" which refers to Durga and the Rani Jhansi who inspire Sudha to save her unborn child at the cost of her marriage. Men, dead or alive, loom large in the landscape of the novel. The most compelling image of the novel is when Sudha visits a temple to pray for a child:

> The women are strewn around the courtyard like plucked blossoms. From their dust wrinkled saris and wilted faces it seems that many have been here for several days. I want to weep too not for me but for us all for rich or poor, educated or illiterate, here we are finally reduced to a sameness in this sisterhood of deprivation. (214)

Compare this sisterhood of deprivation to the sisterhood of fulfillment in *Paradise*. Marriage divides Anju and Sudha, and Gouri Ma's exhortation "no matter who your father was, you are you because ultimately blood is not as important as love" (2000: 246) falls on deaf ears as the novel weaves a monologic discourse about the overpowering presence of men in the lives of women. The novel ends with Anju comparing her husband to "one of those hundred year redwoods you just can't stop yourself from leaning on" (228). Is it 'herstory' or history repeating itself endlessly?

Divakaruni is a wonderful storyteller who lulls you into a dreamless sleep, Morrison is a prophet who fires your blood with dreams of empowerment and change. Divakaruni writes (monologically) about the oppression of women, Morrison (dialogically) writes back to destabilize the center, to question institutions that breed oppression and makes an effort to restructure them. In a nutshell, what does Divakaruni say? Women are objects in India or America, they have to bond together, men are very important in their lives. Morrison's text itself is interrogation, she questions feminine values as a dialogic counter-discourse to masculine values, an open society versus a closed one, Black values as against White ones, the institution of religion, marriage, politics, capitalism, and education. Morrison is an iconoclast who questions the very basis of a liberal humanist American social order. That is why Salman Rushdie in his essay, "Damme, This is the Oriental Science for You" says: "Contemporary Indian literature remains largely unknown in the United States, in spite of its considerable present day energy and vitality." (59)

Morrison, on the other hand, is acclaimed as a classic American writer in the tradition of Twain, Faulkner and Hemingway because, even though there are unifying aspects in her novels, they are not dully repetitive. Each novel reveals the acuity of her perception of psychological motivation, of the female, of the Black particularly, and of the human generally.

What makes the Black women writer cut across the "grid of intelligibility" and use the canon as a site of resistance? Why is the Indian women writer still pandering to the western taste for Oriental exotica? Why is Morrison seen as an American writer and why does Bharati Mukherjee have to call herself an American writer? Why is Morrison an ocean and Divakaruni a pond? Morrison writes back while Divakaruni simply writes about. These are questions that need urgent answers. The trauma of exile and slavery has whetted the Black women's creativity. Taking inspiration from her "female ancestress" who kept the race alive in the face of ethnic cleansing, Morrison and her ilk have used the text to "poach" on malestream America to create a resonant voice that opens the door and points the way. Writing for her is not a private indulgence but a political tool for social transformation.

The Indian woman writer has made a residential choice and relocated herself in America for a materially better life. There is no trauma—merely the pitfalls of acculturation in trying to "straddle two stools." Black 'herstories' validate themselves by opening up the canon because they radically question the values by which literature is traditionally defined; and this leads women outside the academy, in society, in day to day life to open up the interlocking systems that govern social formations. Indian 'herstories' need to validate themselves as something more than mere oriental exotica or a whining lament. They need not merely to state but change.

I would like to conclude with the words of Michel Foucault:

> The real political task in a society such as ours is to criticize the working of institutions which appear to be both neutral and independent. To criticize them in such a manner that the political violence which has always exercised itself obscurely then will be unmasked, so that one can fight them. (1)

Works Cited

Bakhtin, M.M. *The Dialogic Imagination.* Trans. Michael Holquist and Caryl Emerson. Austin: U of Texas P,1981.

Beauvoir, Simone de. *The Second Sex.* Trans. H.M. Parshley. 1952; rpt. New York: Vintage, 1974.

De Certeau, Michel. *The Practice of Everyday Life.* Trans. Steven F. Rendall, Berkeley: University of California Press, 1974.

Divakaruni, Chitra Banerjee. *Sister of My Heart.* New York: Anchor, 2000.

Finke, Laurie A. *Feminist Theory, Women's Writing.* London: Cornell University Press, 1992.

Foucault, Michel. *The Order of Things: An Archaeology of the Human Sciences.* New York: Pantheon, 1970.

Haraway, Donna. "Situated Knowledges: The Science Question in Feminism and the Privilege of Partial Perspective." *Feminist Studies 14*, 1988.

Hawking, Stephen. "Is the End in Sight for Theoretical Physics?" In John Buslough, *Stephen Hawking's Universe: An Introduction to the Most Remarkable Scientist in our Time.* 1985; rpt. New York: Avon Books, 1989.

Jardine, Alice. *Gynesis: Cofigurations of Women and Modernity.* Ithaca: Cornell UP: 1985.

Morrison, Toni. *Paradise.* London: Chatto and Windus, 1998.

Ohmann, Richard. "The Shaping of a Canon: U.S. Fiction;1960-1975." *Critical Inquiry,* 10, 1983.

Rushdie, Salman. *Step across This Line: Collected Non-fiction 1992-2002.* London: Vintage, 2003.

Sere's, Michel. *Hermes: Literature Science, Philosophy.* Ed. Josue' V. Harari and David F. Bell. Baltimore: Johns Hopkins UP,1982.

Within and without Margins: Cross-cultural Spaces in Toni Morrison's *The Bluest Eye* and Kingston's *The Woman Warrior*

SHUKLA SAHA
MMD Govt. Degree, College, Sabroom, Tripura University

Several feminist theorists have debated over the extent to which women share a common culture. Explaining the complexity of the subject Temma Kaplan, for instance, observes, "It is impossible to speak of 'women's culture' without understanding its variation by class and ethnic group. Women's culture, like popular or working class culture, must appear in the context of dominant cultures" (Kaplan: 44). The validity of Kaplan's statement is borne out by reading the works of women from diverse backgrounds. Such books do not simply exhibit the great cultural diversity women experience but also draw forth the discordant definitions of femininity and the incompatible demands a woman is likely to come across as she tries to live in more than one cultural world simultaneously.

Women's worlds may differ widely depending on ethnic background and social class, but it is an undeniable fact that male dominance is a common trend in the societies from which women have written literature. Both Toni Morrison and Maxine Hong Kingston in their first books—*The Bluest Eye* (1970) and *The Woman Warrior: Memoirs of a Girlhood among Ghosts* (1976), respectively—present the contradictions patriarchy creates for women who are at one and the same time subordinated by a culture, and yet, embroiled in its interstices. Women like Morrison and Kingston who are doubly marginal (i.e. not a member of the dominant race or class) are likely to experience this conflict since an affiliation with a minority culture tends to be particularly strong.

While *The Bluest Eye* basically deals with the impact of the predominant white ideas of beauty upon the African American lives of the MacTeers in general and the Breedloves in particular, *The Woman Warrior* vividly depicts the agony of a Chinese-American girl in her quest for identity. Pecola Breedlove, the protagonist of *The Bluest Eye* and Kingston, the protagonist of *The Woman Warrior*, encounter many unpleasant experiences both within and without the family. Within the family, both of them are considered ugly, which naturally prompts them to question their sense of self-esteem. Without the family, Pecola and Kingston have to struggle with the problem of racial and sexual discrimination. Another similarity, which can be clearly perceived, is the effect of migration upon the existence of the family, which in turn affects Pecola and Kingston in shaping their self-perceptions. Finally, born into the abyss between two cultures, both of them are discontented with their respective living environment, as reflected in Pecola's craving for blue eyes and Kingston's bold resistance against her family.

In *The Bluest Eye*, Toni Morrison depicts her protagonist in the form of a dark-skinned young girl, named Pecola Breedlove, who on being rejected by her family and the society at large, embarks on a search for what she apprehends to be an "acceptable" self—the blue eyes of a white girl. Pecola grows up in a family devoid of love and self-worth. Her father Cholly Breedlove, is an alcoholic. He himself was an orphan. Pecola's mother, Mrs. Paulin Breedlove is an aesthetically depleted person. The Breedlove surname is ironic as "love" is just what the family lacks and they are unable to produce more of it as suggested by the word "breed." Instead "breed" becomes an ominous reference to what Cholly ends up doing with his own daughter.

Morrison reveals, through an omniscient narrator, Cholly's family background in order to trace the various incidents in his life that have shaped his tragic fate. Soon after Cholly's birth, his father ran away from home. Four days later his mother dumped him in a junk heap. The parentless infant was rescued and brought up by his Great Aunt Jimmy. Cholly later learnt from her that his mother was somehow insane and his father had gone to Macon. But to the child Cholly, Aunt Jimmy's age, gender and interests seemed to be so distant from his own that he suffered from a sense of detachment. After the death of Aunt Jimmy one chilly spring, Cholly, then in his teens, undergoes two distressing experiences that augment his feelings of isolation and helplessness.

Soon after Aunt Jimmy's funeral, Cholly and a young girl Darlene, go to pick muscadines in a dry riverbed across an open field. As they both engage in a sexual act, two white hunters with long guns come abruptly on the scene and turn his spontaneous act into a public performance by passing racial remarks: "Hee hee heeee." The sucker was a long asthmatic cough. The other raced the flashlight all over Cholly and Darlene. "Get on wid it, nigger," said the flashlight one. "Sir?" said Cholly, trying to find a buttonhole. I said, get on wid it. An' make it good, nigger, make it good" (*BE*: 117).

Thus, in the midst of asserting his masculinity, Cholly is disgracefully de-sexed in the face of racial oppression. After this incident of bungled sexuality, Cholly decides to flee. He sets out in search of his father with the money that Aunt Jimmy had left behind. To his utter dismay, Cholly is totally rejected by his father. With no one to guide him in life, Cholly becomes "dangerously free. Free to feel whatever he felt, he was alone with his own perceptions and appetites, and they alone interested him" (*BE*: 125-26). He courts and marries Pauline Williams but his marital life is devoid of any charm. As unemployment heightens his mental agony, he takes recourse to drinking. He is unable to maintain a healthy relationship with his children. Hence, one Saturday afternoon, when he in a drunken state sees Pecola scratching the back of her calf with her toe—a gesture that reminds him of his first encounter with Pauline—he rapes her. This horrendous incident was greatly responsible for Pecola's ultimate descent into madness. His rape of Pecola is motivated by detestation. He despises his daughter for loving him because he is painfully conscious of his failures.

Pecola's mother Pauline is also incompetent in nurturing her children with proper care. She herself grows up with a fractured sense of self because of a physical deformity caused by a rusty nail that punched through her foot when she was two years old. Pauline's emigration to Ohio after her marriage intensifies her sense of isolation as she is culturally uprooted. Unable to assimilate into the new society she begins going to movies. While watching the movies, she internalizes the white ideas of physical beauty. This not only vitiates her relationship with her husband and daughter but also impairs her self-worth. She assigns Pecola a bottom category in the scale of absolute beauty: "Eyes all soft and wet. But I knowed she was ugly. Head full of pretty hair, but Lord she was ugly" (*BE*: 100).

Instead of displaying tenderness toward her daughter Pauline rebukes her at the slightest pretext. For instance, when Pecola accidentally spills the deep-dish berry cobbler her mother has prepared for the white Fisher family, her employer, the latter reacts violently: "In one gallop she was on Pecola, and with the back of her hand knocked her to the floor. Pecola slid in the pie juice, one leg folding under her. Mrs. Breedlove yanked her up by the arm, slapped her again." (*BE*: 86). She totally ignores the painful burns Pecola suffers from the hot pie, and cuddles the little white girl who happens to be the daughter of her employer. Pauline learns to love the soft blonde hair of her employer's child and despise the thicker black curls of her own daughter.

In denying her own daughter for the little white girl, Mrs. Breedlove not only distances herself from her daughter but also whets Pecola's desire for a pair of blue eyes, for the latter assumes that blue-eyed girls are adored by the white as well as black adults. The society in which Pecola grows up also intensifies her feeling of unworthiness and she experiences a sense of insecurity and isolation. The behavior of the white grocery storekeeper, Mr. Yacobowski, is a case in point. When Pecola goes to his shop to buy candies, she has a painful experience: "He does not see her, because for him there is nothing to see" (*BE*: 42). Eye imagery permeates the scene, as the shopkeeper cannot "see" Pecola. To see her would be to see her as a person, to confront her subjectivity. To Mr. Yacobowski, Pecola is nothing and she in turn can see in his eyes that she means nothing to him. She soon realizes the reason for this unusual behavior. "The distaste must be for her, her blackness. It is the blackness that accounts for, that creates, the vacuum edged with distaste in white eyes" (*BE*: 42).

In another scene witnessed by Pecola's friends—Claudia and Frieda MacTeer-Pecola is tortured by four boys of her own race who dance a macabre ballet around her: "Black e mo. Black e mo" (*BE*: 55). This outrageous behavior of the black boys, besides revealing their growing self-contempt, also enhances Pecola's awareness of being ugly. Apart from being branded a blackamoor, Pecola is rebuked by a plain, brown woman named Geraldine, who absorbs white middle-class standards. Sexually stifled, Geraldine does not bestow any motherly love on her son Junior. She rather showers all her affection toward a blue-eyed black cat. Once while Geraldine is out, Junior tricks Pecola into coming into his house, where he throws the cat on her face, kills it, and then blames her for it. When Geraldine returns she harshly throws Pecola out of the house. Pecola is once again the victim of other blacks' cruelty, implying that hatred of blackness often comes from other blacks. Geraldine sees Pecola as an abstracted representative of a whole social class, a class she despises, and consequently she is cruel to her. Since blue eyes are a symbol of physical beauty, Pecola feels that if she could acquire a pair of blue eyes, she would not only look beautiful and achieve societal acceptance but the attitude of her parents would also change: "If she looked different, beautiful, may be Cholly would be different, and Mrs. Breedlove too. They'd say, 'why, look at pretty-eyed Pecola. We mustn't do bad things in front of those pretty eyes'" (*BE*: 40). In another instance, Pecola drinks three quarts of milk just because "she was fond of the Shirley Temple cup and took every opportunity to drink milk out of it just to handle and see sweet Shirley's face" (*BE*: 22).

The idea of beauty as embodied in the figural image of Shirley Temple is reified into an object such as a cup, in Pecola's immature mind. In her quest for achieving the blue eyes, Pecola has come to equate "I" with "eye." Judged from such an angle, the title becomes all the more significant, as it shows the interrelatedness among the motifs of race, physical beauty, and identity quest. Desperate with misery, Pecola goes to a pedophilic fortune-teller named Soaphead Church to ask for blue eyes. Soaphead is a self-deceiving person who plays God and declines to deal with the subjectivity of other living things in a meaningful manner. He is the only person to whom Pecola has disclosed her wish, but his racial self-loathing prevents him from offering any sound counsel to Pecola.

Taking advantage of her plight Soaphead asks her to kill an old dog that he detests on the one hand and is identified with, on the other. Pecola believes that the completion of the task would be like a transformative spell. The dog is poisoned as an "offering" for Pecola's prayer for blue eyes to be answered. The violent death scene drives her to madness and in her madness she fantasizes that she has got a pair of blue eyes. Soaphead sees nothing wrong in Pecola's longing to see the world with blue eyes. But it can be easily perceived that eye color does not have an effect on vision. The color of eyes is not for looking. Rather it is for being looked at. Pecola who has gone unnoticed by the eyes of others and so has been unable to see herself, i.e., to conceive of her own worth, now has found a way to see herself. Her imaginary friend is the companion she has never had, as well as an admirer of her blue eyes. Now, she literally sees herself in the most tragic way possible.

While *The Bluest Eye* vividly portrays the woes of a poor black girl loathed by her family and society, *The Woman Warrior* depicts the distressing experiences of a Chinese American girl struggling to find her own self in a bicultural society. Growing up in the Stockton Chinatown community, Kingston notices the glaring sexual discrimination rampant there. She discovers that sexual discriminations start at the very moment of birth. While the birth of a boy occasions a month long celebration, the birth of a girl passes by unnoticed.

Sexist sayings like "girls are maggots in the rice" and "It is more profitable to raise geese than girls" (*WW*: 46), produce in Kingston a mixed feeling of vexation and indescribable fear. Whenever she hears any of these sexist sayings she protests by thrashing on the floor and screaming very hard. She also expresses her indignance either by refusing to do what a traditional Chinese girl is expected to do—domestic work—or by spoiling it purposely. Nonetheless, Kingston also harbors unpleasant feelings, which crop up from her awareness that if she would fail to justify herself worthy of eating the food, her parents might sell her upon their return to China. Kingston's fear emanates from the talk-stories that her mother Brave Orchid relates about her life in China. When she tells Kingston how she had purchased a slave girl in the market and trained her to be her nurse, the latter realizes that girls were sellable items and expresses her anguish. "But I did not want to go to China. In China my parents would sell my sisters and me" (*WW*: 99). Her fear is intensified when her mother tells her of the inhuman practice of killing girl babies at the birth beds.

Kingston also comes to know about the inequitable treatment meted out to women in misogynist Chinese society when her mother tells her the story of her unnamed paternal aunt. Having become pregnant in the absence of her husband the aunt drowns herself in the communal well along with her newborn baby when the villagers pillage her family for her infidelity. Brave Orchid narrates Kingston this forbidden story on the occasion of her first menstruation to warn her against sex outside marriage.

While telling Kingston that she will grow up a wife and slave, Brave Orchid also teaches her the song of Fa Mu Lan, The Woman Warrior of the book's title. According to the ballad, it is Mu Lan's filial sense of duty that induces her to replace her aging father in battles against the emperor's enemies. To Brave Orchid, Mu Lan represents a paragon of filial piety and patriotism whereas Kingston sees her as an emancipator of women. The lesson Kingston draws from it is that women are by no means inferior if granted the opportunity. Hence in the chapter entitled "White Tigers" (*WW*: 20), one can sense she imagines herself as Fa Mu Lan, the heroine of her childhood dream. Accordingly, when she says that "I would have to grow up a warrior woman" (urgency of her desire to fulfill her mother's expectation on the one hand and to transcend the sexual barrier on the other). With this in mind, Kingston imaginatively reconstructs, out of her mother's "talk-story," her own version of The Woman Warrior. Due to her personal ire at the Chinese tyrants who oppress women, Kingston makes the Woman Warrior a female avenger by conquering a petty baron who has tyrannized the village women. Kingston's mother and her maternal aunt Moon Orchid furnish living examples of two diametrically opposed female images. To Kingston, while her mother is a flesh and blood version of the Amazon archetype, her aunt is a living example of the No Name Woman archetype. Just as Fa Mu Lan excels in an arena traditionally closed to women, Brave Orchid too had defied tradition by working independently as a doctor in China—an unusual profession for Chinese women at that time. Moon Orchid after living like a widow in China for about thirty years, comes to America at her sister's behest to reclaim her husband who has bigamously married an Americanized Chinese woman, while becoming a successful medical practitioner in Los Angeles. In a scene mixed with farce and pathos, Moon Orchid sets out with her sister to claim her rightful position as first wife. But in the ensuing confrontation near the Western Palace, the unfaithful husband "looked directly at Moon Orchid the way the savages looked. She shrank from his stare; it silenced her crying" (*WW*: 152). Scared into silence by her husband, Moon Orchid soon goes mad. She suffers the pain of sexual oppression like the victimized No Name Woman, without taking revenge on the man inflicting it. Uprooted and deserted, she eventually dies in an insane asylum.

Toward the end of the episode Kingston expresses through an omniscient voice her determination to repudiate the threatening identity of woman as slave-object as represented by Moon Orchid and No Name Woman: "Brave Orchid's daughters decided fiercely that they would never let men be unfaithful to them. All her children made up their minds to major in science or mathematics" (*WW*: 160). Then as the next episode opens, Kingston reiterates her resolution to withstand the male tendency to subjugate women when she says of Moon Orchid's total silence regarding her husband's bigamy and desertion: "I would've told. If I was his wife, I would've told" (*WW*: 163). "Telling" thus forms an important metaphor in Kingston's search for a viable female identity, for only through "telling" can she hope to gain sexual equality. The tragic fate of her aunt Moon Orchid makes her realize that to shape her identity, she must find a voice of her own. It is this search for her voice that predominates the final episode.

As a child, Kingston had a speech impediment. She suspects that it may have resulted from Brave Orchid's cutting the frenum of her tongue. Kingston remained silent for three years at school, thereby flunking kindergarten. While attending Chinese and American schools simultaneously, she was baffled by the "I" and "here" in the American language, which are so different from the equivalent Chinese ideographs. This no doubt shows that since early childhood she has been trying to grapple with the problem of self and place, identity and home. The pangs of straddling across two cultures culminate in a painful incident where Kingston tries to break the silence of another Chinese American girl by tormenting her in the bathroom of her school. Unlike Kingston, who has overcome her initial silence, this is the "one girl who did not speak up even in Chinese school" (*WW*: 172). The silent girl functions as a nightmare double for Kingston. Her attempts at making the girl speak are, as Martin A. Danahay observes "both an escape from victimization and a turning of the other girl into a victim. She both cajoles the girl into speech and tells her, 'Don't you dare tell anyone I've been bad to you'" (*WW*: 181). She thus enforces the injunction not to speak, just as it was imposed on her by her culture (Danahay: 72).

As she begins to realize the importance of self-articulation, Kingston finds to her utter dismay that her parents attempt to marry her off first to one of the FOBs and then to a rich but mentally retarded boy. The mentally retarded boy at first follows Kingston around at the Chinese school and then comes sitting on the crates at the laundry with his boxes of pornographic pictures, a gesture symbolic of sexual oppression. Kingston eventually finds her voice to drive out the sitting huncher.

> One night my throat burst open. I stood up talking and burbling. I looked directly at my mother and at my father and screamed, "I want you to tell that hulk, that gorilla-ape, to go away. If I see him one more time, I'm going away. I'm going away anyway. I am not going to be a slave or a wife." (*WW*: 201)

Thereafter the huncher disappears. If this act of talking out the sitting huncher is a manifestation of her affinity to her mother, Kingston in lashing out at her mother also expresses her desire for individuation and independence. She has finally chalked out the paradigm of her gender identity—to be a woman warrior in America—as demonstrated both in her refusal to be a slave or a wife and in her decision to go away from home. After yelling at her mother in the climactic scene she is eager for reconciliation. To mitigate her guilty feeling arising from such a rebellious act, Kingston longs for the day when her mother can understand and forgive her. Therefore, during her latest visit home, when her mother bestows on her a sign of understanding and forgiveness, she feels quite relieved.

Significantly, Kingston concludes her text with a story told jointly by her mother and herself. She links Brave Orchid's story of her grandmother, who had a passion for the theater, to hers by saying, "I like to think that at some point of those performances they heard the songs of Ts'ai Yen" (*WW*: 207). Ts'ai Yen was a second century Chinese poetess who was captured by a chieftain of a barbarian tribe, who presented her to another chieftain as a gift. During her twelve-year stay with the chieftain she had two sons who could not speak Chinese. She was ransomed back to China to perpetuate the family line of her father. From the alien land she brought back her "Eighteen Stanzas for a Barbarian Reed Pipe," which touched the hearts of foreigners and Chinese alike. Kingston alludes to this female bearer of culture as she discerns analogous experiences. She is alienated alike from the Chinese world of her parents and the world of white Americans. Moreover, just as the songs speak of Ts'ai Yen's painful experience as a slave and wife, her book uncovers her agonizing experience in confronting sexism and racism. Finally, Kingston as a writer sincerely hopes that her "song" sung with a voice found in the new world, would translate well.

Both Kingston and Morrison have deftly portrayed the effect of migration on the lives of the characters in *The Woman Warrior* and *The Bluest Eye* respectively. In *The Woman Warrior,* Moon Orchid offers an example of the cultural misfit who having misplaced herself, descends into madness and dies a pathetic death. Migration has degraded Brave Orchid's status from a respectable village doctor to a lowly laundress and farm laborer. As a Chinese girl growing up in a ghetto, young Kingston finds herself torn between the force of Chinese heritage and the pull of assimilation into the mainstream. Similarly in *The Bluest Eye*, when after her marriage Pauline Breedlove moves to Ohio with her husband, she suffers from a sense of alienation as she has trouble mixing with both blacks and whites. This affects her role as a wife and mother.

The characters of the mothers, portrayed in both the novels, offer a striking contrast. Brave Orchid is strong-willed, independent and self-confident whereas Pauline is dependent and diffident. Unlike Pauline who fights her husband and beats her daughter, the better-educated Brave Orchid is able to maintain a relatively healthy relationship with her husband and children. The unhappy relationship between Pauline and Pecola is manifested in various ways.

The circumstances surrounding Pecola's first period highlight the susceptibility of her position. She is not even with her mother when it happens. Her mother has not taken care to prepare her for it. It is a family tradition that is passed on from one generation to another. Being segregated from these vital connections to family and lineage, results in becoming alienated from one's own physical self, as witnessed in the scene where Pecola screams and cries at the sight of her own menstrual blood. Pauline's tendency to distance herself from her daughter is revealed in her insistence that Pecola call her "Mrs. Breedlove" instead of "Mama," as her friends call their mother. Her lack of concern for her daughter is testified in her apparent indifference to Pecola's plight when the latter tells her about her father's first sexual transgression; consequently, when he rapes her for the second time, Pecola does not tell her mother about it. Pauline's peculiar attitude not only bespeaks her low self-esteem but also the strained mother-daughter relationship.

Compared to this, the mother daughter tie in *The Woman Warrior* is more stable and intricate. For instance, at the onset of Kingston's menstruation, Brave Orchid relates her the tale of her outcast paternal aunt, an act induced by the mother's concern for her daughter's future happiness. In another instance, when Kingston is down in bed with a mysterious illness for eighteen months, her mother nurses her with great care. Brave Orchid's habit of talk-storying her children into sleep is a gesture of love too. Kingston also feels loved when her mother tucks red money in her pocket on New Year's mornings: "From afar I can believe my family loves me fundamentally" (*WW*: 62). By contrast love is something foreign to Pecola:

> "What did love feel like?" [Pecola] wondered. (*BE*: 48-49)

Throughout her interaction with the society Pecola is time and again taught that there is no one to love her. Later on when someone does love her, it is her father who rapes her. Devoid of family support Pecola lacks the inner strength to withstand racial and class discrimination. Each humiliating encounter with the society further adds up her belief that she is ugly and therefore unworthy. Pecola gradually withdraws from the society and folds inward, which in turn heightens her desire for blue eyes. Rejected by her mother and raped by her father, the emotionally unstable Pecola resigns to the private world of fantasy.

Unlike Pecola who passively resigns to fate, Kingston actively resists such racist attitudes as evidenced in the boss of a land developers' association or the boss of an art supply house. When her parents attempt to marry her off first to an FOB and then to a mentally retarded boy, she protests with her newly found voice and decides to chalk out her own destiny by leaving the family circle as well as the Chinese immigrant community, thereby preventing herself from "being forced into the mold of the victimized No Name Woman or Moon Orchid" (Chua: 51).

As Kingston's rebellion typifies her dissatisfaction with the status quo, so does Pecola's desire for blue eyes. However, while Kingston in rebelling against her family determines to formulate an identity of her own, Pecola in yearning for blue eyes wants to transfigure her own identity. As Wen-ching Ho points out: Kingston's "departure from her community serves to provide her with the vantage point from which to figure out how the invisible world her parents build around her fits in solid America. In other words, to search for her identity, Kingston looks backward in time for "ancestral help." By contrast, Pecola in craving for blue eyes has unwittingly discarded the Afro-American value system" (Ho: 37). In spite of the mother-daughter conflict, which gives rise to feelings of being debased and unworthy, Kingston is able to reconcile with her mother by identifying her expectation. Contrary to this, Pecola's relationship with her mother worsens after the kitchen scene, as is shown by the mother's beating her, which results in her miscarriage on the one hand and contributes to her final lapse into the lunacy on the other.

Works Cited

Chua, Cheng Lok. "Golden Mountain: Chinese Versions of the American Dream in Lin Yutang, Louis Chu, and Maxine Hong Kingston." *Ethnic Groups: An International Periodical of Ethnic Studies*. 4 (1and 2): 1982: 33-59.

Danahay, A. Martin. "Breaking the Silence: Symbolic Violence and the Teaching of Contemporary 'Ethnic' Autobiography." *College Literature.* 18 (3): 1991: 64-79.

Ho, Wen-Ching. "In Search of Female Self: Toni Morrison's *The Bluest Eye* and Maxine Hong Kingston's *The Woman Warrior*." *American Studies.* XVII (3): 1987: 1-44.

Kaplan, Temma. "Politics and Culture in Women's History: A Symposium." *Feminist Studies*, 6 (Spring 1980): 44.

Kingston, Maxine H. *The Woman Warrior: Memoirs of a Girlhood among Ghosts.* New York: Alfred A. Knopf, 1977.

Morrison, Toni. *The Bluest Eye.* New York: Pocket Books, 1970.

Ordonez, Elizabeth J. "Narrative Texts by Ethnic Women: Rereading the Past, Reshaping the Future." *MELUS*, 9 (3) 1982: 19-28.

Wong, Jade Snow. *Fifth Chinese Daughter*. New York: Harper Brothers, 1945.

The South Asian Diaspora vis-à-vis the Ubiquitous Bhangra

SOMDATTA MANDAL
Visva-Bharati University, Santiniketan, W.B.

That the diasporic South Asians in the western world are caught between cross-cultural values is not a new phenomenon. There are innumerable documentaries and mainstream feature films that focus on biracial ethnicity, exploration and South Asian self-identity. Some directors tackle the issue rather lightheartedly (the recurrence of the ABCDs is a pointer), others do the soul-searching with more seriousness, in the cinema-verite style. Amidst the plethora of themes, one common area that has drawn the attention of several filmmakers is Bhangra, the folk music of Punjab, which has come to acquire new political and cultural resonance for the South Asian diaspora.

It is a well-known fact that the *desi*-remix of bhangra occurred in Britain much earlier than it did in the United States or Canada. This probably had to do with the nature of the Indian immigrant and also the period of his immigration. In an interesting report about how the bhangra has gripped the non-resident Indians in the United Kingdom, Lavina Melvani[1] informs us that the new bhangra, born of the rural traditions of Punjab, is very much an immigrant music, incorporating the music played in decaying English industrial cities and Trinidadian neighborhoods. If the immigrants hadn't come to the United Kingdom, this music would not have been created. As Sadie O. observes in *SF Weekly:*

> Ever since Gandhi, Britons have been embracing certain aspects of East Indian culture (like Vindaloo and Bhangra) with relish (or possibly chutney). Like Vindaloo, Bhangra has passed through the

> collective digestive tract of the United Kingdom and emerged profoundly changed. Unlike Vindaloo, bhangra will only keep you up all night in order to dance.

This celebratory music of Punjabi farmers transformed by young Britishers of Asian origin certainly crossed the Atlantic into the American music scene, but not in the explosive way it has hit the United Kingdom. Though there are not so many live bands in the United States as there are in Britain and Canada, yet since the mid 1990s onwards, bhangra in the United States has become extremely popular too. Bhangra, imported from the England via CDs and audio cassettes, is now making such an impact in America that cultural anthropologists are considering the plural dance cultures of the South Asian American diaspora a seminal topic of research.

Immigrants, as they become part of the American culture, incorporate bits and pieces of their own traditions into it and that transforms American pop culture. While modern bhangra may be something very new for mainstream audiences, the ever-growing South Asian community in America has embraced it, especially second-generation Indian Americans. Apart from the scores of names popularized now [a long list of their websites being a ready reckoner], several top names like Apache Indian and Bally Sagoo have been signed by major record labels in the United Kingdom and the United States.

A simple report by Ashley Dawson illuminates the situation further:

> On a sweltering August afternoon in 1996, New York City's *Summer Stage* concert series brought the South Asian dance music known as bhangra to Central Park. South Asian families from all over the tri-state area sunned themselves, jostled for room, and danced in a jam-packed sandy space under the sun-dappled plane trees. New York turntablist DJ Rekha added some hometown flavor, spinning bhangra remixes to much applause before the Safri Boys, one of Britain's hottest bhangra bands took the stage. Although bhangra remix had been transforming South Asian youth culture in the US at least since the release of UK musician Bally Sagoo's pathbreaking "Star Crazy" album in 1991, the concert in

> Central Park was a particular milestone. Here, visible to a broad public, was a display of the compelling cultural forms through which South Asians of the diaspora were articulating new, composite identities. The multiple regional contrasts and tensions that define identity within the subcontinent were harmonized in this diasporic context.[2]

Since 1996 onwards Central Park Summer Stage, which is a project of the City Parks Foundation, has been organizing bhangra concerts in Central Park, drawing 6,000-8,000 people. New York's popular disc jockey Magic Mike spun Bhangra remixes and Caribbean Ricky Jai and singer Najma also performed. Later Safri Boyz performed there to the delight of a mixed crowd, which included every one from American kids to Punjabi grandmothers. What is most interesting to note is that although the audience was principally South Asian, there were also many Americans in the audience. According to Bill Bragin, director of "Summer Stage" at that time, the appeal of bhangra was irresistible due to certain reasons:

> Bhangra has very new sounds for a lot of ears but at the same time its rhythm is very strong for dance halls. It's adaptable and adapting so that it can be combined with a lot of different genres; it bears a lot of reference points for people who are not familiar with traditional bhangra. I think a lot of what's happening with pop music around the world is people who are listening to Western pop and dance music equally with music from their own heritage are trying not to make a distinction between one or the other but are coming to it as an equal influence.

He adds that this new bhangra is more self-consciously crossover, combining with hip-hop, jungle, reggae and rock ôn roll. Just as the young Asian community in the United Kingdom closely mingled with their Caribbean friends, so it was a self-conscious attempt to find a musical form that was distinctly Indian chutney and soca music combined together. This resulted in the hybridization of cultures and the emergence of bhangra as one form of diasporic music. As Hindi film music was also incorporated into the calypso music as well as into the bhangra beat, the traditional bhangra tunes gradually moved to a modernized western version.

As Sadie O. points out: "Bally Sagoo is responsible for a huge chunk of the shift from traditional bhangra to modern multiple stylistic fusion. Rap and reggae merge with vocals by Pakistani devotional singer Nusrat Fateh Ali Khan and these eclectic cuts "are seriously pumped up into mega-mixes for the dance floor, and DJs all over are discovering that they work as well for that purpose as more familiar Western styles."

People's musical tastes are very much a part of their background, and that is especially true for immigrants. They seem to identify with the music of the neighborhoods they grew up in, be it white or Caribbean. In fact deejays have taken traditional, familiar stuff and reinvented it, redefined it via mixes and beats. Nothing is too way out or too obscure, be it Hindi or regional, such as Tamil film music. One of the things which made it so significant and dynamic is that it encouraged exchange of cultures on both sides.

Of course everyone is not equally enthused by the infiltration of bhangra in the New World. For example, Krishneil Maharaj finds deep-rooted implications in the popularity of this art form. According to him,

> A funny thing happens to a people when they immigrate to a new land: they start reminiscing about their old land. Their children, born in the new land, undergo a similar fascination with the land of their parents. South Asian immigrants and their children in the US are no different in this regard.
>
> Over President's Day weekend, hundreds of South Asian youths converged at the Kaiser Convention Center in Oakland for the annual Dhol Di Awaaz Bhangra dance competition. Now, whether they acknowledge it or not, the participants are taking part in a process of historical and cultural revision.
>
> What's interesting about bhangra is that it takes us back to a time in South Asian history, to rural areas, where crops were plentiful, where people were happy and had plenty of causes to celebrate. Now, this pastoral South Asia is an immigrant fantasy borne out of South Asian Americans' dreaming of an idyllic Indian past. What bhangra does, in a way, is to present a conservative inter-

> pretation of Indian history in which the glaring problems in the rural areas are overlooked. Issues like the inequity of landownership, class conflict, the displacement of peasants, a history of famine, and the gross neglect by the Indian state and society of the rural poor are brushed away by the desire of South Asians to dream of their homeland in romantic terms.
>
> You're probably saying: How did you get all that from a dance?
>
> I know it is not the job of entertainment events to educate people. I am well aware that one does not go to a cultural or social event to receive a lecture in history. I wouldn't go to a rap concert and expect to be lectured on Atlantic slavery. But those with progressive vision must acknowledge that the events we hold and the things we celebrate about our culture must make it possible for us to gain a real sense of our history, even the ugliest aspects of it.[3]

Since its launch in 1997, *Basement Bhangra*[4] has forced New York to sit up and take notice of Bhangra, rapidly making the outsider art-form an essential part of the NYC club scene. Although Basement Bhangra's success is built on loyalty to the sensibilities of its core audience, the 1st Thursday of every month finds S.O.B.'s over-flowing with a crowd that comes in every shape and color. The monthly event and the international Bhangra phenomenon it helped spark have received extensive attention from national and international press, making the cover of Billboard magazine, features on Dutch and Japanese television, and most recently on the WB11 News at 10. Another interesting phenomenon is noticed in the New York club called "Mutiny" (opened in 1997) that seeks to foster diasporic affiliation across ethnic differences. Mutiny draws both its aesthetic and its political inspiration from the overtly anti-racist traditions of British Asian youth culture and is an important venue for the forging of trans-Atlantic links between the Asian diaspora in Britain and America. A significant number of "Asian underground" deejays have performed here, including Talvin Singh, State of Bengal, Badmarsh and Shri, and Joi. Although these British performers and their anti-racist ethos played a formative role for the club, Mutiny consciously pairs these British performers with local talent. This a potential mix suggests that the new Black Atlantic ties being woven on the dance floor of the club Mutiny are also helping forge bonds of cultural solidarity among New York's community of color.

Over the last few years, Panjabi MC has played as a live act in Europe and the USA. His reaction of performing in New York City is interesting to note:

> In the States, I have played primarily as a DJ in LA, San Francisco, Washington DC and Chicago but in June this year I did my first stage show in New York where I previewed some new tracks. I took along DJ Chani from P.J.D and vocalist, Kebi (I've worked with him on Mirza and he has great potential . . . he introduced a whole new visual and audio element to my stage set), and we played at a club which is predominantly a World Music club in the heart of downtown New York. My PR manager suggested that it would be valuable exposure but initially I didn't think I had the live set to pull it off, but at the end of the day we just blew the whole place up . . . it was an amazing response . . . totally unique. We managed to get a lot of press from the mainstream media. Sangam Entertainment Group who invited me over to New York did a very thorough media drive . . . we managed to attract a crowd that was largely Indian but at the same time the number of non-Asians there was also hard to believe . . . they were lapping up the traditional tunes![5]

What every bhangra artist lays emphasis on is therefore innovation and remixes. He prides himself on being more listener-friendly than a lot of other producers and re-mixers. Talking about his album called *Steel Bangle* (1999) Punjab MC says:

> This music (Bhangra made outside of India) has wasted so many opportunities. It has always had great lyrics but is often held back by the musical content. Even though I'm using modern technology I'm employing traditional ways of moving people—like songs and chord structures—and a lot of it is built around what the people on the street, the people buying the music, are saying.

Some critics see the westernized bhangra scene in the United States as derivative because it is still dependent on music from the subcontinent and from Britain where most of all the Bhangra bands are still based. In fact, it is one of the factors that forces the desi remix culture in America to remain a subculture. Despite the peculiar power of music to cross borders and break down barriers, the hybrid space on the dance floor is always deeply sedimented with prior and political meanings. Regional and national chauvinism, gender and class inequality, and complex forms of internal and external racism all have an impact on the remixed bhangra being produced.

II

Leaving aside the debate whether bhangra in its hybrid forms enriches or diminishes the popular Indian dance form, I will now focus on four documentary films (coincidentally all made by women) that use the bhangra to show the acculturation process in the New World. Since it began much earlier in Britain than in the U.S., the first documentary is by the well-known director Gurinder Chadha who uses this music as a backdrop in her exploration of various notions of Britishness through the eyes of English, Scottish, Irish and Welsh Asians in *I'm British But . . .* (1990; 30 minutes). Using Bhangra and Bangla music and the testimonies of young British Asians, the video uncovers a defiant popular culture—a synthesis—part Asian, part British. "The evolution of British Bhangra and Bangla music marks the beginning of the end of British national chauvinism for those of us who have been born and brought up here. It has helped us define ourselves as a migrant community with a musical language of our own, created by us, for us, but open for enjoyment by all," says Chadha in her commentary. Thus we have a Scottish-Pakistani sheep farmer, a Bangladeshi woman who lives in Belfast and an Indian girl who lives in Glasgow and has a Welsh twang to her voice. The accents are truly as diverse as possible and there is the unceasing Bhangra beat to make a true 'bhelpuri' of what it means to be British and Asian.

Bhangra Jig directed by Pratibha Parmar (4 minutes, 1991) was originally commissioned by Channel 4 to celebrate Glasgow as the European cultural capital. In this short film Pratibha Parmar continues to explore the Asian-Western encounter with a music video. A Scottish Asian woman, in a leather jacket and a tartan skirt walks through superimposed images of Glaswegian architecture, statues and the inside of a Mosque dome whilst these images are cut with young people dancing to a Bhangra soundtrack. In both images and sound Scotland meets Asia in this absorbing testimony to a multi-cultural Britain.

Nandini Sikand's *Bhangra Wrap* (1994; 20 minutes) is the third energetic documentary about a vibrant South Asian youth subculture that fuses hip hop, rap and bhangra music. Based in Toronto, Canada and New York City, Nandini shows us how bhangra is a mix of old and new and is symbolic of universal cultural transformation for new generations. Bhangra House is propagated through alternative radio, party DJs and hip urban clubs where South Asian youth have carved out their own unique sense of style, identity and voice that is an uncompromised mix of old and new, South Asian and American. "I have noticed that there is a different trend, especially among South Asians who have grown up here. They have become proud of their identity—earlier it was always trying to melt and assimilate," Sikand explained. "Now it's like somebody wearing a Nehru jacket or a bandini scarf and it's just an assertion of that identity. And that's where Bhangra really fits in."

Tejaswini Ganti's *Gimme Somethin' to Dance to (*1995; 18 minutes) is a vibrant documentary on the *desi* remix culture in the United States and it looks at how bhangra produced in Britain with samples and rhythms from other music genres has found a place of prominence in New York's music scene. "It seemed to me in the last two years, bhangra has come to acquire a greater presence in the New York City because it was published about in Manhattan and had an event at the Central Park which is outside the Indian mix so to speak," Ganti said.[6] She made the video, her first, as part of her graduate study in Culture and Media at New York University. In the absence of the documentary at present let me give you a little more details about its contents. Documenting the rising popularity of bhangra music, originally from the Punjab and popularized in England with the addition of Western instrumentation, rap and techno beats, and special effects Ganti shows us how popular over American radio stations, bhangra music brings together ethnic groups within the expatriate Indian community. Featured are interviews with various radio DJs. She interviews Magic Mike and DJ Kucha, who talk about their desire to follow Bally Sagoo's path to a major label recording contract and mass stardom. Ganti then cuts from this scene to an interview with DJ Rekha, who unequivocally states that she feels no need to have her work succeed with the dominant white music-listening public. This juxtaposition of starkly contrast viewpoints reveals a great deal about the forms of capital that circulate in different sectors of the *desi* population in New York. In addition to a politicized critique of the pressure for ethnic assimilation, there is also a kind of sub-cultural capital at work in Rekha's pronouncement. As is true of so many other musical subcultures in the United States, claims to authenticity within *desi* club culture are centrally connected to the evasion of commercial success. That micro-politics of club cultures are clearly at work in this context is implied but not overtly discussed by Ganti.

The fifth documentary is Balvinder D. Mudan's *Desi Remix Chicago Style* (1996; 46 minutes) which interviews Chicago area South Asian American musicians about their music, racism, and reclaiming their South Asian culture. Balvinder became aware of her identity and the conflicts she had with both the white culture and her parents' Indian culture as she was involved with student politics in Great Britain. She started using video to express these feelings. Then she came to New York to undertake further projects in documentary filmmaking. When she moved from New York City to Chicago, she received three grants for her documentary *Desi Remix Chicago Style* which won an award at The Chicago Asian American film Festival. Shot in Chicago and London, this energetic documentary follows three very different Punjabi bands and their attempts to use their music as abridge between competing cultural influences of India and America. They face and deal with racism, discover both *desi* sex and *desi* sexism, look for role models and confront politics, history, religion, and their own multiple heritages.

Closely related to these documentaries on bhangra is Swati Khurana and Leith Murgai's *Desi Dub* (25 minutes, 1997) which explores the Indipop/indofunk music scenes in New York City, as seen through the eyes of a popular Indian woman DJ. Kaizad Gustad's *Cornerstore Blues* (1993/48 minutes) is also about blending through music, though of a different sort than the bhangra. It tells the story of Rahul, a young man from India, who feels trapped working in his uncle's corner store in the East Indian section of Jackson Heights in the New York City borough of Queens and dreams of someday making it as a blues musician—a real black blues musician. Now if he can only overcome his Bombay accent, nagging relatives, immigration papers, infatuation with a Blues singer, and hold a tune long enough to avoid being thrown out of every audition he might just make it. He tries, without success, to incorporate elements of East Indian folk music into American blues.

These different explorations therefore lead us to a better understanding of how the Bhangra, in a mix of the old and the new, becomes symbolic of universal cultural transformation for new generations and how the Asian-American cultural scenario is being constantly remixed into newer forms with every passing day. It also explains how a specifically diasporic cultural politics of nostalgia thus ironically has resulted in a transnational impact. As Ashley Dawson rightly points out, this cultural studies model should not be confused with the dominant sociological approaches of the day, which represents Asian youths as trapped in an "identity crisis" that robbed them of agency. Instead, the styles developed within subcultures should be seen as part of a symbolic repertoire through which young people attempt to win space, in both a literal and figurative sense, in relation to their double articulation.

NOTES

1. Lavina Melwani, "Hum Sab Punjabi" www: //ASANet.com
2. Ashley Dawson, "Desi Remix: The Plural Dance Cultures of New York's South Asian Diaspora." *Jouvert* 7.1: 2002. p. 1.

3. Krishneil Maharaj, "Bhangra: A Political Economic Breakdown" *hardboiled.*
4. See website of www.basementbhangra.com for more details.
5. Jatender S. Heer, "Punjabi MC gives Bhangra a much needed jolt" mcpunjabi@aol.com
6. Vijaya S. Jodha, "Cultural Riches." http: // Welcome to Little India

From Marginalized to Mainstream: An Analysis of Manoj Night Shyamalan's Film *The Sixth Sense*

MANPREET KAUR KANG
Guru Tegh Bahadur Institute of Technology, Delhi

The twenty-two million strong Indian diaspora living across eleven continents no longer conjures up the image of the old-fashioned apologetic Indian. Instead, the image that flashes across the mind is of a newly prosperous non-resident Indian, who has earned respect in the adopted country. There are innumerable success stories of people of Indian origin all over the world in such diverse fields as business, politics, engineering and medicine. The 1.7 million Indians account for 0.8% of the total population and are one of the highest earning, best-educated and fastest growing community. The strong moral values and the importance Indians give to education, sees them excelling everywhere. The Indians have indeed come a long way since the move to the Americas in the mid-90s as indentured labor. The Silicon Valley millionaires and the IT and financial whiz kids have given the diaspora a new respectability.

All these Indians do not form a monolithic group and no single migrant can be a representative of this group. The overseas community is formed of people at varied levels that depend upon the time of migration, the place of origin in India and the country where they settled down. Educational levels, class, age and gender are the other contributory factors. Then there is the difference between the first generation Indian expatriates and the second generation brought up in the adopted country. There are also secondary migrants; people of Indian origin who migrated from other countries, such as Trinidad and Kenya to the U.S. The U.S. Indians live in multiracial societies where they have to adjust, adapt and assimilate with other ethnic groups that make the nation. Racial identity, therefore, is an important factor in multiethnic societies.

Migrant diasporas experience displacement, cultural crisis, rootlessness and marginalization. Fiction, as well as other forms of art, becomes a means to convey their diasporic experiences. According to Dipankar Purkayastha, the Indian Americans are unsure, uncertain and insecure. They have one foot on either side. Their positioning is traumatic. This is definitely the experience of the first generation emigrants but according to Indrani Sengupta, "As relocation in the Western world becomes an ethnically challenging issue for the first generation emigrants, the process is somewhat reversed for the second generation and a glimpse of different mindsets emerges out of their exposure to typically Indian situations." Somdatta Mandal says, "The old Kipling lore that the East is East and West is West is passé and the twain does meet," especially in films, which "have been able to do away with homogeneous notions and the negative stereotypical images of migrants that are portrayed in the mainstream media."

In this essay, I make an attempt to analyze *The Sixth Sense* (1999), written and directed by Manoj Shyamalan, who falls in the category of the emigrants brought up in the adopted country. India-born Shyamalan is a screenwriter-director and is being tipped as the next Steven Spielberg in film reviews. At thirty-two, he is among the younger celebrities and is the highest paid screenwriter in the harshly competitive world of Hollywood. His eerie film, *The Sixth Sense*, became the fifteenth highest grosser of all times in the U.S. and it collected six Academy award nominations. Another of his films, *Unbreakable* (2000), has received a record-breaking sum of five million dollars from Disney Productions for the film's script.

Shyamalan was born in Pondicherry and when he was eight months old, his parents, both doctors, moved to the U.S. He grew up in the posh suburban Penn Valley area of Philadelphia and had an early passion for filmmaking. He was given a Super-8 camera when he was eight years old and he had completed forty-five home made movies by age seventeen. His movies depict strong family bonds, themes of family and parenting—these are the subjects that are dear to his heart. Most of his movies have supernatural overtones and he seems obsessed with the unknown (*Signs, Unbreakable*). His first film, *Praying with Anger*, the story of an Indian exchange student who finds himself a stranger in his homeland, was named the Debut Film of the Year at the American Film Institute in Los Angeles in 1993. His second film, *Wide Awake* (1998), was a huge success at the box office.

His third film, *The Sixth Sense,* based on his childhood fears about ghosts, is a psychological horror film. The eerie pace is maintained by psychological details and not with gory or extravagant special effects. "People take time to get into details but it resonates with the viewer," feels Shyamalan. He says that as a filmmaker, one cannot assume that the audience "is coming from the same emotional place as you . . . you have an onus on you to build that through the film . . . and not go under the assumption that if I'm crying because I wrote the scene, then clearly everyone else will be crying." He gives us an example of the trauma of the mother in *The Sixth Sense* to elaborate this point. He states that many people will cry when the mother cries when she sees her son suffering but many people may say:

> We don't attach that much [significance] to our moms, because our mom wasn't there for us. So you gotta tell me why I need to feel for this particular mom, not go under the assumption that you feel for moms because everyone feels for their mom, right? . . . I have to give you the reasons why—even the smallest of things.

The mother in this movie is overheard talking about her son in her sleep and she says, "If somebody tries to hurt you I'm going to kick their asses." The crowd laughs at this endearing statement and thinks, "Even in this woman's sleep, . . . she's ready to protect her child." And then when she cries, when she breaks, the crowds cry with her.

Based on a paranormal phenomenon, the film is deeply emotional. In an interview Shyamalan says, "Everyone's goal is to emotionally engage the reader and the audience. It should touch a chord with people." His film has definitely touched the hearts of mainstream audiences who flocked to the theatres, making *The Sixth Sense* the top earner for the summer of 1999. What are the factors which helped him, an Indian American, transform a movie into a cult object? Umberto Eco says that

> for transforming a book or a movie into a cult object. . . . The work must be loved obviously but this is not enough. It must provide a completely furnished world so that its fans can quote characters and episodes as if they were aspects of the fan's private sectarian world, a world about which one can make up quizzes and play trivia games. . . . Naturally all these elements (characters and episodes) must have some archetypal appeal.

In his analysis of *Casablanca* he further comments, "One can ask and answer questions about the various subway stations of New York or Paris only if these spots have become or have been assumed as mythical areas." *The Sixth Sense* has been shot in Shyamalan's hometown, Philadelphia, and we see haunting images of the city. The church and the school are important landmarks the audiences can connect with. Shyamalan says, "I don't care about the box office. I want to be a phenomenon where the audience feels some connection." The story should "have a universal resonance, thematically . . . where everyone can relate to what's going on, in their own way and take something from it." Whereas many Indian writers wish to highlight the Indian experiences in their work, Shyamalan focuses on the universality of the theme in his works.

In the film, the main character is Cole Sear, an eight-year-old Philadelphia boy who feels there is something lurking around in his home when he is alone and will not say why. He finds comfort in his room, under a tent, in the company of religious figures and toy soldiers. He is sensitive to them and wants help. The help comes in the form of Dr. Malcolm Crowe (played by Bruce Willis), a child psychologist who is dedicated to helping people after a traumatic experience with one of his former patients. The doctor wants the boy to tell him his secrets. He sets out to find why this young boy is so disturbed and obviously deranged . . . or is he? Cole resists, but finally confesses: he sees dead people who scare him and hurt him. There is more misery for the Cole family. Cole's father has left him, and his mother (Toni Collette) is frustrated by her inability to comprehend her son's stories. She feels her son's problems are psychological. The film has long conversations between Cole and Crowe, and a relationship of trust develops between the two. The most poignant scene is when a dead girl gives Cole a videotape that reveals the identity of her murderer.

Eco further states that "in order to transform a work into a cult object one must be able to break, dislocate, unhinge it so that one can remember only parts of it, irrespective of their original relationship with the whole. . . . It should display not one central idea but many." There must also exist "inter-textual frames," by which he means "stereotyped situations derived from preceding . . . tradition such as the narrative situation in which the hero fights the villain and wins" or "the story of the *verge sonillee* [dishonoured virgin]." These frames should not only belong to a "sort of" tradition, but should "also display a particular fascination." These "inter-textual archetypes" serve "only to indicate a pre-established and frequently reappearing narrative situation . . . provoking . . . a sort of intense emotion accompanied by the vague feeling of a déjà vu, that everybody yearns to see again."

Keeping in mind the above observations, I found a number of 'inter-textual frames' in my study of *The Sixth Sense.* Towards the beginning of the film, Dr. Crowe, the psychoanalyst, is confronted by an extremely disturbed patient who shoots at the doctor. The genres of violence and psychodrama are both invoked in this one incident. Soon after, we see Crowe take up the case of Cole and there is a focus on the doctor-patient relationship, which is a theme often explored in films. We then observe the relationship of the doctor with his wife taking a downturn as he has little time for her—the story of the self-sacrificing, committed doctor and the disillusioned wife. She begins to see someone outside her marriage that invokes themes of betrayal, marital infidelity and the spurned husband.

The film revolves around Cole having supernatural powers, the power to see the dead which is a gift and a curse. The film thus rests on the psychic, occult frame. The silently suffering Cole and the trauma of his mother make the film a story of pain and suffering. Eco says that "the extreme of pain" leads to "sensual pleasure." Cole in addition to his other problems is emotionally hurt by the school bully and the insensitive attitude of the schoolteacher. The travails of single parenthood and the consequences of a broken marriage on the mother and child are additional concerns highlighted in the film.

In the movie, the theme of childhood fear is expanded into the theme of communication. Dr. Crowe and his wife Anna, are not communicating properly, Lynn (Cole's mother) and Cole are also not communicating properly and the ghosts are also not able to communicate with Cole. Everyone is learning to communicate in the proper way, to speak the things that are important to him or her. Finally we come to the climax of the story, which is an amazing anti-climax—another archetype in films. Dr. Crowe realizes that he has been dead ever since the deranged patient had shot at him, but he had not known it. Cole, of course, could see him and converse with him because of his sixth sense. He then sadly reflects, "I think I can go now. I think I needed to help someone. I did it."

Works Cited

Applied History Research Group, The. "Asian and African Labour: Indenture and Beyond," http://www.ucalgary.ca/applied_history/tutor/migrations/home5.html. 1999-2000.

Apun ka Choice Bureau. "Shyamalan: The Next Spielberg," August 1, 2002.

Argent, Daniel. "The Writing Sense: Excerpts from an Interview with M. Night Shyamalan," http: //www.shyamalan.

Chohan, Satinder. "When Holly met Bolly," *The Guardian*, December 2, 1999.

Deoshi, N.K. "Manoj Shyamalan spins another Eerie Yarn," http://www.apunkachoice.com/scoop/bollywood/20001130-1.html, Nov. 30, 2000.

Eco, Umberto. "*Casablanca*: Cult Movies and Intertextual Collage," *Modern Criticism and Theory: A Reader*, ed. David Lodge. London: Longman, 1988: 445-55.

Hill, J. "The Appeal of Contemporary Blockbusters," *Unorthodox Reel*, http: //www.un-reel.co.uk/bloc.htm. 2000.

_____. "How do you Make a Genre Film Interesting?," *Unorthodox Reel*, http.//www.unreel.co.uk/genrehtm. 2000.

_____. "Point-of-View Shots in Horror Films," *Unorthodox Reel*, http:/ /www.unreel.co.uk/psycho.htm. 2000.

Lal, Vinay. "Reflections on the Indian Diaspora, in the Caribbean and Elsewhere," *Manas: Reflections on the Indian Diaspora*, http: //www.sscnet.ucla.edu/southasia/Diaspora/reflect.html.

Mandal, Somdatta. "Abstracts" for MELUS-India National Seminar on Asians in the U.S.: The Diasporic Experience, April 2003.

Mathew, Jayant Mammen. "Haunting Hollywood: Manoj Night Shyamalan makes a top grosser out of childhood fears," *Guardian Unlimited*, October 10, 1999.

Purkayastha, Dipankar. "Abstracts" for MELUS-India National Seminar on Asians in the U.S.: The Diasporic Experience, April 2003.

Sengupta, Indrani. "Abstracts" for MELUS-India National Seminar, April 2003.

Sinha, Vimmy. "The Great Indian Diaspora," *HT Sunday Magazine*, January 5, 2003.

MELUS: Where Shall We Go from Here?*

MOHAN RAMANAN
University of Hyderabad

This is only my second Presidential address but my third to this forum. In each of my statements I have tried to address the question of what the relevance of American Studies to this country could possibly be, and in particular, what possible points of convergence with Indian concerns a forum like MELUS, dedicated to the study and analysis of ethnicity, margin and collectivities, could have. This is an important question given the existential angst of scholars in American Studies in this country. By a fine irony we find ourselves meeting in the very Institution which was for more than three decades synonymous with American Studies in India and today that Institution, already forced by the exigencies of Indian academic life and the politics surrounding it to change its avatar to emphasize its Indian character, is now undergoing yet another change which might, if good counsel does not prevail, marginalize American Studies altogether. That we are meeting here today is a question of chance and it provides yet another opportunity to us, particularly from this country, to ask why we do America here and how in these critical times we propose to do it in the future. The first point I want to make is that the various organizations concerned with American Studies in this country do not speak to one another, else I cannot understand why the initiative Sachidananda Mohanty, Gholam Sarwar Chaudhuri and I took to establish a nodal organization to be called South Asian American Studies Association received only lukewarm support and I, at least, did not have the courtesy of replies from functionaries in the other organizations. I mention this only to point to the less than serious attention American Studies receives in this country. Things have not improved after 9/11 and American intervention in Iraq has only hardened the attitude of those who matter in Government and elsewhere when it comes to pleading the cause of American Studies in India. It is this context that I would urge you to keep in mind when we are debating the various familiar issues of ethnicity, multiculturalism, marginality, periphery, expatriate sensibility, exile, home and abroad and trans-cultural encounters in the coming sessions. Our discussions will be meaningful only when we colour our statements with this crucial interrogation of the relevance of what we are saying. To my American friends who have taken the trouble of travelling so far it is equally important that they ask what it is that they are promoting and how they propose to make a mark in countries like ours which now seem to have a pathological distrust of what America is and stands for.

For a beginning let me recall a point I made in my first Address about the Commonwealth of Literature we enjoy by seeing our own Indian writers in America as part of the rich and braided tapestry which multiethnic writing in the United States is. I focused on the poetry of Indran Amirthnayagam, an American diplomat stationed at Monterrey, who writes in Spanish and English. He is a Sri Lankan Tamil by origin and has lived in America since he was eight and he writes not only of America but also about Sri Lanka and the difficulties of the Tamils there. His poetry is suffused by the bicultural nature of exile and provides a paradigm for the writings of our own writers who are abroad and who speak of exile and the kingdom, of loss, and of the ecstasy of longing for home. I could have taken a Hispanic writer or an Amerindian or an African American for my model but I chose an American who is Sri Lankan and made the point that he explains through comparison and contrast the quality of the writing of Indian American writers like Rushdie, Mistry, Alexander, Lahiri, Mukherjee and Vikram Chandra. I believe this is instructive. It tells us of the mutual interdependence of writers, all of whom are in a similar, if not identical, existential situation. It further compels us to break down narrow disciplinary walls, partisan and contingent categories, and forces us to ask if ideas like MELUS are relevant anymore and if there is not a need to revaluate the usefulness of such categories. I do believe that MELUS has, and is still performing an important role and the work done so far is not negligible. It has sharply distanced itself from mainstream American writing and concentrated on the canons which are now enabled by ethnicity and race and multiculturalism. From a postmodern perspective it has been an unexceptionable enterprise but is it not time for us to review our work and if necessary move on in directions to which both postmodernism, and its cousin postcolonialism, inexorably draw us? I think there is a need. What I am hinting at is the clear signals we now seem to be receiving regarding an exclusive ethnic identity which refuses contact with other ethnicities, other collectivities and in a word with what Wordsworth called the widest commonality of Man. Let me hasten to add that invoking categories from an obviously white canonical figure need not be shunned. This is a needless sentimentalism and I believe that we at MELUS are strong enough to accommodate ideas from the mainstream also, without prejudice to our main objectives.

What has postmodernism taught us? I think in a brief essay like this, I cannot effectively summarize the whole of this intellectual enterprise with which American Studies has been implicated. However a selective analysis is possible and I would claim that postmodernism has been at the cutting edge of our intellectual enterprise and that it is only natural to see MELUS as an offshoot of this intellectual provenance. It made it possible to question the given paradigms of American Studies because postmodernism encouraged us to question UR narratives, the Center, the essentialist formulations which created a hegemonic aura around the existing paradigm of American Studies. These included ideas of America's Manifest Destiny, the notion of America as "a City on the Hill," the view that Americans were an exceptional people. American myths of the expanding frontier, the American Adam, the Virgin Land, the innocence of the American, especially the innocent Abroad, and the idea of an American Pastoral in many ways defined the Nation and the people. Crevecoeur's view of America as the melting pot civilization, which in a sense gave coherence to these varied American motifs was effectively challenged by the new multiculturalism represented in the writings of Toni Morrison, an Alice Walker, a Momaday, a Welch, a Lahiri, a Divakaruni, or a Kingston, and their "Braided Lives" gave a local habitation and a name to so many writers in the periphery and the margins of American culture. American culture had to come to terms with these nay-sayers and had to expand itself to include this medley of new voices.

It taught us the value of "Difference" and it asked important questions about the local and the specific and allowed us to test the UR narratives with a commitment to small histories or to put it in Indian terms to interrogate, if not supplant, the "Margi" with the "Desi." Thus we were able to see the problems of a Momaday character as the particular offshoot of a particular reality and we resisted the tendency to assimilate all this in a pan American narrative. Plenitude and pluralism became our watchwords and we began to empathize with human experience that was other to us in a variety of ways instead of obliterating its specificity in a futile quest for uniformity, but in the process we were not quite grasping the point that unity is necessary in our common pursuit. I shall have something to say about the distinction between uniformity and unity by and by but suffice it to say that perhaps we are at a point when we seem to have carried the question of difference too far, so much so, that we are not able to see the need to effect coalitions with other groups and forge a sustained campaign for the unity of such groups which must come together to reinforce the lessons of postmodernism. We are lapsing into a solipsistic world where no argument is possible and nobody can dare invade a privacy, a sublime essential universe, which to my mind is no different from the tyrannies of an oligarchy or even a fascist state. What ought to be a democratic expression of difference becomes, by a stroke of irony, an expression of a new essentialism which warns everyone off and gives a slogan to its acolytes—"We speak for ourselves, about ourselves, and to ourselves." Can we not see the danger of this exclusivity? MELUS must address this question.

When it came to the reading of texts we did not always understand the postmodern insistence about inter-textual reading and we more often than not in our commitment to identity politics allowed the notion of the Work and the Author to go unchallenged. Too much of our criticism assumed the stability of the work and the author because we could not allow ourselves to abandon faith in meaning and the power of interpretation. Thus in even what ought to have been radical discourses involving African American writers we tended to take the old Liberal Humanist line and even while mouthing slogans of race, class, gender and ethnicity, we tended to do so in the framework of Liberal Humanism. Clearly this has meant that we were contradicting ourselves and oblivious to the irony of the situation or simply not able to carry the logic of postmodernism to its inevitable end. This end to a large measure, I believe, is conducive to a greater expansion of the imaginative franchise and in its acceptance of the open-endedness of texts and the possibility of poetic apertures which refuse any easy assumption of the organicity of a text, enables a genuine humanism to reassert itself. Bakhtin's ideas of the dialogic text, the sheer multivocalism automatically conferred on all kinds of writing, and his suggestive categories of the carnivalesque and the democratization of literary culture are prescriptions for a Humanism heavily touched by postmodern concerns. It is and will no longer be innocent but actually inclusive and accepting. I have elsewhere spoken of a Liberal Humanism under correction, and by this I should imagine that this Humanism will respect difference and celebrate gendered narratives, speak up for Race as an important critical category and certainly assert the vital perspectives of Class in our discourse. In the Indian context this would mean a greater sensitivity to Dalit issues and an acceptance of Tribal and other voices as a necessary part of our enterprise. The fragments of the nation, to use Partha Chatterjee's catchy phrase, is our business. But having said this I must also repeat that this foregrounding of difference and the local and the specific will have meaning only if it is in the service of a truly Humanist project of the kind I have identified. MELUS would need to sort out its commitment to difference without losing the larger perspectives which a Humanism under correction enables. That is, MELUS should not hesitate to see a work as a text, an author as a writer and the critic as reader. This would allow greater play to dialogism in texts, a more exciting analysis of discourse rather than the tired explication of individual works which many indulge in now, even while purporting to concern themselves with ethnicity and race.

A proper convergence of the postmodern and the postcolonial ('pomo' and 'poco') ought to be our agenda for the future and I shall try to give an outline of how that agenda should appear. For a start, I think, we ought to move beyond identity politics to a more comprehensive framework for MELUS. We have made a modest beginning by asking our delegates to include the Canadian experience as well. There are obvious differences between American and Canadian experience but there are also similarities and the main point of convergence as I see it is that both countries have an aboriginal experience that cannot in all fairness be seen as radically dissimilar. Thus, I should imagine that we can encourage more actively than we have done Aboriginal Studies in MELUS. That immediately raises the question of the relevance of narrowing down such studies to only North America. Are we to keep out Aboriginal Studies in Australia or for that matter Aboriginal or Tribal Studies in India in MELUS in the conviction that our interest is America and America alone? I do not think we can sustain these artificial barriers too long because the kind of expansions I am advocating will compel us to be more self-consciously comparative in our perspective and that would imply that the study of a Welch can be effectively done only if we were to place him in relation to a Canadian indigenous writer or even a Tribal writer like Laxman Mane from India. Then again America and Canada have a large expatriate population and from our point of view in India the Indian Canadian and the Indian American experiences clearly have a lot in common with one another and with the Expatriate Indian writer's experiences in Fiji, Canberra, or in the UK. To do one to the exclusion of the others is a drastic curtailment of academic freedom and a damper to the critical enterprise. MELUS cannot participate in this kind of academic fascism. As a mark of our rejection of fascism I propose that we make a deliberate departure from previous practice and encourage studies in our own Dalit and tribal cultures in relation to the American. And this clearly means that we cannot confine ourselves to writing in English but move to the languages of our country and welcome translation activity as a necessary concomitant of comparative studies. The extraordinary literary provenance in our Indian *bhashas* is waiting to be tapped by MELUSians who by temperament and training are most likely to profit from such forays.

In our studies so far ethnicity has been a dominant concern and this was natural given MELUS' identity. But the time has come for us to go beyond ethnicity and identity questions and to ask the kind of questions Alice Walker has been asking. *The Color Purple* is an extraordinary novel for a variety of reasons. For me it is Martin Luther King's ideas being given fictional form and it appeals to me for its great compassion and the power of love it emphasizes. But from the point of view of our immediate task its appeal is precisely because it cuts through the category of race and ethnicity to inform it with the concerns of gender, and within gender, it asks us to become even more specific than we have ever been by focusing on the gender question in relation to Celie, the African American woman. This degree of specificity in a way cuts at the root of the Feminism advanced by white women like Elaine Showalter and encourages us to break down the dominant UR Feminism of White America and to make space for Womanism which is both culture specific and which allows us to make common cause with all women everywhere who are threatened and exploited. The adherence in Walker to a generous Humanism is in keeping with my idea of a new Humanism which accepts the widest commonality of Man. On the one hand, Walker is challenging us to go to the root of things and not to accept large narratives that tend to obliterate the vital differences in race and gender experience and this holds a lesson for us in MELUS. But the whole tendency of Walker's novel is to reinterpret the spiritual message of Martin Luther

King which spoke of unity, not division, forgiveness, not revenge, accommodation not exclusiveness. To us in this country influenced by the thought of Mahatma Gandhi, King and Walker must surely have important resonances. While we must henceforth continue studying literature by women not as an essentialist monolith but as specific to the locale and the identity of the writer, we must nevertheless not forget that no individual writes in a vacuum and that putting such writing in context and in relation to other similar writing alone will be adequate. This means that we can and should study a white feminist like Adrienne Rich and we can do so profitably only when we can see her in all her human quiddity as unique and different from the black Nikki Giovanni. To take the logic of this argument further we can and should in MELUS now study white writers with profit and Jewish writers too. This must come as a shock to those who wrote off Jewish ethnicity in the name of MELUS. We can further study Indian diasporic women writers and if we can dilate on Bharati Mukherjee, Jhumpa Lahiri, Meena Alexander, Chitra Banerjee Divakaruni who live in the USA we can by the same logic write about women writers like Shashi Deshpande, Nayantara Sahgal, Shobha De, or Arundhati Roy who have not migrated within the confines of MELUS. Why not? They provide an important contrast to our expatriate writers and a comparison of these writers with our native writers must not only be useful but necessary. Again we need not take Salman Rushdie's provocative remark about Indian English writing coming from India being the most valuable literature coming from the subcontinent too seriously. It was, as everyone will readily grant, a remark made out of ignorance or arrogance or both and in any case MELUS cannot provide Rushdie medication for 'Rushdieitis.' We should do the logical thing and that is, read translations from our native provenance. If we can do this for India we can do this for Canada and America, wherever an indigenous literature exists.

I think I have said enough to indicate why and where we must go. I believe that this is the only natural course open to us and if we do go in these directions, we might find ourselves participating in a dialogue between cultures, which after all was what America stood for. In the revised scenario I can see Bellow supping with Kingston and Lowell doing business with Meena Alexander or Tennessee Williams making common literary cause with Vijay Tendulkar. In this way we will expand our literary franchise, we shall honour difference, and each separate collectivity or fragment of the nation or nations will have its place in our scheme of things, but we shall only make one demand of our MELUSians and that is whatever they do they should not forget the commonality of man and while honouring difference they should also move in the direction of Unity. Unity honours difference and has no fear of multiplicity or plurality. It can accommodate and it does this by acutely being conscious of the ills of an older Humanism which participated in the totalizing narratives of the West and was implicated in the project of modernity, which in turn had hegemonic designs and was clearly the ideological justification for colonialism. We reject neo-colonialism and its attendant global discourse but we shall not abandon the intellectual quest for unity that respects nationalities, cultures, and peoples. In this lies our relevance (for our country) as scholars of American Studies. Thank you.

*This is the text of the Presidential Address delivered to the MELUS Conference held in Hyderabad in January 2004. I have retained the flavour of the speech and not made any substantial alterations.